UNPALATABLE

INGRID G. HOUCK SERIES IN FOOD AND FOODWAYS

UNPALATABLE

Stories of Pain and Pleasure in Southern Cookbooks

Carrie Helms Tippen

UNIVERSITY PRESS OF MISSISSIPPI / JACKSON

The University Press of Mississippi is the scholarly publishing agency of
the Mississippi Institutions of Higher Learning: Alcorn State University,
Delta State University, Jackson State University, Mississippi State University,
Mississippi University for Women, Mississippi Valley State University,
University of Mississippi, and University of Southern Mississippi.

www.upress.state.ms.us
Illustrations by Lindsey Cleworth

The University Press of Mississippi is a member
of the Association of University Presses.

This is derived, in part, from an article published in *Food, Culture, and Society* on September 30, 2021, available online: https://www.tandfonline.com/doi/full/10.1080/15528014.2021.1984659. An earlier version of "Keep Southern and Cut the Fat" originally appeared as a blog post on FoodFatnessFitness.com.

Copyright © 2025 by University Press of Mississippi
All rights reserved
Manufactured in the United States of America

∞

Library of Congress Cataloging-in-Publication Data

Names: Tippen, Carrie Helms, author.
Title: Unpalatable : stories of pain and pleasure in Southern cookbooks /
Carrie Helms Tippen.
Other titles: Ingrid G. Houck series in Food and Foodways.
Description: Jackson : University Press of Mississippi, 2025. |
Series: Ingrid g. houck series in food and foodways |
Includes bibliographical references and index.
Identifiers: LCCN 2024036138 (print) | LCCN 2024036139 (ebook) |
ISBN 9781496854797 (hardback) | ISBN 9781496854803 (trade paperback) |
ISBN 9781496854810 (epub) | ISBN 9781496854827 (epub) |
ISBN 9781496854834 (pdf) | ISBN 9781496854841 (pdf)
Subjects: LCSH: Cooking—Psychological aspects. | Food writing—Southern
States—History. | Cookbooks—Social aspects—Southern States. |
Food writers—Southern States. | Cooking, American—Southern style—
Social aspects. | Rhetoric—Social aspects. | Southern States—Social life and customs.
Classification: LCC TX644 .T577 2025 (print) | LCC TX644 (ebook) |
DDC 641.300975—dc23/eng/20240907
LC record available at https://lccn.loc.gov/2024036138
LC ebook record available at https://lccn.loc.gov/2024036139

British Library Cataloging-in-Publication Data available

CONTENTS

Preface vii

Acknowledgments ix

"Party with a Purpose":
Celebration, Suffering, and Social Justice 3

The Urgency of Pleasure:
Theorizing a Rhetoric of Pleasure in Cookbooks 18

"A Lot of Past to Reckon with":
Grappling with Slavery and Racism 50

Making Do:
Pain of Poverty and Pleasure of Resilience 88

A Season of Sweetness:
Gardening, Canning, and Women's Labor on Farms 121

Keep Southern and Cut the Fat:
Body Fat and Illness in Wellness Cookbooks 154

"Useful in a Fearful Time":
Responding to Grief and Death in Funeral Cookbooks 191

Towards a Conclusion:
Intersections and Implications 227

Index 239

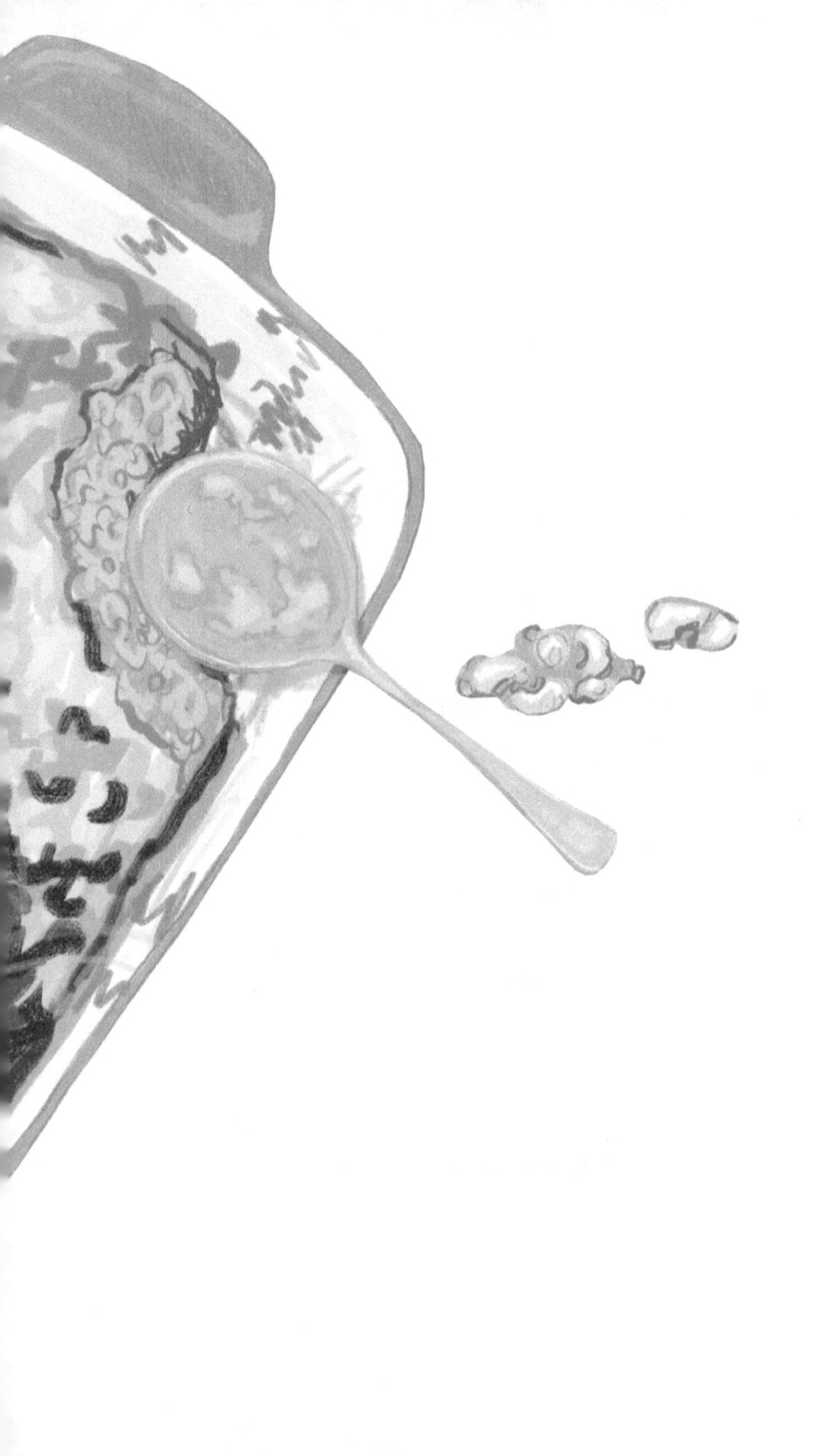

PREFACE

> Corn, till it have past through the mill and been ground to powder, is not fit for bread. God so deals with his servants: he grinds them with grief and pain till they turn to dust, and then are they fit manchet for his mansion.
> —ANNE BRADSTREET, MEDITATION #19

My interest in this topic of suffering in southern food narratives comes in part from a personal place. Thus the chatty openings of each chapter and this maudlin preface. I hope you'll bear with me a moment.

My partner and I tried unsuccessfully for a few years to have a biological child. I started seeing a therapist for the first time when it seemed clear that we would need medical intervention to conceive and that my ambivalence about having children at all would have to be resolved, one way or the other. I needed help thinking the unthinkable and speaking the unspeakable. It wasn't just the unthinkability of a thirty three-year-old, mostly cisgendered, mostly heterosexual, married woman rejecting motherhood that I struggled with. It was the unspeakable hypocrisy of giving up on a challenge. How could I quit now, *now*, after so many tears and so much time? To quit now would just make all that suffering for naught.

In conversations with my therapist, I discovered that one of the many things that kept me pushing against inevitable defeat long past the point where my desire for a biological family was exhausted was a narrative that suffering was a quality of goodness and strength, a key component of the story of femininity which I had heard all my life. Women suffer for beauty, for family, for work. Think about Ginger Rogers, in the old cliché (oft attributed to my personal paragon of southern womanhood, Texas governor Ann Richards), doing everything Fred Astaire did, but backward in high heels. Women suffer, and they do it with style. I worried that I had not suffered with style through my ordeal. I had gained weight, yelled at my husband, withdrawn from my friends, lied to my family, stalled on writing projects, neglected my students.

I was jealous and furious all the time. My thoughts were nasty. I wanted to be one of those ducks serenely floating on the surface but paddling like mad just underneath (another cliché attributed to another tough lady I could not effectively emulate, Eleanor Roosevelt), only I kept making these ugly, rage-filled splashes. I wasn't, as Eleanor also quipped, a tea bag that showed its hidden strength in hot water. I boiled dry. I was no Steel Magnolia, risking it all for "twenty-minutes of wonderful." I wilted. In the stories I heard and witnessed, suffering was a chance to grow, a chance to prove your worth, a chance to be purified and made whole. It had nearly broken me.

I spent a lot of my time with my therapist thinking about metanarratives I had internalized, and since my day job at the time was moving a book about southern identity and authenticity to press, I could not help but connect the dots. There was something specifically southern in the lore about enduring suffering. From *Steel Magnolias* to the Lost Cause mythology, southerners are presented as beset on all sides with adversity and still just on the cusp of a return—all with hair that is holding up beautifully.

This book is based on a principle of pleasure and the basic assumption that to avoid suffering is no less noble or brave than to drive directly into it. I feel the urgency of pleasure and the need to interrogate the purpose of suffering. It may seem naïve to focus on pleasure in what may well be the twilight of the Anthropocene. Perhaps if pleasure were as serious an undertaking as suffering, we'd find ways to end the suffering of our fellow beings that much faster.

May all beings be happy and free, and may my life contribute in some way to the happiness and freedom for all.

ACKNOWLEDGMENTS

Not long after I began to formulate this project, I interviewed Catherine Keyser for an episode of the podcast *New Books in Food*. Cat described her book *Artificial Color: Modern Food and Racial Fictions* as "a project of pleasure." Cat explained: "My academic career thus far has followed the things that I get the most enjoyment out of . . . I tend to tackle topics that people think of as unserious and then try to recuperate the urgency of those pleasures." I thank Cat for lending me that phrase "the urgency of pleasure," for demonstrating the seriousness of literary food studies, and for showing me how to let the pleasure of curiosity drive my professional agenda.

Thanks go to Jamie Birdwell-Branson, Tyler Branson, and James Chase Sanchez who were there when I discovered that the three articles that I was failing to complete on our writing retreat were really three chapters of a book. Jamie stood with me at the Big Post-It with a Big Sharpie and helped me form the outline that has never changed since it emerged perfect and whole in that Airbnb in Detroit. Thank you, friends.

Thank you, Erica Abrams Locklear, for agreeing to be my long-distance writing partner midpandemic, even though we still have not managed to meet in real life. Thank you for being my first reader for many parts of this project and offering your brilliance. Thanks to the many panel and event organizers who have given me a chance to share this work in progress at conferences and lectures: Michal Choinski, Marzena Keating, Molly McGeehee, Courtney George, Brita M. Thielen (twice!), Emily Whittington, Evangelia Kindinger, Alice Julier, Wesley Beal, and David A. Davis.

Katie Keene and Emily Bandy at UPM have been a pleasure to work with. Thank you for taking on this project with so much enthusiasm and shepherding it so efficiently into print, and thanks always to the reviewers whose thoughtful feedback shaped the final product in vitally important ways.

Special thanks go to my partner, Jay Tippen, who has fed me ever so many dinners during this season. To my parents Eddy and Joburta Helms and my sisters Melinda Huddleston and Andra Vaughn, who all gracefully let me skip family Christmas to finish this manuscript. To my parents-in-law, Philip and Pamela Tippen, who make me believe that food can be love language after all.

UNPALATABLE

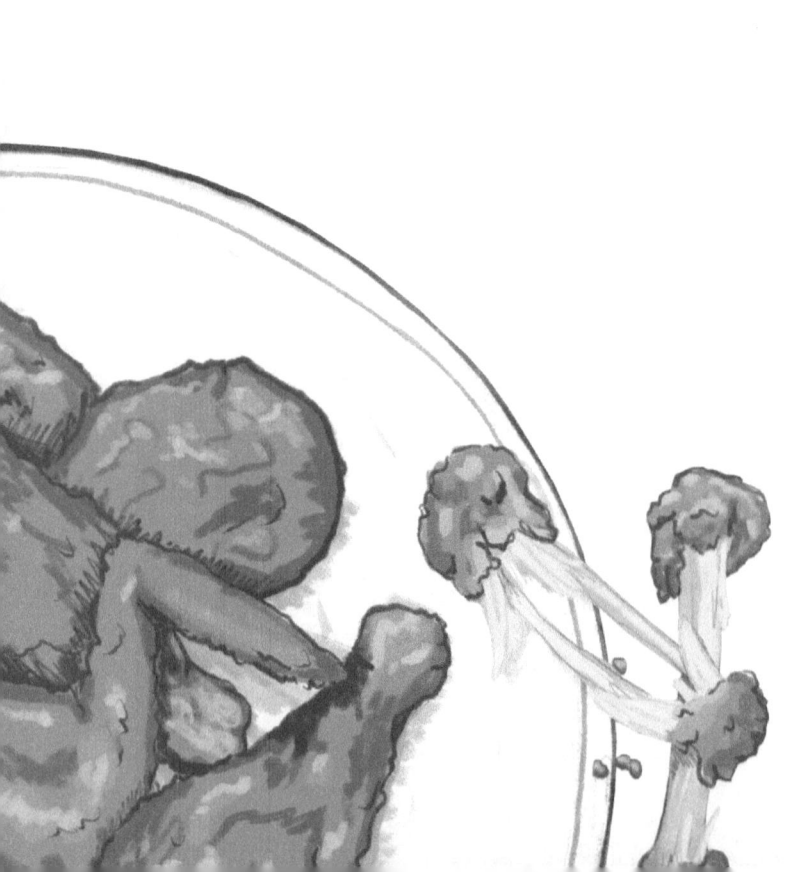

"PARTY WITH A PURPOSE"
Celebration, Suffering, and Social Justice

In a literature course I call "Food and American Identity," I assign an unusual pair of texts from the anthology *Hunger and Thirst* edited by Nancy Cary. The first is a prose poem called "Suicide," by Trissy McGhee. The speaker addresses the deceased person directly in apostrophe, describing the process of finding out about the death, gathering with family to mourn, and eating and drinking with loved ones while the dead person "no longer needs anything, just some time and a place to dissolve." The grotesqueness of the dead body is placed alongside tactile descriptions of preparing shortbread: "I press beads of butter between my fingers. At the viewing, I touch your arm plumped with Perfect-tone." The feeling of butter between the fingers is immediately connected to the feeling of dead flesh; the mourner's need for food to function is contrasted with the dead body's peace that is past physical need. The speaker of the poem bakes joylessly, almost automatically like so many other things that happen in the poem to the speaker's body, now "a dumb thing ... to be fed and watered." At the conclusion of the piece, the mourners eat the shortbread and drink whiskey by the casket, an irreverent reflection of the sacrament, tasting the blood and body of Christ, toasting whiskey and eating the cookie that has reminded them of the flesh of their loved one. The speaker invites the dead person's spirit to "follow the crumbs" of these cookies back to the places where their loved ones live, where the spirit will be invited in for tea (239).

The second text is a recipe for shortbread provided by the author of the preceding poem. "Selina's Shortbread" directly follows the poem in the anthology after a turn of the page. The "note" at the bottom of the recipe indicates, through a reference to McGhee's grandmother's suggestion that the dough be made by hand, that this is the recipe for the same "Gram's shortbread" from the poem. The ingredients are few, and the process is relatively simple. "Knead, knead, knead," the speaker of the recipe urges, echoing the theme of "needing" from the poem. The final instructions in the recipe say to "take a bite and then sip a bit of whiskey or tea. Repeat" (240), mirroring the final scenes of the poem, eating the cookies while drinking whiskey and inviting the ghost to tea.

I present these texts to my students with a question: Do you want to use this recipe? I ask them what they would think about while making the shortbread. Would they be replaying the scene from the poem in their heads? I ask them if they'd think about how dead bodies might feel to the touch. Would they ever touch butter in flour again without thinking about dead bodies? They quiver with disgust; their faces show it. I ask them what the shortbread would taste like, how it would feel in their mouth. I think about a line from the poem: "everything turns to ash in my throat" (239). I imagine that pasty feeling of a rich but dry cookie sticking to my teeth, the roof of my mouth, the sides of my throat. I can't even imagine swallowing. I ask them: If you served this shortbread to guests, your family, your coworkers in the break room, what would you tell them about where it came from? This is usually where the morbid sorts get excited. They see themselves shocking and horrifying their friends, seeing the joke play out. The rest conclude that it wouldn't be polite to present this suicide shortbread and its story in a place of business. Why is this so weird?

I cannot imagine this pair of texts occurring together anywhere else other than a *literary* anthology on food and drink. They mimic the conventional cookbook page of today: a short, personal narrative headnote followed by a list of ingredients and a procedure for preparation. Though the prose-poem-as-headnote breaks convention by addressing an audience that is not the reader, it does use a second-person pronoun that is typical of cookbook construction. And yet, everything about it seems wrong, almost perverse, for a cookbook. That turn of the page from poem to recipe may be an accident of publication, just how the pages fell when placed in the layout, but it creates a feeling of surprise, something completely unexpected to follow the poem, another tiny shock to the system after the emotional ride of the poem. When have you ever seen a recipe follow a poem about the violent death of a beloved person? Just imagine a cookbook of recipes, each accompanied by stories of suicide and mourning with no optimistic turn towards healing. Or, if you prefer, a book of stories about death and grief, each paired with a recipe that does not intend to make you feel any better about what you've read. It would defy the central defining feature of most American cookbooks as a celebration of cuisine or culture and instructions for pleasure, success, or improvement.

Until I began this project, this was something that I felt rather than understood. Cookbooks are fun to read and browse, fun to talk about, fun to give and receive and collect. Of the cookbook plot structures and themes that Anne Bower identifies in her taxonomy in *Recipes for Reading*, all are oriented around success and pleasure, whether it is the plot of "integration," the attainment of social acceptance and cultural achievement (38), or "differentiation," the celebration of the unique aspects that separate a group from the dominant culture (40). "One of the most consistent and enduring plots in community cookbooks," according to Bower, is "the plot of moral or religious triumph" (43) with instructions for the reader to share in this character improvement. Bower argues that the recipe is itself a predictable narrative of success: a mere list of scattered ingredients transformed into a harmonious final dish, the ordering of chaos into "voila!—a dish to please the tummy and the tongue" (37).

With their rhetorical focus on convincing readers to cook and eat along with the narrator, cookbooks are typically more oriented toward pleasure and convenience as persuasive strategies than toward pain and responsibility (Warren Belasco's "culinary triangle" of identity, responsibility, and convenience is another key concept I use with my students to talk about food choices [7]). Though some cookbooks do seek to convince readers to use recipes aligned with their moral and ethical convictions (think of the now-classic *Diet For a Small Planet* from 1971 or Calvo and Esquibel's *Decolonize Your Diet* from 2015), many more appeal to readers through gorgeous glossy photos, delicious sensory descriptions, and assurances that cooking their recipes will lead to pleasures at the table and in their relationships to others. *The Joy of Cooking* remains a perennial favorite for just this reason, promising joy right there in the title. Contemporary cookbook readers have come to expect a story from their cookbooks wherein they may play the role of a coprotagonist with a wise guide on a path to pleasure, whether that pleasure comes from cooking and eating or just imagining those processes. The conventions of the cookbook genre prime readers for pleasure.

I felt this orientation to pleasure while writing my first book, *Inventing Authenticity: How Cookbook Writers Redefine Southern Identity*. I suggested in that book that one of the central tensions in new southern cookbooks is a general squeamishness about discussions of the past that might bring up painful subjects like slavery, poverty, violence, and other injustices. I considered that the pain might be felt by white southerners in the form of guilt or shame, but it could just as easily be felt by southerners of color in the form of rage or grief, another in the myriad of micro- and macroaggressions that alienate them from the metanarrative of (white) southern history and identity. I argued that this discomfort leads writers away from narrating a "burdensome" southern history in recipe origin stories as the primary method for suggesting authenticity, leaning instead on the "smaller" and more pleasant histories of family networks and personal memories. One of the basic assumptions of that book is that southern cookbook writers cannot rely solely on history and tradition for evidence of authenticity because the southern past can be too painful, too potentially alienating for an essentially persuasive genre. It seemed obvious to me then that the cookbook—especially a southern cookbook—needed to minimize pain to reach its intended audience.

In fact, popular southern food culture garners a great deal of criticism for being ahistorical or apolitical, avoiding difficult subjects, whitewashing the past, or rushing to a naively optimistic vision of a "welcome table" where southern food is a great equalizer and unifier. In the summer of 2020, the Southern Foodways Alliance (SFA) came under fire with public calls for its long-time director, John T. Edge, to step down. *The New York Times* headline from June reads: "A White Gatekeeper of Southern Food Faces Calls to Resign." Though Edge and the SFA are praised in the article for being founded on a "subversive" mission to "help heal a tortured racist history" and for taking (sometimes awkward or halting) steps toward amplifying diverse voices in southern food (Severson, "White Gatekeeper" par. 5), many of the people calling for Edge's resignation cite too much celebration and not enough critical engagement as key problems with the organization's practices. Though large events featured BIPOC chefs and writers, some participants like Asha Gomez felt the spectacle of the event clouded the more noble purpose of the gatherings. Gomez told the reporter, "You are a prop in what felt like a dog-and-pony show" (qtd. in par. 33). Toni Tipton-Martin, author of *The Jemima Code* and the first working president of the SFA, argues in the article that the annual symposium had lost its focus on critical engagement in favor of celebration: "The party with a purpose that we created left attendees with the idea that something powerful had happened, but *it didn't hurt*. Over the years it morphed into the party appearing to be the most important thing. I understood the slope we were on" (emphasis mine, qtd. in par. 56). Critique implies pain; it should *hurt* to look closely with *purpose*. There is the possibility of a "party with a purpose" that balances celebration with examination, but Tipton-Martin notes that the pleasure of the party has overshadowed that critical engagement.

The charges that southern food writing in general, and the SFA in particular, are too celebratory are not new. In a 2017 profile of Edge and the SFA, also written by Kim Severson, under the headline "A Powerful, and Provocative, Voice for Southern Food," Severson notes that "Even some fans find his take on Southern history wrapped in too much romance, his style too ego-driven or his perspective sometimes skewed by his race, gender and power" (par. 7).

Severson describes the annual Symposium as "the organization's version of a Burning Man festival," but acknowledges that all the food and fanfare are "presented with a wry twist and academic scaffolding, and always with an eye on larger social issues" (par. 18). Many of the same critical voices from the 2020 article show up in the 2017 article, raising many of the same concerns with "blind spots" (Purvis qtd. in par. 8) and difficulties of grappling simultaneously with a brutal southern past and white/male privilege. As Marcie Cohen Ferris succinctly summarizes: "There are many ghosts and ancestors that tap on his shoulder, as they do particularly all white Southerners, and he has to learn to push them into place" (qtd. in par. 12). Critics of southern food culture continuously call for more critical engagement with the more painful parts of the region's past and present, finding the emphasis on pleasure to be somewhere between a distraction and an insult.

In Severson's 2017 article, Scott Romine points to exactly why cookbooks and popular food media often do not take on the darker parts of history: "Think about the bodies that died in those South Carolina rice fields.... You don't want to pay $12.99 for heirloom Carolina Gold rice if that's the image you have behind it" (qtd. in par. 24). If the goal of a cookbook is ultimately commercial—to sell cookbooks, establish a chef-author's brand, drive traffic to their restaurant, encourage readers to buy certain products, as well as offer a path to pleasure—then it would be counterproductive to that mission to remind readers of the bodies in the rice fields without also offering them a way forward into a pleasant present. Similarly, in his chapter from *Ecocriticism and the Future of Southern Studies*, Daniel Spoth critiques both southern food media and southern foodways scholars for seeing in food discourse "what they—and, potentially, their readers—*want* southern foodways to represent: a fondly recalled, unproblematic communion with the landscape" (131; see also Spoth's 2023 book *Ruin and Resilience: Southern Literature and the Environment*). Spoth argues that these narratives don't stay in their bound pages but influence environmental policy by "obscur[ing] the centuries of poor environmental stewardship that preceded" the new wave of farm-to-table southern chefs (132). While it seems clear that acknowledging the suffering of the oppressed, including the degradation of the environment, is the right thing for a writer to do, building an identity around suffering without overcoming (whether your southern forebears were experiencing or inflicting it) is hardly a successful marketing tool.

Much cookbook criticism—my own included—has read the southern cookbook genre's emphasis on pleasure and celebration as naivety at best and willful ignorance at worst. However, it is not my contention that pleasure is a uniquely southern invention to solve a peculiarly southern problem. As

I will explain in the following chapter, the cookbook genre encourages the erasure of pain through its orientation toward pleasure. Pleasure is at the core of the cookbook as a genre, regardless of its regional affiliation. Therefore, all cookbooks must negotiate with pleasure and pain, fantasy and reality, nostalgia and history, as they attempt to convince readers of their rhetorical purpose. Southern cookbooks may be naïve in their representation of the pleasures of food, but they are not uniquely or even especially so.

However, cookbooks of the contemporary South must negotiate a unique tension between the cookbook genre's essential requirement for pleasure with the South's essential narrative of pain. How they choose to balance these contradictory essences is up to each cookbook author and responds to their particular rhetorical purpose for writing. The underlying assumption of Romine's argument in the quotation above is that the essential experience that defines Carolina Gold rice is pain: human bondage and the forced labor and death of Black people. All the other pleasurable experiences of rice cannot stack up against the burden of pain enough to move the needle of rice's essential meaning. The overarching narrative of the US South is often one of pain, loss, privation, exploitation, poverty, and suffering of all kinds. Consider the great southern invention of the blues, a tradition steeped in suffering and expressing pain through music. Or the South's most loved and hated media shorthand *Gone with the Wind*: a story of a great fall followed by an even greater climb, marked all along with loss. Consider William Faulkner's *oeuvre* and imagine Quentin Compson rehashing the tragic tale of Thomas Sutpen and muttering to himself in "the iron New England dark" of a Boston winter that he doesn't hate the South (303). Think of Flannery O'Connor's cavalcade of grotesques. Of the apocalyptic hellscapes of AMC's *The Walking Dead* and the first season of HBO's *True Detective*. Literary and literal stories of the southern past are marked with physical and psychic pain. Though scholars of the US South recognize that "'South' is an imagined location, an inherently unstable unit of space" and "each 'South' is the creation of a particular historical moment," (Guterl par. 1), Matthew Pratt Guterl argues that the imagined South of the 1950s and 60s "when this place seemed most monolithic and uniform" was a place of exceptional suffering:

> This particular South was assumed to be sexualized, tropical, and horribly violent; it was the low-slung id to the North's preening superego. It was, most of all, a melodramatic conflation of the antebellum slaveholding South with the South of Jim Crow, featuring Bull Connor's wild dogs and water hoses, and bloodied young black men and women, all battling for their lives in a location whose borders

were presumed to be unchanged from the days of the old Confederate States of America. (par. 2)

The history of slavery, white supremacy, violence against people of color, poverty, and intellectual "backwardness" that characterizes the imagined South described by Guterl intersects with a history of literary renaissance and culinary innovation. At the same time that white landowners kidnapped and enslaved Africans for their own profit, people who were enslaved innovated some of the most famous dishes of southern cuisine (chronicled thoroughly in Kelley Fanto Deetz's *Bound to the Fire*). While the South imagined by today's cookbooks is created in a different moment, the New South necessarily responds to this violent old South, even as it attempts to define itself in opposition to it. To write about new southern food is to invoke a history of suffering, even if the purpose of writing is to represent an "unsuffering" present.

This is where I left the discussion of suffering in my first book. Two unexamined assumptions are at work here: first, that a cookbook was created for pleasure in some essential way so that talking about pain would be antithetical to its very nature, and second, that southern history and culture are so defined by suffering that they are incompatible with the cookbook genre. Of course, the continued existence and popularity of southern cookbooks and other food media is proof that they are not, in fact, incompatible, but that they require a certain amount of rhetorical skill to navigate in ways that would be acceptable to an audience. To make an argument for southern authenticity, then, a writer must encounter and resolve the paradox of a suffering South in a pleasure-oriented genre.

In the next chapter, I return with a more nuanced approach to my original thesis that the rhetorical function of cookbooks cannot accommodate stories of pain. First, I interrogate the assumption of the connection between the cookbook and pleasure on the most basic genre level. Rather than accepting this premise at face value, I present in this chapter an interdisciplinary theory about the rhetoric of pleasure in the cookbook genre and the way that this orientation toward pleasure affects readers' expectations and constrains writers' choices. Being oriented to pleasure does not compromise the genre's ability to resist and subvert oppressive norms or dominant ideologies. In fact, as Sherrie Inness has argued, the very nature of the cookbook as "trivial" or "domestic" means that the genre can transgress norms without catching the attention of unintended audiences who might be critical of the messages (4). Therefore, contemporary writers of southern cookbooks have a choice to follow convention and present narratives of the southern past without struggle or to resist that convention and address past pain that continues to manifest in the present.

The rest of this book seeks to answer just one question: If pleasure is so important to the cookbook genre, why do southern cookbook writers bother with stories of suffering? If my theories of the genre are viable, then it follows that the admission of suffering into a cookbook narrative is an optional authorial choice, one that may open up a writer to a dangerous rhetorical exercise that could misfire. Given the cookbook genre's need to deliver pleasure, it is significant that southern cookbooks make any mention of past pain, even (or perhaps especially) if that pain results ultimately in pleasure. While these stories of suffering often find easy resolution in the delights of the kitchen, which may strike some audiences as undermining the force of that suffering, the presence of suffering at all is a significant departure from convention worthy of examination.

The expectation that cookbooks and other popular southern food writing would abandon the celebratory convention of the genre altogether is unrealistic. Black, Indigenous, and other people of color in the South could not be true to themselves (the only definition of authenticity that I believe is possible or desirable) without the rhetorical option to speak the truth of their painful experiences to powerful audiences. Nor should these writers be hesitant to highlight their own creativity, resilience, and strength of character and culture. There are also examples of white cookbook writers who are resisting conventions and using the acknowledgement of suffering of BIPOC communities as an opportunity to make space for reconciliation, reparation, or apology for past wrongs. Current tensions notwithstanding, John T. Edge writes in "Debts of Pleasure," a 2013 article for *Oxford American*, "To do good work in the world of Southern food, I've come to believe, we have to start by paying down the debts of pleasure we owe to the men and women who sustain our society" (par. 19). Edge is specifically talking about unnamed and unacknowledged kitchen workers and waitstaff, mostly people of color, past and present. Their suffering (and creativity) has made the pleasure of consuming southern food and food discourse possible, generating a debt that must be paid through recognition, storytelling, humility, and gratitude. For white southerners especially, the final step in paying down that debt may be the most expensive one of stepping aside. While John T. Edge is still listed as part of the SFA staff as "Founding Director," he is literally at the bottom of the list. Melissa Booth Hall and Mary Beth Lasseter, interim codirectors, sit at the top ("Staff"). Still, the very fact of naming suffering in a cookbook narrative may be an act for social justice that subversively defies conventions of the genre.

With its baked-in mandate to give pleasure, the genre of the cookbook doesn't lend itself easily to nuanced discussions about suffering. When writers do talk about suffering in southern cookbooks, it tends to take the form of overcoming or moving past pain, ultimately finding pleasure in food and the performance of an authentic identity. While some critics have read these narrative moves as minimizing or erasing real pain (and perhaps some writers have had this intention in mind), it is possible to see both the moments of suffering and the turn to pleasure as unique windows to explore southern identity-creation.

An examination of these rhetorical strategies may open up possibilities for cookbook writers to find new models for paying down "the debt of pleasure" accrued by the suffering of so many. Is reconciliation best accomplished over narratives of shared suffering or shared pleasure? Is it possible for suffering and pleasure to exist simultaneously without one overshadowing or undercutting the other? How might southerners grapple honestly with suffering and pleasure at once? This investigation is at least partially my own search for the best models that we might hold up to the cookbook publishing industry as exemplars of the kind of arguments that could satisfy the very real concerns of scholars, the conventions of the genre, and the expectations of cookbook readers all at once. On the other hand, part of my responsibility is to identify storytelling techniques that undermine the reality of that painful past in ways that are harmful or even violent. How might storytelling—both stories of suffering and stories of pleasure—be a tool for not just truth and reconciliation but reparation?

The following chapters examine the complex negotiation of the genre's expectations of pleasure and the region's identification with pain in some specific categories of suffering: slavery, segregation, and ongoing racial violence; poverty, scarcity, and resourcefulness; gendered divisions of labor and physically painful agricultural and domestic work; grief, death, and loss; and diabetes, heart disease, and obesity represented as an illness. In each category, the distinctly southern experience of this kind of suffering is mediated through the genre's expectation of pleasure. How do cookbooks use these stories of suffering to define an "authentic" southern experience or identity, and what are the implications of accepting or rejecting this narrative as essential to southern identity? How do cookbooks turn that story of pain into moral triumph or the pursuit of pleasure to meet the conventions of the genre?

In the chapter "'A Lot of Past to Reckon with': Grappling with Slavery and Racism," I tackle the most obvious and ubiquitous story of southern suffering which garners the most criticism in southern foodways scholarship. This chapter examines narratives written by white writers and writers of color who discuss the suffering of slavery in the past and racism in the present in order to discover the variety of rhetorical approaches to accepting or rejecting slavery as an "authentic" southern experience. While chattel slavery was never practiced exclusively in the US South, slavery has left an indelible mark on the region, its culture, and its identity, becoming an essential characteristic of the South and a symbol of "authenticity." As Rafia Zafar argues in *Recipes for Respect*, a headnote explaining that a dish was invented by enslaved cooks or contains ingredients that enter the cuisine through African slave trade suggests that a historical origin in the practice of slavery is evidence of a distinctly southern dish (18). One of the most serious critiques leveled at southern cookbooks is that texts by white writers and chefs erase, obfuscate, or minimize a history of slavery in the South, which means erasing the contributions of Black southerners to southern culture (and by extension, denying them membership in the regional identity) as well as erasing white southerners' complicity in slavery and ongoing racial discrimination and violence. Scott Romine's comment above about ignoring the bodies in the fields to sell expensive rice is characteristic of this criticism. I leveled a similar charge myself in *Inventing Authenticity*. The cookbook genre's rhetorical orientation towards pleasure explains why cookbook writers would want to eliminate slavery entirely from their narratives, but it does not explain why southern cookbook writers choose to reference slavery as a painful era in the South's past when they do not have to. It is in these narratives that we see some of the most egregious examples of using the suffering of the past for present profit as Romine suggests, but I also discover some examples of writers who are purposefully using these moments as opportunities for truth and reconciliation.

Like slavery, poverty is not exclusive to the South, but poverty became associated with the South in popular imagination through the photography of the Farm Services Administration and Works Progress Administration of the New Deal era, through Robert Kennedy's life-changing "poverty tour" of the Mississippi Delta in the 1960s, and pop culture touchstones like *The Beverly Hillbillies* and White Trash Cooking of the 1980s. The chapter "Making Do: Pain of Poverty and Pleasure of Resilience" examines stories in contemporary cookbooks that describe southern food traditions born of poverty (like hoe cakes, moonshine, or foraged greens), now "upgraded" for fine dining. Cookbook writers also draw on stories of past poverty, their own and their ancestors', as evidence of their personal connection to "authentic" southernness. These stories are supported by visual cues that connect to a recognizable history of southern poverty through material objects like mason jars, homespun fabric, distressed wood, and cast iron. I argue that markers of suffering in southern poverty have been repurposed for communicating a form of "down home" southern "authenticity" that rejects the pretensions of contemporary gourmet food culture which have led to distaste for the term "foodie" and its connotations of exclusion. The stories of suffering in poverty turn toward pleasure through narratives of upward mobility, perseverance, resilience, and resourcefulness. The combination of stories and images in these cookbooks suggests a down-home unpretentiousness that links simplicity, age, and personal connection to southern authenticity. While some stories of poverty romanticize dire conditions without moving to relieve them, I examine other narratives of poverty where the turn to pleasure may also offer a model for resisting a capitalist system through social entrepreneurship, sustainable living, and valuing working-class knowledge and skills.

The third chapter, "A Season of Sweetness: Gardening, Canning, and Women's Labor on Farms," addresses an aspect of authentic southern suffering that emerges from questioning my own personal relationship to southern womanhood and suffering. Popular representations of southern women, as in my all-time favorite film *Steel Magnolias*, tend to rely on characterizations of women overcoming suffering with silent grace and strength, patiently enduring difficulty, or actively choosing paths of pain that ultimately lead to higher pleasures. In the kitchen, women's food practices that are time- or labor-intensive draw the admiration of cookbook writers, especially the activities of gardening, tending animals, and preserving vegetables and meats. These activities are intense in the amount of planning and attention they require, in addition to heavy lifting, high temperatures, specialized knowledge, and high risk. This toil pays off, however, in delicious foods as well as security for the family when fresh vegetables are out of season. Canning and preserving—presented in these texts as essential and authentic southern practices—especially associate women's sacrificial kitchen labors with the pleasures of natural abundance and nourishment at the expense of women's physical and emotional suffering. In *Inventing Authenticity*, I briefly examined the figure of the southern grandmother as an authority in the kitchen whose culinary innovations could be used as evidence of authenticity. I return to that figure again to examine how the suffering of women can be employed as evidence of southern identity alongside their creativity, or in some cases, as the source of their creativity. Drawing on primary texts authored by writers of all genders, this chapter engages with feminist theories of pleasure and pain to examine the significance of turning women's labor into their own pleasure, not merely the pleasure of others.

"Keep Southern and Cut the Fat: Body Fat and Illness in Wellness Cookbooks" examines narratives of suffering and pleasure in cookbooks that are oriented toward weight loss or the relief of symptoms of an illness. Southern foods most often identified as "authentic" or canonical tend also to be perceived as fattening or unhealthy. Representations of the "deep-fried South," render the South as uniquely susceptible to diabetes, heart disease, and having fat bodies. In contemporary cookbooks, this "unhealthy" version of southern food is often characterized as "inauthentic," a cheap fast-food caricature of a deeply complex, vegetable-centric, naturally seasonal cuisine that has been coopted by capitalist outsiders for their own profit. By redefining the source of southern authenticity and remaking the canon of southern foods, cookbook writers suggest that the truly "authentic" southern food is a solution to the problems of poor health, not the cause of them and that southerners can experience the pleasures of good health, good food, and authentic southern identity simultaneously. In this chapter, I examine southern cookbooks focused on a "healthy" diet and reducing fat, sugar, meat, salt, and other "unhealthy" ingredients like Virginia Willis's *Lighten Up, Y'all* (2015), *Paula Deen Cuts the Fat* (2015), and *Southern Living's Slim Down Cookbook: Eating Well and Living Healthy in the Land of Biscuits and Bacon* (2013). Though this author rejects the assumption that a thin body is synonymous with good health, these cookbooks are predicated on illness, including body fat, as a specific kind of suffering in need of a unique solution that will maintain southern identity while bringing pleasure in the form of "health," the relief of symptoms, weight loss, and recovery—and almost always pleasure in the form of good flavor. While the narratives suggest that fat and illness are typical of the South (and that fat itself is an illness), they also argue that illness is not "authentic," or that health is not a threat to "authenticity." The narratives promise that readers can keep their authentic "southerness" but lose their suffering from illness without sacrificing pleasure from cooking and eating. In some ways, marking the disabled or fat body as a source of suffering undermines moves in disability studies to destigmatize illness, and especially fat, as problems in need of correction. However, it is possible to interpret the turn to pleasure in eating on the way to healthfulness as a revolution in the relationship between sick bodies and food, allowing space to consider food and taste as sources of pleasure and identity performance for all people and not exclusively as medicine or poison for unhealthy bodies.

The final chapter, "'Useful in a Fearful Time': Responding to Grief and Death in Funeral Cookbooks," examines narratives of the emotional suffering of grief and personal loss. As with other forms of suffering, southerners do not experience grief or death more often than any other region, but southerners tend to represent their funeral rituals and rites as distinct from other regions of the US. As Joshua Graham argues in "Funeral Food as Resurrection in the American South," "the handing down and sharing of funeral food recipes, lore, and memories both help maintain strong family community bonds and stave off individual social death," allowing the deceased to continue to "exert agency over and with the living" (89). Narratives about death and the dead in cookbooks invoke stories of suffering, but they "have the net effect of resurrecting the social influence of the long-dead" in ways that may have a positive effect on projects of social justice (89). I examine a niche subset of southern cookbooks that provide instructions for proper feeding, behavior, and rituals for southern funerals like *Being Dead Is No Excuse: The Official Southern Ladies Guide to Hosting the Perfect Funeral* (2013) and *The Southern Sympathy Cookbook* (2018). Cookbooks like these argue that southern funerary traditions are distinct among Americans while promising delicious food, fellowship, and the metaphorical resurrection of the dead as a balm for suffering death in a community. While these cookbooks empathetically describe the painful feelings that must accompany a death, they also offer advice and recipes to ease the social awkwardness of grief, providing comfort and a path to the end of suffering through culinary pleasure. This chapter examines both the suffering of grief and the pleasures of cooking as an embodied practice that relieves emotional pain through alimentary pleasure.

This project considers the complexities of suffering and pleasure in the context of intersectional identities, power structures, and dominant ideologies of the South. For white southerners, narratives of pleasure tend to relieve feelings of guilt and the "burden of Southern history." In many ways, all of the turns toward pleasure discussed here have the capacity to relieve white southerners of the burdens of guilt and shame: guilt for slavery, shame for poverty, pity for their grandmothers, mortification of social awkwardness in grief, and the indignities of illness. Critics of the genre suggest that these burdens of guilt are not so easily relieved by mere caloric intake, and certainly, that is correct. Implicit in the "debt to pleasure" argument is a warrant that white southerners have not earned the privilege of relief from their burdens in reconciliation until they have first spoken the truth and made reparations. Stories of southern suffering may be a place to begin speaking the truth. But they are not reparations.

The same turn to pleasure can be revolutionary for marginalized and oppressed individuals and groups. For Black southerners, taking pleasure in the contributions of their enslaved ancestors need not erase the suffering they experienced but may honor it as a valuable inheritance to build a pleasurable future. For the working poor, taking pleasure in their own resourcefulness provides a basis for pride and resistance to alienation from their work. For women and nonbinary folks, taking pleasure in physical labor and its delicious fruits is to claim territory reserved for cismen. For the grieving, taking pleasure in cooking is to practice radical self-care and reify the social influence of individuals who may have had far less power in life. For humans with sick or fat bodies, taking pleasure in eating is to resist an ableist and fat-phobic narrative that tells them to mistrust pleasure and choose self-loathing. While many of the texts I examine in this work are still problematic, at the very least they show that a market exists for a cookbook that grapples openly and honestly with the incomplete work of civil rights and social justice and resists the impulse toward potentially toxic positivity.

I no longer see the verbal tip-toeing around pain in southern cookbooks to be something disingenuous or cowardly. Instead, inviting critique of the painful past into cookbook narratives is a rhetorical choice that has to negotiate some challenging and contradictory expectations; the bravest and boldest of these acts ought to be recognized as a model for how the limits of the genre may be tested in service of social justice. For writers of southern cookbooks who are so often criticized for not speaking of suffering *enough* or for placing the party before the purpose, this framework highlights rhetorically effective moves that could serve as blueprints for speaking of suffering *more*.

WORKS CITED

Belasco, Warren. *Food: The Key Concepts*. Berg, 2008.

Bower, Anne. "Cooking Up Stories: Narrative Elements in Community Cookbooks." *Recipes for Reading: Community Cookbooks, Stories, Histories*, edited by Anne Bower, U of Massachusetts P, 1997, 29–50.

Calvo, Luz and Catriona Rueda Esquibel. *Decolonize Your Diet: Plant-Based Mexican-American Recipes for Health and Healing*. Arsenal Pulp Press, 2015.

Deen, Paula. *Paula Deen Cuts the Fat: 250 Recipes All Lightened Up*. Paula Deen Ventures, 2015.

Deetz, Kelley Fanto. *Bound to the Fire: How Virginia's Enslaved Cooks Helped Invent American Cuisine*. UP of Kentucky, 2017.

Edge, John T. "Debts of Pleasure." *The Oxford American*, 15 Sep 2013, https://www.oxfordamerican.org/magazine/item/278-debts-of-pleasure.

Faulkner, William. *Absalom, Absalom!* Vintage International, 1990.

Graham, Joshua. "Funeral Food as Resurrection in the American South." *Dying to Eat: Cross-Cultural Perspectives on Food, Death, and the Afterlife*, edited by Candi Cann, U of Kentucky P, 2018.

Guterl, Matthew Pratt. "South." *Keywords for American Cultural Studies*. NYU Press, 2007. https://keywords.nyupress.org/american-cultural-studies/essay/south/.

Inness, Sherrie. *Secret Ingredients: Race, Gender, and Class at the Dinner Table*. New York: Palgrave MacMillan, 2006.

Lappe, Frances Moore. *Diet For a Small Planet*. Ballantine Books, 1971.

Magness, Perre Coleman. *The Southern Sympathy Cookbook: Funeral Food with a Twist*. Countryman Press, 2018.

McGhee, Trissy. "Suicide." *Hunger and Thirst: Food Literature*, edited by Nancy Cary, et al., San Diego City Works Press, 2008, 239.

McGhee, Trissy. "Selina's Shortbread." *Hunger and Thirst: Food Literature*, edited by Nancy Cary, et al., San Diego City Works Press, 2008, 240.

Metcalf, Gayden and Charlotte Hayes. *Being Dead Is No Excuse: The Official Southern Ladies Guide to Hosting the Perfect Funeral*. Hachette Books, 2013.

O'Neil, Carolyn. *Southern Living's Slim Down Cookbook: Eating Well and Living Healthy in the Land of Biscuits and Bacon*. Oxmoor House, 2013.

Rombauer, Irma S., et al. *The Joy of Cooking: 2019 Edition Fully Revised and Updated*. Scribner, 2019.

Severson, Kim. "A Powerful, and Provocative, Voice for Southern Food." *The New York Times*, 9 May 2017, https://www.nytimes.com/2017/05/09/dining/southern-food-john-t-edge-profile.html?searchResultPosition=1.

Severson, Kim. "A White Gatekeeper of Southern Food Faces Calls to Resign." *The New York Times*, 29 June 2020, https://www.nytimes.com/2020/06/29/dining/john-t-edge-southern-foodways-alliance.html.

Spoth, Daniel. "Southern Foodways and Visceral Environmentalism." *Ecocriticism and the Future of Southern Studies*, edited by Zackary Vernon, Louisiana State UP, 2020, 128–39.

Spoth, Daniel. *Ruin and Resilience: Southern Literature and the Environment*. Louisiana State UP, 2023.

"Staff." *Southern Foodways Alliance*, 9 Oct. 2023, www.southernfoodways.org/about-us/staff/.

Tippen, Carrie Helms. *Inventing Authenticity: How Cookbook Writers Redefine Southern Identity*. U of Arkansas P, 2018.

Willis, Virginia. *Lighten Up, Y'all: Classic Southern Recipes Made Healthy and Wholesome*. Ten Speed Press, 2015.

Zafar, Rafia. *Recipes for Respect: African American Meals and Meaning*. U of Georgia P, 2019.

THE URGENCY OF PLEASURE
Theorizing a Rhetoric of Pleasure in Cookbooks

In the opening chapter of *I Know Why the Caged Bird Sings*, Maya Angelou writes: "If growing up is painful for the Southern Black girl, being aware of her displacement is the rust on the razor that threatens the throat" (4). The memoir places pain upfront as the defining experience of Black southern girlhood, focusing on Angelou's early life in Stamps, Arkansas, where she and her brother Bailey lived with their grandmother and uncle, separated from their mother. While Angelou describes warm memories of her loving family, the general store owned by her grandmother, and the Black community and church around her, she and her family also experience racism and the threat of violence, culminating in an evening when Uncle Willy must hide in a bin of potatoes to avoid being lynched by the KKK for some other Black man's imagined insult (17–19). After the children are reunited with their mother in St. Louis, seven-year-old Marguerite is raped by her mother's boyfriend (78–79). When the crime is discovered, her rapist is arrested, put on trial, convicted, and sentenced. He is released the same day, but then he is murdered, presumably in retribution for the crime (84–86). Marguerite blames herself both for the rape and for the man's death. In her childlike and traumatized calculus, it was her speech that cost the man his life, and in response, she stops speaking:

> I had sold myself to the Devil and there could be no escape. The only thing I could do was to stop speaking to people other than Bailey. Instinctively, or somehow, I knew that because I loved him so much I'd never hurt him, but if I talked to anyone else that person might die too. Just my breath, carrying my words out, might poison people and they'd curl up and die like the black fat slugs that only pretended. (87)

Though the memoir recounts great suffering and pain, it is also story of resilience and recovery, with moments that emphasize the kindness, love, and support of Angelou's community and family; a life-sustaining love of language, reading, writing, art and dance; and her journey to owning, knowing, and trusting herself.

Angelou's 2004 cookbook *Hallelujah! The Welcome Table* repackages some passages from Angelou's well-known memoirs along with a few new stories into a new genre accompanied by recipes. Comparing the same stories in these two related but distinct genres reveals how genre conventions make subtle differences in storytelling, especially the discussion of pain and pleasure. The chapters of the cookbook are each organized around a single narrative followed by recipes that make a menu of related dishes. The first seven narratives of the cookbook coincide with the same period of Angelou's childhood covered in *I Know Why the Caged Bird Sings*, but the stories in the cookbook are heavily edited from their original versions to emphasize pleasure and minimize pain.

For example, the cookbook chapter, "Liver to Grow On," starts with a retelling of chapter 4 from the memoir, which describes making sausage and crossing the color line of the segregated town to buy liver from a white butcher. The first three paragraphs of the cookbook narrative are nearly identical to the memoir, with a few sentence-level changes that significantly alter the tone of the story. In the memoir, Angelou writes: "In Stamps the custom was to can everything that could possibly be preserved. During the killing season, after the first frost, all neighbors helped each other to slaughter hogs and even the quiet, big-eyed cows if they had stopped giving milk" (25). The cookbook's revision assigns specific gender roles where the memoir was vague: "In Stamps, women preserved everything that would submit to the process," and "men killed the hogs and cows selected for slaughter" (45). The phrase "during the killing season" is dropped, along with the anthropomorphized and sympathetic description of the "quiet, big-eyed cows." These subtle changes remove some of the horror of animal slaughter, but they also add in some expected gender norms. The passage preserves some of the gory descriptions of women with "their arms elbow deep in the [raw] ground meat" and "blood popp[ing] to the surface" of salted hams, but these are wrapped around with delicious descriptions of "choices on the shelves that could set a hungry child's mouth to watering. Green beans, snapped always the right length, collards, cabbage, juicy red tomato preserves that came into their own on steaming buttered biscuits, and sausage, beets, berries and every fruit grown in Arkansas" (*I Know* 25, *Hallelujah!* 45). The pleasures of the senses are highlighted in the cookbook while the suffering of animals is minimized.

The major differences between these two versions of the story concern the children's unaccompanied trip twice a year to the butcher in the white part of town at Momma's insistence that the growing children should have fresh, not preserved, meat. In both genres, Angelou describes crossing that line into "whitefolksville" (a phrase only used in the memoir, 25) as a frightening experience: "We were explorers walking without weapons into man-eating animals' territory" (*I Know* 25, *Hallelujah!* 46). The cookbook records the indignities of waiting to be served last, even after a Black maid or cook because "her order was intended for white people" (46). The story in the cookbook ends with the children crossing "back across the white zone I considered a frozen tundra" and into "the black residential area where every house seemed to sing 'Welcome' and on to the store and Momma and the hot skillet" with its delicious smells of frying bacon and onions. Momma and Willie sacrificially take smaller portions of meat for the good of the young, growing people, and the narrator speculates in the final line of the essay: "we chewed and swallowed it, and it helped us to grow, and maybe it did make us into better human beings" (46). Though the cookbook story addresses a moment of fear and discrimination, the stakes seem to be low. The children never actually encounter the "man-eating animals" that they fear. The prejudices that they meet with are dehumanizing and personally painful, but they aren't enacted by any particular person or with any particular malice. The butcher serves them eventually. No blood or tears are shed. They are rewarded with familial love, and any suffering is ultimately character-building, making them healthy, strong, "better human beings."

In the memoir, however, this story ends with the narrator speculating on the inhumanity of white people. Angelou is much clearer about the sources of the fear the children experience:

> In Stamps the segregation was so complete that most Black children didn't really, absolutely know what whites looked like. Other than that they were different, to be dreaded, and in that dread was included the hostility of the powerless against the powerful, the poor against the rich, the worker against the worked for and the ragged against the well dressed. I remember never believing that whites were really real. (25)

Even as a child, Angelou can sense that the "differences" of race and racism are artificial, exaggerated, and unfair. She notices that white people's underwear (and therefore the body parts they cover) are just like Black people's.

Even as a child, she isn't fooled into internalizing the racism she experiences. But while the cookbook's story highlights the temporary and easily soothed dehumanization of the Black children, the memoir dehumanizes, flattens, and stereotypes white people:

> I couldn't force myself to think of them as people . . . Whitefolks couldn't be people because their feet were too small, their skin too white and see-throughy, and they didn't walk on the balls of their feet the way people did—they walked on their heels like horses . . . These others, the strange pale creatures that lived in their alien unlife, weren't considered folks. They were whitefolks. (26)

The cookbook provides a narrative of overcoming suffering that ends with the pleasures of family and home. The memoir provides no such pleasant resolution. The narrator emerges from her encounters in whitefolksville embittered and more aware of and irritated by the pointlessness of segregation and racism. She has taken up the weapon white folks used to justify ignoring her and turned it on them, making them not-people, not real, not worth thinking about.

Why can't the cookbook story end this way? I think the short answers are genre and audience expectations. The long form of the memoir invites sustained meditation on difficult subjects; the short form of the recipe headnote may clip attention to nuance. Memoir readers expect to be challenged; cookbook readers expect to be pleased. While the cookbook title invokes the "welcome table," the passage from the memoir purposefully and quite literally alienates white readers. As genres, the cookbook and the memoir have much in common. *Hallelujah! The Welcome Table* intentionally aligns itself with the memoir genre through the reminder of Angelou's reputation as memoirist on the cover, identifying her explicitly as the author of *I Know Why the Caged Bird Sings*. The subtitle of *A Lifetime of Memories with Recipes* foregrounds memory before recipes, suggesting the primacy of the stories. *Hallelujah! The Welcome Table* rejects standard cookbook organization around courses of a meal in favor of a chronological order around story making it structurally more like a memoir than a cookbook. Finally, the intertextuality of the cookbook text with the memoir signals just how similar the conventions of the personal narrative recipe headnote are to the personal narrative essay. Still, the memoir and the cookbook remain very different rhetorical situations, as evidenced by the editorial changes to this passage for its new genre and audience.

In this chapter and as a foundational premise of this book, I argue that pleasure is a convention of the cookbook genre and an agreement between readers and writers which makes the genre essentially distinct from all other lifewriting genres. Further, I contend that cookbooks promise many types of pleasure with high-stakes consequences: not merely the pleasure of good tasting food, but also the promise of intangible social and cultural capital that may have significant effects on the lived experience of cookbook readers and users. Finally, combining theories of genre from rhetoric and literary studies with theories of pleasure and suffering from women's and gender studies and other fields, I argue that these high-stakes pleasures serve as a meaningful form of resistance. Theorizing a rhetoric of pleasure in cookbooks posits the interplay of suffering and pleasure not as a contradiction, backpedaling, or folding to the pressures of an uncritical audience, but as a rhetorical strategy for delivering important messages of resistance into unexpected, and until recently, underexamined places.

PLEASURE AS GENRE REQUIREMENT

Many of the earliest scholars of cookbooks connected the genre to life writing, memoir, and autobiography as a way to understand cookbooks as literary and historical documents (see Lynne Ireland's 1981 essay "The Compiled Cookbook as Foodways Autobiography," Anne Bower's 1997 collection *Recipes for Reading*, and Janet Theophano's 2003 monograph *Eat My Words: Reading Women's Lives Through the Cookbooks They Wrote*, and many more). This link to memoir and autobiography has been a useful entry point to making ostensibly nonliterary texts legible and acceptable to literary scholars. Genre theories in the field of autobiography and life writing are also helpful in thinking critically about the cookbook as a genre related to but distinct from memoir.

In addition to the formal similarities between the narrative passages of most of today's cookbooks, which focus on the memories of their first-person author-narrators, and long-form memoir or personal essay, the relationship between cookbook writers and readers is analogous to the "autobiographical pact" theorized by Phillip Lejeune in the 1970s and built upon by scholars of autobiography and memoir. The autobiographical pact describes an unspoken agreement between the writer, publisher, and reader that by labeling the text "memoir" or "creative nonfiction," or by having a first-person narrator with the same name as the writer, the writer and publisher are offering a true representation of real people and events, as best as the writer is able to remember. The reader, then, agrees to believe that the story is true and that it is being told in good faith, even as the reader allows the writer freedom to dramatize and fill in the gaps of imperfect memory. This agreement creates the "paradox at the heart of memoir," as G. Thomas Couser argues: the more fictional tools a writer uses (dialogue, setting, scene), the more realistic and believable the memoir appears (80). The autobiographical pact baked into the genre—an unspoken agreement that essentially distinguishes narrative nonfiction from narrative fiction—allows the writer the flexibility to fictionalize and dramatize for effect, while readers "acknowledge that the memoir's reliance on memory renders it fallible" (81). As long as the writer is using their imagination in good faith, in service of that capitalized Truth, then the reader agrees to suspend their disbelief when appropriate. If the reader will give the writer latitude to report an entire conversation in dialogue or describe a setting that they most certainly are recreating from an unreliable memory, the reader will be rewarded with a pleasurable reading experience that engages their imagination and access to Truth.

A similar kind of agreement seems to be at work in the cookbook. In order for the cookbook writer to win the trust of the reader, both parties have to agree that the contents of the cookbook are "true," in the sense that the formulas supplied will lead to the outcomes described. The writer is offering recipes in good faith, and the reader can take them at face value, assuming that what is presented as fact is fact: that subjecting flour, sugar, fat, and eggs to heat will produce cake. Pleasure is also a key part of the agreement. The reader can trust that following the procedures will lead to safe and delicious food. Even though the cookbook writer may use metaphor to describe the taste of a dish or hyperbole to convince the reader of the superlative ease of the recipe, the reader must believe that the writer would not intentionally give the reader formulas that are harmful, disgusting, or scientifically impossible. Like a memoirist, the cookbook writer dramatizes and embellishes but does not lie. A cookbook that lies will fail. A cookbook that does not promise or provide pleasure will fail. Implicit in the genre is an agreement that the reading experience will pay off in pleasure.

The autobiographical pact in life writing exists because readers of memoir and autobiography are encouraged to alter their attitudes and actions based on the lessons that they intuit from their reading. Benjamin Franklin's famous autobiography (1793), oft touted as the model on which the whole of the American memoir tradition is built, is certified by letters from friends begging him to put his life story into print so that the youth of the new republic might follow his example for self-improvement. It is important to the reader that the story be True in case they decide to change their very lives in response to their reading.

Perhaps the only genre where a reader is more likely (and literally) to change their lives after reading is the cookbook. Cookbooks often begin with similar claims that someone else wants or needs this information more than the writer wants to provide it for their edification and pleasure. Angelou's dedication addresses "O [maybe, Oprah?], who said she wanted a big, pretty cookbook. Well, honey, here you are" (vii). Jennifer Cognard-Black writes of the "embodied rhetoric" of the recipe and the unique ability of the recipe to turn from mere text to an emotional and physical experience, taking the text into the body and making it part of the reader's character and constitution. When a recipe is "actually cooked and not just read about, the material world beyond the text is changed—fiction becomes reality.... A reader doesn't just imagine herself or himself as a cooking character in this setting of kitchen things. A reader actually becomes that character" (Cognard-Black 39). Even though the actual cooking experience rarely lives up to the idealized representations in cookbooks, the stakes in this performance are high. Recipes may be taken into the body, and the stories that accompany them may be taken into the character of the reader. They may become the center of social rituals like family meals, or over time may even become disconnected from their original source and identified with the cook as a part of their persona.

The promise of truth and pleasure creates the trust between writer and reader that makes it possible for the reader to become cook and participate in the drama of the recipe. Without narratives, a collection of recipes would still come with an unspoken assumption of pleasure, but the narratives and text around the recipes make those promises of pleasure explicit, building an argument on the ethos of the speaker, hailing the audience and attempting to persuade them with strategic appeals. Violation of this trust in memoir leads to scandals so infamous the name of the offending party becomes a shorthand warning to avoid the pitfalls of the genre (i.e., James Frye). Violation of this trust in a cookbook renders that book obsolete as a usable technical guide (admittedly its primary purpose) or as a script for a social performance or a marketing tool for its creators. It might continue to function as an art object, a status symbol for semipublic display in the home, or an imaginative reading experience, but then it becomes some other genre, no longer a real cookbook.

A TYPOLOGY OF PLEASURES

Though the genre of the cookbook is clearly designed to give pleasure "to the tummy and tongue," as Anne Bower writes, this is not the only pleasure promised by the genre. Implicit in the cookbook genre is an agreement that the reading experience will pay off in at least one of many kinds of pleasure: delicious food, an entertaining process, an impressive social display, happy fellow diners who give the cook their love and respect, a delightful imaginative experience that is at the heart of reading as a practice. Special subgenres of cookbooks may also explicitly promise control over body weight and appearance, the relief of symptoms of an illness, moral superiority through ethical behavior, self-confidence in mastering a new skill, connection to a distant culture or community, the seamless appearance of belonging or assimilation into a desired community. I will examine some of these pleasures in the following pages, moving from the more concrete to the more abstract. To organize this discussion, I'll draw examples from a wildly popular recent American cookbook, Samin Nosrat's *Salt, Fat, Acid, Heat*. I've chosen this book almost at random from my shelf to be representative of the genre as practiced in the United States to demonstrate that the expectations to center pleasure are not unique to southern cookbooks which will be the focus of the rest of the book. Nosrat is not doing anything particularly special with pleasure here, though the rhetorical purpose of the book may lead her to emphasize certain pleasures over others, like any author would tailor the genre to their particular persuasive goals. From this example we may be able to generalize about the genre.

THE PLEASURE OF FLAVOR

Most obvious among the pleasures promised by a cookbook is delicious food. While the precise meaning of "delicious" is subjective, all cookbooks—through implication or direct statement—promise that the recipes they provide will taste good. They may even use superlatives in the titles and headnotes that promise it will taste the best, the most, the truest. The first words of Nosrat's introduction to *Salt, Fat, Acid, Heat* are: "Anyone can cook anything and make it delicious" (5). Nosrat may be more attentive to flavor and taste than some other cookbooks because the premise of the book is that these four elements—"salt, which enhances *flavor*; fat, which amplifies *flavor* and makes appealing *textures* possible; acid, which brightens and balances *flavor*; and heat, which ultimately determines the *texture* of food"—are key to perfectly preparing just about anything (5, emphasis mine). Nosrat claims these principles will show readers "which ingredients to use, how to cook them, and why last-minute adjustments will ensure that food tastes exactly as it should ... allow[ing] all great cooks ... to cook consistently delicious food" (5). Nosrat describes how her training at Alice Waters's famed California restaurant Chez Panisse prepared her to discern what is delicious and how years of experience and experimenting taught her how to achieve it: "The idea of making consistently great food had seemed like some inscrutable mystery, but now I had a little mental checklist to think about every time I set foot in a kitchen: salt, fat, acid, heat" (9). These four "compass points," Nosrat says, "have set me on a path to good food every time I cook" (10). While I already accept as a part of the cookbook compact that the author won't try to trick me into eating bad-tasting food, the cookbook writer purposefully declares these intentions to deliver great taste to solidify that trust through the promise of pleasure.

THE PLEASURE OF PROCESS

A second level of pleasure promised by cookbooks is an enjoyable cooking process. The ends are delicious, but the means to those ends will also be pleasant on their own. Nosrat explicitly promises a lot of pleasure in the journey of learning to cook her way: "You'll find yourself improvising more and more in the kitchen. Liberated from recipes and precise shopping lists, you'll feel more comfortable buying what looks best at the farmer's market or butcher's counter, confident in your ability to transform it into a balanced meal" (5). These good feelings have nothing to do with the way the food tastes, but in how the cook feels about the process of cooking and about themselves as competent cooks. Creativity, liberation, trust in your instincts and abilities, inspiration: all of these pleasures come from the process of reading and using this cookbook. Nosrat is perfectly clear in the "How to Use This Book" section: "Remember to have fun! Don't forget to enjoy the pleasures, both small and large, implicit to cooking and eating with people you love!" (13). A statement like this is typical of almost any cookbook. Even in cookbooks that take a more negative stance on cooking as a practice, like the famous *I Hate to Cook Book* by Peg Bracken (rereleased in a 50th anniversary edition in 2010) and the more recent *What the F**K Should I Make For Dinner* by Zach Golden (2011), there is a promise that cooking will be more tolerable, if not pleasant, if you use these books as guides. Golden's introduction acknowledges that while cooking "in addition to being a necessary activity can be a hell of a lot of fun," the unpleasant part is choosing what to cook. His cookbook provides the solution to eliminate this unpleasantness through a choose-your-own-adventure-style guide to browsing, while also making the reader laugh at the grumpy tone of the instructions and the blue comedy of titles like "Eat my balls, and if that doesn't sound appetizing, try some fucking Roast Chicken" (14) (if you find that sort of thing funny). Readers are encouraged to imagine themselves having a pleasant experience before they ever begin cooking in order to persuade them to make that leap from consumers of a text to producers of food.

THE PLEASURE OF TASTE

Most cookbooks are based on the assumption that the reader is cooking for an audience of more than oneself. Unless the book is explicitly about cooking for one or possibly two (like Anita Lo's 2018 book *Solo: A Modern Cookbook for a Party of One*), the assumption is that the reader is seeking guidance from the cookbook for making an impressive social display of taste in the kitchen—an abstract form of pleasure rarely promised explicitly in cookbook texts. Even if all of the diners are related members of the cook's household and not guests from outside the home and immediate family, there is an element of displaying and performing identity as those familial bonds are defined and solidified through commensality. Scholars have long understood the kitchen and dining room as semipublic spaces in the home where the domestic meets the social. Sociologist Angela Meah figures the kitchen as part of an "emotional geography" of the home, where "the materiality of the kitchen figures as crucial in processes of identification, negotiation, and relationality" and where "one's sense of being in the world is magnified rather than diminished" (56). Urszula Niewiadomska-Fils borrows from Mary Lousie Pratt's definition of a "contact zone" to argue that the eating and food preparation spaces of the home may be thought of as a place where "disparate cultures meet, clash, and grapple with each other, often in highly asymmetrical relations of domination and subordination" (Pratt qtd. in Niewiadomska-Fils 40). Alice Julier's sociological study, *Eating Together: Food, Friendship, and Inequality* explores the kind of meals where a cookbook would be the most helpful: communal meals shared with people from outside of the family unit in the family home. These "social meals" create conditions where differences in gender, race, and class may become more visible. As Julier explains:

> The meals and relationships they describe are tied up in particular understandings of difference and inequality, understandings that emerge from the historical and contemporary configuration of gender, race, and class.... Put simply, people with greater access to resources that accrue from gender, race, and class privilege have access to more variety and more nutritionally rich food and can focus on the meal as a *social accomplishment* rather than a necessity. (3, emphasis mine)

When we figure a meal as a "social accomplishment"—as the public display of taste and distinction as defined by Pierre Bourdieu—and as an extension of privilege and power, the high stakes of the cook's performance become clear. Bourdieu includes "cookery" in the list of areas where "cultural competence" can be "revealed in the nature of the cultural goods consumed, and in the way they are consumed" (13). Taste is on display at mealtimes whether the meal is reinforcing and reproducing taste within a closed family group or openly performing for friends and strangers welcomed into the cook's home. Communal eating is necessarily social, though Bourdieau is wise to remind us that the food itself is not responsible for making meaning: "Most products only derive their social value from the social use that is made of them" (21). The rituals of dinner establish and elaborate hierarchies of power in any group. A meal cooked in the home distinguishes those who labor from those who benefit from labor, those whose tastes are considered and those whose tastes aren't considered.

Much is at stake in this kind of social performance, especially for the cook who may be displaying the whole family's class status or ethnic and cultural identity to guests whose reactions may have far-reaching consequences. In these moments of high-stakes, semipublic, social performance, a home cook might look to the authority of a chef-authored and commercially published cookbook for a script that would help them minimize and obscure differences and inequalities. Bourdieu suggests that taste in cooking, like taste in cosmetics, clothing, or home decor can be "opportunities to experience or assert one's position in social space, as a rank to be upheld or a distance to be kept," becoming part of an "art of living" that communicates class (57). This kind of taste education might look like a cookbook that demonstrates how to cook gourmet food cheaply to hide a lack of cash resources, or it might explain the proper way to serve a dish to prevent the cook from making an error in manners that a "true" member of that class would have absorbed through exposure. To be received as legitimate that taste must erase its acquisition and appear as "the practical affirmation of an inevitable difference," since "each taste feels itself to be natural" (56). Perhaps less charitably, the cookbook script could help a cook to subtly exaggerate and reify their social superiority by demonstrating "natural" taste.

Drawing on the concepts of capital and distinction first established by Bourdieu, Peter Naccarato and Kathleen Lebesco define "culinary capital" as a set of food-related practices that signal social status. Culinary capital explains "how and why certain foods and food-related practices connote, and by extension, confer status and power on those who know about and enjoy them.... As individuals assert the value of certain dietary preference and food practices over others, they engage in the quest for culinary capital" (4). Cookbooks function as a source of culinary capital as well as a manual for deploying that capital in a social performance. They provide the information to "know about" food, the words to say to deploy that knowledge, and the promise to "enjoy" it.

The process of turning cookbook text into cultural and social capital is made possible through storytelling and performance. In addition to instructions for performance in the kitchen through recipes, cookbooks provide a script for the reader-user to perform at the table through narrative headnotes. The headnotes give the cook something to say as they place the dishes in front of their dinners. A good story preinterprets the meaning of the meal for the diner, allowing the cook to control the outcome of the social interaction with storytelling, even if they cannot always fully control the outcome of subjecting ingredients to cooking. The cook might simply mention the book or famous chef they got the recipe from, thereby reinforcing the "culinary capital" as it borrows the ethos of the source to lend credibility and status to the meal. Perhaps another promised pleasure of the cookbook genre is pleasant conversation, the confidence of knowing what to say in awkward social situations, a way to understand a meal as a pleasurable community experience.

Nosrat is not particularly explicit about how cooking in her way can impress diners in a social situation, but she does offer a lot of text that a reader can use in this kind of conversation. "Insider" information about how professional chefs cook might become culinary capital in the form of specialized knowledge or "a bit of sophistication" that nonprofessional cook-readers can "bank and invest later in a social situation in which it is important to raise your stature," to borrow a phrase from Lisa Heldke's *Exotic Appetites* (16). Nosrat delivers the most impressive scripts in passages about the science of cooking. The first chapter includes five pages on the types of salt including illustrations of the crystal structures (21–25), followed by a full page describing the differences between *taste* and *flavor* and how "salt helps release the flavor molecules that are bound up in the tomato's proteins" causing it to "taste more intensely of tomato" (26). An extended discussion on osmosis and diffusion, under the title "How Salt Works," explains how salt affects different proteins and vegetables on a cellular level (29–37). The illustrations also add to this cerebral view of cooking. A table comparing the measurements of different kinds of salt needed to reach equivalent salt flavor delivers a lot of information, but the table is colorful and hand drawn to take some of the intimidation out of the wall of numbers. The kind of scientifically informed cooking in Nosrat's cookbook isn't new (the home economists and domestic scientists of the late nineteenth and early twentieth centuries knew as much), but readers of *Salt, Fat, Acid, Heat* can use this scientific information to demonstrate their vast knowledge of food to their diners in an impressive display of culinary capital.

Whether scientific knowledge about how cooking works, cultural knowledge about how certain groups of people eat (i.e., Nosrat's "World of Flavor" wheel in the center of the book [194]), or the social capital of appearing to share a personal social network with Samin Nosrat, the capital mined from the raw material of a cookbook can be invested in social situations to increase one's status in the group. Not a small amount of pleasure accompanies social belonging, and certainly, avoiding the pain of broadcasting perceived social inferiority and "poor taste" is a hard-earned kind of pleasure.

THE PLEASURE OF AFFECTION

A related abstract pleasure in cooking for an audience is the opportunity to give and receive love and affection. In this admittedly cynical-sounding analysis, affection becomes a subset of social capital, a "sentimental currency." I borrow this term from other literary scholars who describe sentimental currency as feelings or expressions of emotion that might be exchanged for economic security and support. For example, in "Marketplace Transactions and Sentimental Currencies in Fanny Fern's *Ruth Hall*," Jennifer Harris argues that the "ideology of separate spheres" and "Cult of True Womanhood" that pervaded nineteenth-century America left women with little access to economic capital or any valuable social capital to exchange for money, as evidenced by Ruth Hall's inability to enter the marketplace as a young widow and her near total dependence on the financial support of her in-laws and her father. Ruth's upbringing, though, has given her a surplus of sentimental currency and soft skills like decorating, cleaning, and flower arranging that would help her to earn affection and approbation from a partner. As Harris explains, this market of sentiment fails Ruth, whose domestic labors cannot earn the affection or support of her in-laws, father, or brother after her beloved husband dies. Sentimental currency may never replace the buying power of actual currency or protection under the law that would grant equal access to economic capital, but it's not nothing, either. In her successful marriage, Ruth's domestic labor earned her a great deal of love and pleasure, and had her husband lived, she could have found satisfaction and safety in that economy for life, Harris suggests.

Twenty-first-century food culture is not a direct analogy to nineteenth-century domestic fiction, but the concept of sentimental currency aptly describes what happens when we think about "cooking with love" as both a social transaction and a pleasure-centered experience. Just as Ruth Hall labored to make a pleasant domestic space in exchange for the love and protection of her husband, contemporary cookbooks promise a script to perform a domestic task that will ensure an equitable exchange: a labor *of* love *for* love. No doubt this is a cynical way of thinking about the transaction, but it is one that elucidates the high social stakes. In *Salt, Fat, Acid, Heat*, Nosrat focuses narrowly on how the cook will feel about themselves when they cook her way (self-love is still love, as Anita Lo's cookbook-for-one suggests), but implicit in all the discussions about good cooking and delicious food is the idea that you'll be "cooking and eating with people you love!" (13). This implied promise of receiving love might show up as the explicit promise of other people's pleasure: a recipe with something for everyone, a crowd pleaser, something even picky children will eat. The implied logic is something like this: your diners will love the food, and they will love you for giving it to them.

There is pleasure in showing love without the expectation of return, but in the market of sentimental currency, one of the pleasures of cooking for others is getting their love, respect, and appreciation in return. However, just as this economy of feelings fails Ruth Hall and reifies an inequitable and oppressive system of gender segregation, sentimental currency in twenty-first-century food culture has the same potential to misfire and perpetuate harmful gendered roles and expectations. Essayist Sarah Miller writes about the precarious exchange of food for love in a personal essay alternately titled "Cooking for Others Can Be Selfish," and "Why Cooking Sucks." The premise of the essay is that the author is frustrated with cooking and the pursuit of culinary perfection, especially because that perfection doesn't seem to matter to the people she is cooking for. Miller writes about a particularly disappointing dinner: "When I finally went to bed after hours of cooking and cleaning up, having achieved absolutely nothing—having impressed no one, including myself, with the food I made—I said to my boyfriend, 'Cooking is really stupid'" (par. 3). By highlighting its absence, Miller articulates the kind of sentimental pleasure that is promised by cookbooks but not at all guaranteed in the act of cooking. Cookbooks as a genre may offer a pathway to earning the love of others, but in reality, the exchange depends much more on the actions of the diners than on the performance of the cook. Miller equates the vulnerability of cooking for others to that of sex:

> For each [cooking and copulation], you put the very core of yourself out there in a very pointed attempt to give someone a one-of-a-kind sensual experience, and to differentiate yourself, to declare, "Please

notice and appreciate my singular talent," and when at your urging they sample and reject, well, it is not good. (par. 9)

Miller makes explicit the risk inherent in cooking to receive affection when she describes her mother's frustrated attempts to win her family's love and attention by baking perfect pies. "The prize was not the pie but being the wonderful person who had made the pie," Miller explains, "and this seemed like a stressful situation, as you could guarantee the existence of the pie, but not sufficient praise and attention as to make the pie worth creating" (par. 17). In the end of the essay, Miller gives up cooking as too risky, too inefficient of a method for receiving love, particularly from unreliable and unfaithful partners (par. 29–30). But cookbooks broadly suggest that there is a method for success that will ensure that the product will be so good that praise will have to be forthcoming, and the process will be easy enough that the amount of sentimental currency earned will be commensurate to the amount of effort put in. While Miller's essay concludes that these promises of earning love through cooking are delusions, the essay also suggests that the delusions are powerfully convincing and hard to shake from metanarratives of what it means to cook.

Nosrat's insistence that the simple rules in *Salt, Fat, Acid, Heat* will make cooking easier and more instinctual includes this promise of pleasure in the form of happy diners. The science of cooking advanced by Nosrat seems also to imply that the risks Miller describes can be mitigated. "You can make anything taste good," Nosrat encourages. "Keep reading, and I'll teach you how" (11). In "How to Use This Book," Nosrat directly addresses new cooks, reassuring them that they "will quickly catch on to the basics—each element is organized by its flavor and its science, guiding you through both the *whys* and the *hows* of good cooking" (12). The implication of scientific cooking is that it is not mysterious. Though Nosrat retains the drama and romance of food that seems miraculously delicious in narratives, she reveals quickly that the miracle is easily discovered. Why did simple lunches at the beach taste so magically good? Salt (19). Why does food in Italy taste so different in each region? Fat (58–59). What appears to be ineffable and intangible *terroir* is actually very simple and not at all a secret to those who are paying attention. Part of the appeal of making cooking easy and enjoyable is to increase the likelihood of a good return on emotional investment: minimal risk, minor investment, predictable product, outsized returns. Good food is not a mystery; there is a guaranteed path to success. The reader-user can make a pie (or roast chicken) worth creating that is all-but-guaranteed to make them the wonderful person who made the pie.

THE PLEASURE OF IMAGINATION

On the continuum of concrete to abstract pleasures, perhaps the most abstract is the pleasure of a delightful imaginative experience. The pleasure of any kind of reading is the pleasure of imagining the text that is unfolding in front of you. Those people who keep cookbooks on their nightstands and coffee tables as well as kitchen shelves know that there is a kind of pleasure to be taken in reading something that asks a reader to tap into their visual, aural, tactile, and olfactory sense memories to build a scene in the movie of their mind. In an article from *The New Yorker* titled "The Pleasures of Reading Recipes," food historian and critic Bee Wilson describes the delights of reading "stories of pretend meals" in the recipes—including both the headnotes and the procedures—that the reader has no intention of ever attempting to make:

> Don't be fooled by the fact that they are written in the imperative tense (pick the basil leaves, peel the onion). Yes, you might do that tomorrow, but right now, you are doing something else. As you read, your head drowsily on the pillow, there is no onion, but you watch yourself peel it in your mind's eye, tugging off the papery skin and noting with satisfaction that you have not damaged the layers underneath. (par. 1)

The recipe itself, Wilson argues, is a "story arc" oriented toward pleasure and a happy ending from "the tricky early prepping stages via the complications of heat and measuring before you arrive at the point of happy closure where the dish goes in the oven or is sliced or served" (Wilson par. 6). There is a distinct kind of pleasure in imagining yourself as capable and effective, a hero in the story arc of the recipe. The recipe form encourages this kind of audience participation in the role of protagonist of the narrative.

Like all cookbook authors, Nosrat writes using the imperative mood and the personal pronoun "you," implicitly and explicitly hailing the audience as an active participant. In a section titled "Balance, Layering, and Restraint," Nosrat instructs the reader in the process of creating a meal. Not only does that passage make the reader the subject of sentences and protagonist in a scene, it is also jam packed with adjectives:

> Garnish soft comfort foods with crunchy crumbs, toasted nuts, or crisp bits of bacon to make things interesting. Serve rich meats with bright, acidic sauces and clean-tasting blanched or raw vegetables. Serve mouth-drying starches with mouth-watering sauces, and recognize that a well-dressed, juicy salad can serve as both a side dish and a sauce. . . .

> Pair delicate ingredients that could easily be overwhelmed with clean, bright flavors—light broths, tender herbs, a squeeze of citrus at the end, no browning. Think of spring peas and asparagus, delicate salmon or halibut, or a salad of summer fruits. Other times, the weather, the season, or the occasion demands depth of flavor: aggressive browning of both the aromatics and the meat in a braise, rich stocks, cheeses, mushrooms, anchovies, and other savory ingredients rich in umami. (195)

Nosrat directly invokes imagination: "Think of spring peas." I quote at length to offer my reader a chance to experience the pleasure of reading directly. Notice how the compounding of sensory descriptions affected you, reader. Nosrat certainly provides much for the reader to imagine, especially in her attention to descriptions of flavors and textures.

Similarly, Nosrat invites the reader to imagine themselves successful and independently confident. "These are the four notes of the culinary scale; learn your way around them," Nosrat advises. "Verse yourself in the classics, and then begin to improvise like a jazz musician, putting your own spin on the standards" (200). The book is meant to be only a temporary guide to accessing the instincts of a trained chef: "These resources are kind of like training wheels: use them until you feel comfortable cooking without them. Then abandon them, using only the four elements of good cooking as a guide. They are all you will need" (200). Imagine yourself in the ecstasy of an improvising jazz musician or the freedom of flying downhill on a big-kid bike. These are the equivalent pleasures of cooking with confidence, but *imagining yourself feeling them* is a shadow of that pleasure.

It's a fun read. Cookbooks rarely state outright that they hope you like reading these "pretend stories," or that you'll enjoy all the adjectives and metaphors they'll use, but that pleasure is implied by the strategies that writers use to make their recipes and recipe narratives stories that can be executed in the mind as well as the kitchen. Twice Nosrat encourages readers to read the whole book beginning to end before attempting to cook from it (12, 193), though she admits that demanding that kind of linear reading is not expected from "your typical cookbook" (12). In the center of the book is a gatefolded page with a decision tree titled: "What Should I Cook?" The first question is "Have I read this book?" and if the answer is "no," the reader is instructed to do so: "Ok. I get it. But this book is really about the journey, not the destination, so maybe stop trying to skip ahead in life and head back to the beginning. XO" (193). Though clearly this is meant as a gentle joke (the kiss and hug at the end to balance the acid with sweetness), the message is that cooking may be the end result of reading this book, but it is not the first priority of the writer. In fact, there are only four recipes before page 224 in a separate section: "Part Two: Recipes and Recommendations." The recipe section is preceded by an orange page with a white handwritten note: "and now that you know how to cook . . ." (201). The implication is that you have learned to cook by reading about and imagining cooking. The recipes are almost superfluous: training wheels to be discarded (12, 200). Though of course her purpose in writing is that you will be the hero of actual cooking, much of the book is set up to foreground reading and imagining as pleasures on their own.

Certainly, the balance of text is toward nonrecipe text. The kind voice of the encouraging narrator is itself pleasant. In part one of the book, each element has only a single recipe represented visually in a two-page spread with hand-drawn illustrations and handwritten instructions. The tone of these four recipes is more humorous than the more formal and traditionally formatted recipes in part two of the book. "To Make a Mayonnaise and to Fix a Broken Mayonnaise" is particularly conversational and purposefully entertaining as a reading experience. The first step to fix a broken mayonnaise is to "Stop. Take a deep breath. It happens to everyone" (87). The speaker of the recipe follows this gentle encouragement with more direct instruction: After adding "the hottest water your tap can muster" to a clean bowl, the cook should "start whisking like your life depends on it. Then, just like you did earlier with the oil, add that sad, broken mayonnaise, *drop by drop* and for heaven's sake, *keep whisking*. Then when you've whisked about ½ of the mixture, ask yourself, 'Is this working?'" (emphasis in original, 87). The recipe is clearly meant to be instructional and useful to the mayonnaise maker, but the writer has chosen to deliver it here in a method that is both artistically appealing to the eye with hand-drawn lettering and graphics and artfully appealing to the reader with a creative voice and tone. While Nosrat is explicitly positioning *Salt, Fat, Acid, Heat* as a utility text, she also instructs us to experience it as a pleasurable literary text first.

Returning for a moment to the example from Maya Angelou's cookbook that started this chapter, it is easier to see now why Angelou's story is altered as it moves between genres. What pleasures does the text promise in exchange for our trust? Both the cookbook and the memoir emphasize pleasant smells, tastes, and textures. Those are preserved across the genre line. Neither suggests that butchering animals to make sausage is fun or easy, but the cookbook narrative lowers the stakes for the process of shopping for liver in a segregated southern town. While it seems that feeding the children liver is a way for Momma to show concern for her grandchildren's physical growth, the cookbook highlights her maternal affection and concern for their moral growth, as well. What the cookbook offers that the memoir does not is a script for performance. The reader can both perform the recipe in the kitchen and retell the story at the table. The cookbook provides a script for making the exchange of food for social capital (I am well read and have intimate knowledge of an important cultural figure like Maya Angelou) or sentimental currency (you should love me for giving you this food like Angelou loves her grandmother for giving her this same food). Though Angelou does not attempt to make a hard sale of liver's delicious flavors and textures, there is still pleasure in the emotional and imaginative experience. Anything that would distract from that pleasure (i.e., the reminder of dead and bleeding animals or the cruelty of white people inflicted upon Black people) is not unexpectedly minimized. While cookbooks become with each passing year more attuned to the pleasures of reading, the genre is still primarily oriented toward the eventual move into the kitchen, and Angelou's cookbook narrative simply offers more pleasure than the memoir's narrative. Cookbooks are unique not only in the conventions of the genre but in the relationship of speaker to reader and story to reality, and so cookbooks must be evaluated based on how an individual writer chooses to negotiate with these unique genre conventions and expectations.

Taken together, I've outlined a framework that prepares us to better appreciate why pleasure is a key element of the cookbook genre as well as the high stakes of those pleasures. The act of reading and using a cookbook is an interactive experience between a writer and a reader that is special among genres of informative and imaginative writing. In exchange for the reader's trust and intimate participation in the story of the text, cookbooks promise pleasure, explicitly in their persuasive statements and implicitly in their rhetorical purposes. Those pleasures are personal and social, as small as an entertaining reading experience and as important as securing the love of a partner or belonging in a community. They are concrete and abstract, visible and invisible, some lasting just as long as it takes to read the page or digest the meal and some indelibly shaping how the cook is seen in the world. It is easy to dismiss cookbooks and other recipe texts as pleasant ephemera, but thinking of the genre-deep pleasure pact with the reader in this way reveals that there is also serious business at work in these delights.

THE URGENCY OF PLEASURE: PLEASURE AS RESISTANCE

To be clear, being oriented toward pleasure does not compromise the genre's ability to resist and subvert oppressive norms or dominant ideologies. In *Secret Ingredients: Race, Gender, and Class at the Dinner Table*, Sherrie Inness argues that cookbooks have a long history of hiding the "recipes for revolution" in plain sight: "Cooking literature teaches lessons about race, class, and ethnicity; none of these issues is absent from a cookbook, including one that might appear to be nothing more than a collection of recipes" (3). Though Inness admits that cookbooks may be complicit in "perpetuat[ing] socially conservative and traditional roles for women and men" (3), she argues that "cooking literature plays more political roles than we might assume" by "promulgating certain agendas, while undermining others" (4). The very nature of the cookbook as "trivial" or "domestic" means that the genre can transgress norms without catching the attention of critical audiences. The orientation toward pleasure can be a convenient carrier for subversive messages, including messages about human suffering, who may bear responsibility for that suffering, and how that suffering may be alleviated.

The idea of pleasure as resistance is already firmly established in feminist theories, though typically associated with sexual pleasure as a resistance to patriarchy, especially cisgendered women's experience of pleasure in heterosex, prioritizing or insisting on her own pleasure (over reproduction or her male partner's pleasure), or being an agent of her own pleasure. Even admitting the existence of her pleasure has been presented as a revolutionary act that resists and undermines oppressive gender roles for women. Michel Foucault posits in *History of Sexuality* that the repression of sex is the negation of pleasure and that revolution and pleasure go hand in hand:

> What sustains our eagerness to speak of sex in terms of repression is doubtless this opportunity to speak out against the powers that be, to utter truths and promise bliss, to link together enlightenment, liberation, and manifold pleasures; to pronounce a discourse that combines the fervor of knowledge, the determination to change the laws, and the longing for the garden of earthly delights. (7)

In two monographs, *Queer Political Performance and Protest: Play, Pleasure, and Social Movement* and *Play, Creativity, and Social Movements*, Benjamin Shepard explores the ways that social movements use music, dance, word-play, improvisation, humor, absurdity, and a carnival-like atmosphere of fun (sometimes including food) in public protests, demonstrations, and political actions. Shepard argues that play and pleasure have the effect of binding protesters together in a common feeling of joy and inviting "once-passive spectators" to join. However, Shepard is clear in his conclusion:

The fun of social change works best as part of a holistic approach to organizing which includes a clear goal or question, a great deal of research on an issue, accompanied by a coherent approach to communicating a goal, mobilization around it, a legal strategy, direct action to achieve it, and sustainability strategies to keep the campaign going. Here, play is but one ingredient of a larger mix of strategies which help create power. (*Play* 261)

Pleasure alone, in the sheets or in the streets, is unlikely to dismantle power on its own. But the nature of play and pleasure are disarming and destabilizing, working as rhetorical appeals and easy-to-accept invitations into allyship.

Critical race theory and Black feminism also offer a strong foundation in imagining pleasure as a subversive tool. In these fields runs a current of theorizing about what it means for people of color to dare to express feelings of love or joy, or to seek pleasure, while simultaneously acknowledging the reality of pain and suffering, especially as a result of systemic racism. In their examination of expressions of "Black Joy" in online spaces, Jessica H. Lu and Catherine Knight Steele outline a myriad of strategies for "everyday resistance" among African Americans practiced historically and in the present, including music and singing, signifying and word play, and humor and satire that critique and resist dominant structures of power (825). In researching the hashtags #carefreeblackkids, #carefreeblackkids2k16, #freeblackchild, #blackboyjoy, and #blackgirlmagic, Lu and Steele find that the use of these hashtags peaked in response to publicized acts of racism as "intentional acts of resistance to mainstream news cycles demonizing Black children and proliferating coverage of Black death" (828). The authors conclude, "The joyful posts shared via these hashtags celebrate Black life in ways that challenge mainstream media's attempts to fix Black people and Black life into a position of death and despair; assert Black people as fully human, capable of experiencing and expressing a full, dynamic range of emotion; and capture, share, and circulate expressions of Black life without concern for the white gaze" (829). Expressions of Black Joy as resistance are not intended for white audiences, but, as Lu and Steele argue, make meaning to other Black viewers and readers.

Javon Johnson similarly posits that the visibility of Black pain in media often has the consequence of benumbing audiences and flattening the conversation to "bottom line blackness" (180) that erases nuance: "I do not want to think about invisibility and inaudibility as antithetical to visibility and audibility. The in/visibility and in/audibility of Black pain are often one and the same" (178). If publicizing pain does not ensure visibility, then publicizing joy may be an antidote. In his essay, "Black Joy in the Time of Ferguson," through an examination of his own experience and through a survey of contemporary Black poetry, Johnson figures Black joy as one of many responses to state-sanctioned violence: expressing fury in poetry, marching in street protests, and experiencing the joy of falling asleep listening to music "because I wanted to be happy and black." Johnson figures Black joy as a productive resistance:

> More than a method to endure, however, black joy allows us the space to stretch our imaginations beyond what we previously thought possible and allows us to theorize a world in which white supremacy does not dictate our everyday lives. . . . In this way, black joy provides another set of political tactics to "make do" and use the in/visibility and in/audibility of black joy as a site with which to operate outside of white supremacy. (180)

I will return to these ideas of Black Joy as resistance in the following chapter as I examine stories of slavery in southern cookbooks, but the possibility of pleasure as an effective tool for social justice begins here.

Johnson and Lu and Steele all emphasize that these expressions of joy only work as resistance when they come organically from Black creators and circulate among Black audiences. Whether pleasure is protest or propaganda depends entirely on its rhetorical situation: who is speaking, to whom, and to what ends. Indeed, as all of the voices above remind us in chorus, pleasure is but one tool in the protester's arsenal. It is an energizing force that may carry on a movement, as Shepard explains. Pleasure alone is unlikely to topple regimes, but its value as rhetorical tool for resistance and protest in the hands of oppressed groups remains undervalued and under examined.

Taking joy in food, cooking, and eating may be one method for resistance to oppression. Psyche Williams-Forson, writing about African American foodways, suggests that Black women's narratives about food and its meanings are a method for exercising power in culture:

> In their ability to control the "symbolic language of food," and to dictate what foods say about them and their families, women often negotiate the dialectical relationship between the internal identity formation of their families and the externally influenced medium of popular culture. In this way, they protect their families against social and cultural assault as well as assist in the formation and protection of identity. (92)

Celebration of food as delicious and culturally valuable can be a way of building solidarity and distinction that can extend to other art forms and arenas. Forson positions this identity formation as a defense against assault from the outside and a prevention of suffering as well as a pleasure on its own.

Building from these strong backgrounds in feminist theory and critical race studies, we can begin to see the cookbook's orientation toward pleasure as potentially subversive. However, it also seems clear from these foundations that the effect of pleasure as resistance depends mostly on the identity and intentions of person wielding it. Particularly in the US South, where eliding the suffering of the past means silencing people of color, make no mistake: emphasizing white pleasure at the expense of Black pain is a cultural violence that reproduces and naturalizes white supremacy. It is this kind of pleasure-centered erasure by white writers that rightfully earns the ire of food writing's critics and scholars. For some white writers and some cismale writers, taking pleasure is at best an expected outcome and at worst a gross kind of victory lap. The cookbook genre encourages erasure of suffering through its orientation toward pleasure. This project will unflinchingly confront those moments of racism, sexism, and classism as they appear.

Being oriented to pleasure does not disqualify the cookbook genre as a whole as a meaningful tool for resistance in the hands of other writers with other rhetorical goals. For writers of color and women writers, the act of acknowledging pleasure of any kind is already a kind of resistance, a kind of protest that acknowledges their value. To skip over suffering may be a way of claiming a more powerful high ground for making an argument about their valuable contributions to cultural and regional identity. The poet Judith Ortiz Cofer described this rejection of suffering in Latinx women as a gender-neutral *macho*: "the arrogance to assume that you belong where you choose to stand, that you are inferior to no one, and that you will defend your domain at whatever the cost" (4). Cofer is talking about the right of women to claim the space and time to write and create art rather than submit to martyrdom by subsuming themselves in family responsibilities and caretaking. But I think it applies here, too. To assert a right to pleasure (sometimes known as "the pursuit of happiness") is to lay claim to belonging in the body politic. To assume that pleasures are urgent, important, and vital to the project of equity is to assume a position not on the suffering margins but in the powerful center of authority. By contrast, narratives of suffering begin the story by reminding the audience of a time when the speaker was marginalized or powerless, without the authority to speak. Skipping that suffering and beginning the story with the assumption of a completed victory places the speaker in that powerful position of belonging where they choose to stand as a self-authorized voice.

In short, silence about suffering in cookbooks or any other medium is not always an erasure or aporia that needs to be filled; sometimes it is a rhetorical strategy for establishing the ethos of the speaker, for identifying with the audience, and for recruiting allies in the fight. The analysis that follows will examine the rhetorical possibilities for resistance and persuasion that are opened when speakers in cookbooks choose pleasure over or alongside narratives of suffering.

SUFFERING AGAINST GENRE EXPECTATIONS

The question at the heart of this project is about how writers work within the cookbook genre's expectation of pleasure to discuss the reality of pain. We have established that pleasure is a convention of the genre and that pleasure itself can be a significant act of resistance when used strategically. However, just as interesting to this study are the moments when writers break conventions to discuss pain and suffering. In a genre so controlled by convention like the cookbook, it is hard to break expectations and keep connection with the audience. How and why would cookbook writers address past pain when the conventions of the genre do not call for it?

When I have floated the idea of a cookbook of suffering in conversations and conference papers, people remind me of *In Memory's Kitchen: A Legacy from the Women of Terezin*. The collection, published in 1996 and edited by Cara De Silva, is made up of recipes, poems, and letters composed by Mina Pachter, a woman who was interned in the Jewish ghetto/concentration camp of Terezin or Theresienstadt during the Nazi occupation of Chekoslovakia. There is evidence that the recipe collection may have been a collaborative project of many women who were confined together (xxix), but the archive of material was bequeathed from Pachter to be delivered as a personal and cultural inheritance to her adult daughter Anny who fled to Palestine (xxv). The recipes represent foods that could not have been available to Pachter and her fellow prisoners at that time, instead comprising memory foods and aspirational foods. "Born out of the abyss," De Silva writes in the introduction, "it is a document that can be comprehended only at the farthest reaches of the mind" (xxvi). De Silva identifies many such collections of fantasy-recipes, reporting that this common practice of remembering foods and imagining their preparations had a name in internment camps: "cooking with the mouth" (xxix). De Silva argues that thinking, discussing, and writing about food was an important defense against the humiliations, deprivations, and dehumanization of occupation. De Silva cites a number of survivors who agreed that imagining the pleasures of food helped them survive (xxviii).

Though the book was composed in a time of great scarcity, hunger, and fear, the recipe section of the book is not a record of that suffering. The poems and letters that describe the suffering of the ghetto are physically separate from the recipes: "Many poems were written in Terezin, often sad or grim," the editor explains. "Mina's came on separate sheets, not part of the cookbook" (81). This suggests a purposeful separation of pleasure and suffering by literary genre as well as literal space. Two separate resistances seem to be mounted here. In the poems and letters, there is a refusal to remain silent about suffering, to record it in detail, to ensure that there is an unflinching account of the reality of their situation. But in the cookbook, the pleasures of the imagination announce a bright and uncrossable line where Nazi torture has not entered and cannot enter. In the bunker of imagination, disguised as innocuous and impractical, a mere collection of recipes, Pachter and her comrades experienced pleasure in defiance. De Silva imagines that the cookbook is born out of a search for pleasure amid pain: "Did setting down recipes bring comfort amid chaos and brutality? Did it bring hope for the future in which someone might prepare a meal from them again? We cannot know" (xxvi).

The saddest cookbook we can imagine is actually a book about pleasure, hope, resilience, and resistance to oppression; the sadness and suffering are the context rather than the content. De Silva follows the unanswerable questions above with this statement: "certainly the creation of such a cookbook was an act of psychological resistance, forceful testimony of the power of food to sustain us, not just physically but spiritually" (xxvi). Laura Shapiro writes in her 1996 review of the book for *Newsweek*, "to write [the recipes] down was to insist on a real-world future, to insist that their daughters would receive their inheritance. The manuscript they labeled simply Kochbuch was a powerful symbol of their resistance to annihilation." Scholars agree. In her chapter for the collection *The Politics of Traumatic Literature: Narrating Human Psyche and Memory*, Lauren Cirina emphasizes the cookbook's transformative power for resistance and community, finding "respite [from trauma] through their imaginations and memories" (261). *In Memory's Kitchen*—at least, the *kochboch* section of it—is not, in the end, a book of suffering, even as it emerges from great pain. The suffering is detectable only as subtext and context, not in the text of the recipe collection.

This juxtaposition of pleasure and pain is partly understood by distancing the recipe collection from the genre of the cookbook. In a review for *The New York Times*, Lore Dickstein calls it "not a cookbook." The startling title of the review, "Hell's Own Cookbook," places it out-of-bounds of the genre, even perverse, a dark shadow to some other sublime ideal cookbook (Dickstein). Even the foreword from Michael Berenbaum makes clear "this work—unlike conventional cookbooks—is not to be savored for its culinary offerings but for the insight it gives us in understanding the extraordinary capacity of the human spirit to transcend its surroundings, to defy dehumanization, and to dream of the past and the future" (xvi). Shapiro suggests that the proper way to read the books is "as a Holocaust document, of course, not as a guide to making strudels and tortes." Despite this declaration, Shapiro does describe making and eating a chocolate torte from a recipe in the collection. Rona Kaufman describes her reaction to Shapiro's use of the cookbook with horror:

> I have to admit that when I read that Shapiro was going to eat the cake that came from the recipes, I felt a little sick to my stomach. I imagined that she was eating not Pachter's torte but Pachter's body . . . . I suppose it is this insistence on use that strikes me, that sickens me. I tend to see these recipes not as useful, practical guides but as testimony. I'm tempted to call these recipes sacred text—therefore untouchable, unusable . . . . Read and honor—but do not touch. (427–28)

To consider the recipe collection as a useful, salable commodity (as the genre of the cookbook demands) is insulting and inappropriate in Kaufman's reading. If *In Memory's Kitchen* is indeed a book of suffering, then using its recipes (i.e., treating it as a cookbook) is antithetical to the point of being disgusting. In her article "Testifying, Silencing, Swallowing: Coming to Terms with *In Memory's Kitchen*," Kaufman struggles to define exactly how a reader should relate to the collection, a struggle which emerges from its indeterminate genre, alternately considering it as a sacred text, testimony, diary, memoir, monument, and antimonument—anything but cookbook. I suspect that these readers are excepting and exempting the recipe collection from the genre of cookbook because its connection to pain and suffering makes it unusable as a set of instructions for pleasure.

Furthermore, Kaufman reiterates that the suffering memorialized in *In Memory's Kitchen* is all in the "frame" of the book provided by De Silva in the introduction and Michael Berenbaum in the foreword, which preinterprets the recipes. "Without that frame, without the preface and introduction, the recipes testify to nothing," Kaufman argues, "They never say, 'This is what happened.' They never name their trauma—their recording comes out of trauma—but without the book's frame, it is impossible to recognize it as such. We need a story to point, to show, to explain" (434). Kaufman resists this editorial framing of the recipes as either a resistance to oppression or as evidence of suffering. In the end, *In Memory's Kitchen* may be neither a cookbook nor a book about suffering.

And yet, the inability to pin down its genre is evidence of the point I am attempting to make here: the defining difference between the genre of the cookbook and the genre of the memoir is pleasure. Memoirs can be centered on the reader's pleasure, but cookbooks must be. This explains why the *kochboch* portion is silent on the subject of suffering and why imagining recipes, "cooking with the mouth," can bring such pleasure to its practitioners. It also explains why the frame of suffering provided by the letters, poems, and editorial commentary make the book into something else, ineligible for membership in the cookbook genre as it is practiced today. As the shelving suggestions on the back cover remind us, *In Memory's Kitchen* is a book of Jewish studies and history, not cookery.

The last few years, however, have seen a handful of recipe collections clearly marketed as cookbooks that specifically invite feelings of pain into their rhetorical purpose while also maintaining that their recipes are meant to be used as a conventional cookbook. *Feed the Resistance* by Julia Turshen and *Protest Kitchen* by Carol J. Adams and Virginia Messina both clearly identify themselves as reactions to the 2016 election of Donald Trump to the US presidency, tapping into the anger, fear, and disappointment of many that followed. Turshen opens her book with a scene one week after the election at a community meeting for immigrants and allies to learn about their rights in the face of the president's proposed travel ban, capturing a sense of fear and urgency to protect vulnerable citizens. Each moment, Turshen explains, new information symbolized by the relentless pinging of news alerts on smart phones around the room increases the feeling of danger: "It felt as if no matter how quickly we rallied to find a solution, the problem itself wouldn't even stand still" (9). Turshen describes the climate as one of increasing anxiety, a "new world, which in some ways is not a new world at all and is just the old world without the guise of false security;" it is "a time of upheaval," dangerous as "a match just struck" (9). Turshen becomes leader of "the Food Team," charged with organizing meals for protestors (11). In spite of all the negative feelings that inspire the cookbook, it presents the recipes in the book as both pleasant and useful. The cookbook provides advice for "Practical Activism" (16–19) as well as useful recipes that can be easily made and even carried to protests. Food is still presented as a "balm" and "a constant reminder of transformation and possibility," a comforting solution to the painful feelings that inspired the book (12).

Similarly, Adams and Messina's *Protest Kitchen* emerges from "an unsettled time in politics" where "it's easy to feel overwhelmed" by concerns for "basic human rights, social justice, climate change, and the very future of our democracies" (1). Adams and Messina link the regressive politics of the Trump administration to a nostalgia for a 1950s-like world, including 1950s-era attitudes toward women and people of color as food producers for a white supremacist patriarchy (14–15). In addition to being a balm for the emotions or fuel for the bodies of protesters, Adams and Messina argue that eating itself can be a protest, an act of resistance against systems of oppression (namely, capitalism and climate change, food insecurity, misogyny, racism, exclusionary politics). From feelings of uncertainty and anger come active solutions and positive support for concrete social change, inclusive democracy, and compassion. In this collection of recipes, food may not be explicitly presented as a source of comfort, but it is a source of positive feelings: "During a time when you feel disempowered, your food choices can be a source of empowerment" (5). Again, these painful feelings are channeled into positive actions and emotions.

Yet another collection of recipes and stories, titled *Rage Baking: The Transformative Power of Flour, Fury, and Women's Voices*, is framed as a reaction to the testimony of Christine Blasey Ford in the hearings for Supreme Court nominee Brett Kavanaugh, particularly the futility of that painful testimony to stop his nomination from becoming an appointment (xiii). The title of the book sparked controversy, as the term "rage baking" was originated by Tangerine Jones in 2015 as a hashtag, website, "personal practice" of self-care, and collaborative social action (Jones, "The Privilege of Rage" par. 4). Rage baking, for Jones, was specifically a response to racial violence and injustice. As a self-identified "Black woman born and partly raised in the South," Jones considers kitchens to be "sacred, powerful spaces," where she could safely discharge feelings of rage and "channel it" into something more pleasant, but more importantly, concretely productive (par. 2). The rules of #ragebaking, as set down by Jones, include turning the results of baking outward in service of others and the struggle for equity: "whatever you make must be shared, preferably with strangers. Pass it out. Mail it. Throw a party. Take it to the nearest shelter. Set up a #ragebaking stand." This is rule number one ("Fundamentals of Rage Baking" par. 1), and Jones herself reports sharing her efforts with a social justice nonprofit for an entire year ("The Privilege of Rage" par. 5). While Jones ultimately acknowledges that #ragebaking is about finding joy (or at least releasing suffering), it begins with a feeling of pain that is difficult to express, particularly for African American women:

> Black folks are never allowed to admit when we're tired and why and we're certainly not afforded our legitimate and justified rage. I didn't just want to take out my anger, hurt, and frustration. I wanted to

channel it and move through it. I wanted to get my heart right, renew my hope and find a way forward. ("The Privilege of Rage" par. 1)

As the title of Jones's article suggests, the privilege of expressing rage is more easily extended to white women and professional writers like Kathy Gunst and Kathy Alford, editors of the cookbook *Rage Baking* and regular content creators for the Food Network and NPR, who do not share credit with Jones or acknowledge her as the originator of the term or concept of rage baking (though they have since released a statement declaring "The intent has never been to claim ownership of the term 'rage baking,' nor to erase or diminish the work of others using the phrase" (qtd. in Saxena par. 18). However, Gunst and Alford still address the very real pain of women at large. There are women of color represented among the contributors, though Jones remains uncredited. The privilege of whiteness is that their pain and rage are somehow more tolerable, less threatening, easier to swallow than other forms of pain. Perhaps this is one of many reasons why Gunst and Alford have a cookbook—a genre intolerant of unresolved pain—and Jones has a social movement. As Jones commented to a reporter from the online publication *Eater*, "I don't think the publishing world is ready to deal with or package black women's anger in ways that are easily digestible and commodified" (qtd. in Saxena par. 14).

Still, Gunst and Alford recognize that a cookbook built on women's rage is an anomaly in the genre. Kathy Gunst describes a lifetime of suppressing strong emotions (xiii) and feeling "a level of rage I rarely experience explode within me" when provoked by a friend at a dinner party (xiv). Gunst reacted to this friend's dismissal of her feelings in response to Ford's testimony by "[weeping] with fury" in the bathroom until she could return to the table to do "what well-behaved women all over the world do: I apologized for getting upset" (xiv). The political climate is described as "an unrelenting tornado" of bad news (xv). The only action that seems to soothe Gunst's anger is baking. But the soothing is temporary: "Did the baking stop the rage? Hell no. Did the baking make all the lies and deceit and behind-the-scenes dealings feel less menacing? No. Did the baking make me feel less afraid of the erosion of democracy I was witnessing as I listened to the evening news? No, it didn't really do any of those things" (xv). Like Turshen, Adams and Messina, and even Jones, Gunst presents cooking as something to do on the way to the fight and as a part of the fight. But even Gunst and her coeditor Alford, both veteran cookbook writers and food journalists, recognize that something about a cookbook built on rage as an organizing principle is a challenge to the genre: "we knew it had to be much more than a 'regular' cookbook," but "we weren't quite sure what that might look like" (xvi). The unsoothed and unsolved anger of women, Gunst argues, is hard to handle in any circumstance; it may be especially hard to comprehend in the genre of the cookbook where pleasure is the primary goal.

While each of the books described above acknowledges strong feelings of pain, suffering, fear, anger, and urgency for action, they also provide a pathway to pleasure in the form of empowerment, comfort, meditative practice, fantasy, memory, connection, sweetness. Even cookbooks that begin in pain usually end in some kind of pleasure. Together, these books present a challenge to the genre of the cookbook as only delivering pleasure. They all stand out as something not quite "regular," something counter to a basic convention of a highly conventional genre. A book of recipes so oriented to pain can't quite be called by the name "cookbook" without some explanation or resolution. These books, and the southern cookbooks that I will examine in the chapters that follow, demonstrate two things: first, that to carry the name of cookbook a recipe must in some essential way make a promise of pleasure in the imagination and in the material world of the kitchen, and second, that the genre of the cookbook is not, in fact, intolerant of suffering altogether, only suffering without hope of relief. The turn to pleasure is not always erasure, obfuscation, or admission of defeat. It may be one ingredient in a recipe for revolution.

WORKS CITED

Adams, Carol J., and Virginia Messina. *Protest Kitchen: Fight Injustice, Save the Planet, and Fuel Your Resistance One Meal at a Time*. Conari Press, 2018.

Alford, Katherine, and Kathy Gunst, editors. *Rage Baking: The Transformative Power of Flour, Fury, and Women's Voices*. Tiller Press, 2020.

Angelou, Maya. *I Know Why the Caged Bird Sings*. Bantam Books, 1997.

Angelou, Maya. *Hallelujah! The Welcome Table*. Random House, 2004.

Bower, Anne, editor, *Recipes for Reading: Community Cookbooks, Stories, Histories*. U of Massachusetts P, 1997.

Bourdieu, Pierre. *Distinction: A Social Critique of the Judgement of Taste*. Translated by Richard Nice. Cambridge: Harvard UP, 1984.

Bracken, Peg. *I Hate to Cook Book: 50th Anniversary Edition*. Grand Central Publishing, 2010.

Cirina, Lauren. "A Revolt of the Spirit: Defiance, Preservation, and Sisterhood in In Memory's Kitchen: A Legacy from the Women of Terezin." *The Politics of Traumatic Literature: Narrating Human Psyche and Memory*, edited by Önder Çakırtaş, Antolin C. Trinidad, Şahin Kızıltaş. Cambridge Scholars Publishing, 2018, 252–70.

Cofer, Judith Ortiz. "The Woman Who Slept with One Eye Open: Notes on Being a Writer." *Sleeping with One Eye Open: Women Writers and the Art of Survival*, edited by Marilyn Kallet and Judith Ortiz Cofer. U of Georgia P, 1999.

Cognard-Black, Jennifer. "The Embodied Rhetoric of Recipes." *Food, Feminisms, Rhetorics*, edited by Melissa A. Goldthwaite. Southern Illinois UP, 2017, 30–47.

Couser, G. Thomas. *Memoir: An Introduction*. Oxford UP, 2012.

De Silva, Cara. *In Memory's Kitchen: A Legacy from the Women of Terezin*. Rowman and Littelfield, 2006.

Dickstein, Lore. "Hell's Own Cookbook." *The New York Times*, November 17, 1996, Sunday, Late Edition. https://www.nytimes.com/1996/11/17/books/hell-s-own-cookbook.html

Franklin, Benjamin. *Autobiography of Benjamin Franklin*. Henry Holt and Company, 1916. Project Gutenberg. https://www.gutenberg.org/files/20203/20203-h/20203-h.htm.

Foucault, Michel. *The History of Sexuality, Volume I: An Introduction*, translated by Robert Hurley. Pantheon Books, 1978.

Golden, Zach. *What the F*@# Should I Make for Dinner?: The Answers to Life's Everyday Question (in 50 F*@#ing Recipes)*. Running Press Adult, 2011.

Harris, Jennifer. "Marketplace Transactions and Sentimental Currencies in Fanny Fern's Ruth Hall," *American Transcendental Quarterly*, vol. 10, no.1, March 2006, pp. 343–59.

Inness, Sherrie. *Secret Ingredients: Race, Gender, and Class at the Dinner Table*. Palgrave, 2005.

Ireland, Lynne. "The Compiled Cookbook as Foodways Autobiography," *Western Folklore*, vol. 40, no.1, Jan 1981, pp. 107–14.

Johnson, Javon. "Black Joy in the Time of Ferguson," *QED: A Journal in GLBTQWorldmaking*, vol. 2, no. 2, 2015, pp. 177–83.

Jones, Tangerine. "Fundamentals of #RageBaking." *Ragebaking.com*, 11 July 2016. https://www.ragebaking.com/2016/07/11/ragebakingrules/.

Jones, Tangerine. "The Privilege of Rage." *Medium.com*, 14 Feb 2020. https://medium.com/@tangerinejones/the-privilege-of-rage-e5b2cb53d238.

Julier, Alice. *Eating Together: Food, Friendship, and Inequality*. U of Illinois P, 2013.

Kaufman, Rona "Testifying, Silencing, Swallowing: Coming to Terms with *In Memory's Kitchen*," *JAC*, vol. 24, no. 2, 2004, pp. 427–45.

Lo, Anita. *Solo: A Modern Cookbook for a Party of One*. Knopf, 2018.

Lu, Jessica H., and Catherine Knight Steele. "'Joy is Resistance': Cross-platform Resilience and (Re)invention of Black Oral Culture Online," *Information, Communication & Society*, vol. 22, no.6, 2019, pp. 823–37, DOI: 10.1080/1369118X.2019.1575449.

Meah, Angela. "Materializing Memory, Mood, and Agency: The Emotional Geographies of the Modern Kitchen." *Gastronomica*, Summer 2016, pp. 55–68.

Miller, Sarah. "Cooking for Others Can Be Selfish," *Café.com*. 2016. http://www.cafe.com/r/9b514042-a7f9-47b5-93da-ffeb0b2a1a97/1/how-cooking-for-others-can-be-selfish.

Niewiadomska-Fils, Urszula. *Live and Let Di(n)e: Foodscape and Race in Southern Literature*. U of Arkansas P, 2020.

Naccarato, Peter, and Kathleen LeBesco. *Culinary Capital*. Berg, 2012.

Nosrat, Samin. *Salt, Fat, Acid, Heat: Mastering the Elements of Good Cooking*. Simon and Schuster, 2017.

Saxena, Jaya. "The 'Rage Baking' Controversy, Explained." *Eater*, 19 Feb 2020, https://www.eater.com/cookbooks/2020/2/19/21142732/rage-baking-tangerine-jones-racial-injustice-controversy-explained.

Shapiro, Laura. "Review of *In Memory's Kitchen: A Legacy from the Women of Terezin*." *Newsweek*, vol. 128, no. 11, 9 Sept 1996, p. 73.

Shepard, Benjamin. *Play, Creativity, and Social Movements*. Routledge, 2013.

Shepard, Benjamin. *Queer Political Performance and Protest: Play, Pleasure, and Social Movements*. Routledge, 2010.

Theophano, Janet. *Eat My Words: Reading Women's Lives through the Cookbooks They Wrote*. Palgrave Macmillan, 2002.

Turshen, Julia. *Feed the Resistance: Recipes + Ideas for Getting Involved*. Chronicle Books, 2017.

Williams-Forson, Psyche A. *Building Houses out of Chicken Legs: Black Women, Food & Power*. U of North Carolina P, 2006.

Wilson, Bee. "The Pleasures of Reading Recipes." *The New Yorker*, 26 July 2013, https://www.newyorker.com/books/page-turner/the-pleasures-of-reading-recipes.

"A LOT OF PAST TO RECKON WITH"
Grappling with Slavery and Racism

As you make your way through this book, you'll notice that I have just one artistic move for opening a new chapter: the charming personal anecdote. This is in part due to my past as a creative writing student and teacher, but it is also a pretty common strategy in scholarly food writing, too. How could it not be? Everybody is part of a food culture of some kind, and no doubt the audience has experienced personally exactly the thing that the writer is about to unpack. The reader will be so surprised when they discover the quotidian thing of cooking and eating that they have done without thinking all their lives is actually a very complex and meaningful activity. I joke with my family and friends outside academia that they can read the first eight pages of each chapter and know enough about what I do without getting bored or mired in scholarly complications. The personal anecdote is my rhetorical strategy for inviting a general audience to my lecture. It's also an authenticity argument I learned from writing my first book; I'm offering you a true-to-myself, one-of-a-kind glimpse at the *real me*.

But this chapter is not one that I can easily start with a personal narrative. It's a chapter about stories of slavery and racism in cookbooks. As a Nice White Lady, I know that centering myself at a time like this is missing the point. I'm tempted to take the advice of the woman who sold me the best barbecue rib tips and Delta tamales of my life from a former Quizno's in Clarksdale, Mississippi; when her daughter suggested she call up Guy Fieri to put her business on *Diners, Drive-ins, and Dives*, she replied, "Go sit down someplace." Sometimes that's best thing an ally can do.

But "sitting down someplace" and letting writers of color do all the work of critiquing a harmful system is precisely the problem I want to address in this chapter. White writers of southern foodways have often avoided engaging with the painful past and present of racism in food culture by simply staking their territory elsewhere. I argued in *Inventing Authenticity* that the main reason that southern writers do not rely on historical narratives to prove the authenticity of their recipes is that the past is painful, particularly for black and indigenous southerners who have simultaneously created southern cuisine and been excluded from southern identity (69–70). To meet the cookbook genre requirements of pleasure and to avoid potentially alienating readers through representations of suffering in the past, writers—even writers of color—may erase the history of slavery or obscure it in euphemisms or complicated sentence structures. When they do bring up the past, writers tend to share credit widely to tell the pleasant story of a peaceful southern melting pot of crosscultural collaboration, or conversely, they focus on the safer route of the personal, representing only themselves in a pleasant family story rather than the potentially unpleasant public history of the South at large. When it comes to the legacies of slavery, many of today's white writers tend to choose "sitting down someplace" over the potential risk of walking through the difficulties of discussing race from their privileged position. I won't make that mistake, though I acknowledge that I may make many others before the end of this chapter.

There are serious limitations to "sitting down someplace" as a strategy of avoiding pain. Telling a pleasant story requires silencing and ignoring other facts of the past and present. It is, at its core, a convenient reemplotment that selectively chooses which facts to tell. It is necessarily incomplete as a representation of the past, present, and future. This is perhaps the bottom line of the criticism aimed at popular southern food writing. As a writer imagines a pleasurable story of the South and experience of southernness, that writer not only fails to grapple with the South's complicated past—especially slavery, racial violence, and discrimination based on race—they rewrite that past and perpetuate mythology.

While it seems clear that acknowledging the suffering of the oppressed is the right thing to do, building an identity around pain without the possibility of overcoming suffering (whether your southern forebears were experiencing or inflicting it) is not a successful marketing tool. Folks who are concerned about the loss of southern distinction or closing the market for distinctly southern products, experiences, and narratives have a stake in making sure that *a southerner* is something everyone wants to be. Narratives of a South without the suffering of slavery and racism make southern history and identity easy: easy to hear, easy to bear, easy to wear on a t-shirt or ballcap, easy to share in a recipe. Without the burdensome complications of a history of pointless pain—or worse, a history of purposefully inflicted pain—it becomes easier for audiences to buy the version of southern identity on offer.

It's also really difficult to talk about race in America, full stop. I genuinely hate the term "cancel culture," but it's hard to deny that making a mistake—even a well-intentioned one—can have outsized consequences for a career lived in public. I don't need to rehash Paula Deen's egregious (and not well-intentioned) acts of racism that ended her meteoric rise to fame and curtailed her empire. Nor do I need to describe again the long battle fought on Twitter and blogs and in food magazines between Sean Brock and Michael Twitty and a host of other commentators about who can and should represent and sell Gullah cuisine (summarized in *Inventing Authenticity*, 143–47). Even John T. Edge and the Southern Foodways Alliance, whose founding mission is explicitly about diversity and inclusion, are not immune from getting it wrong, stepping out of bounds, and being called to the carpet for spending too much time standing at the center amplifying and not enough time sitting down someplace and listening.

Even when not explicitly discussing the complexities of race, celebrity chefs and food personalities may unexpectedly find themselves in hot water. Alison Roman, who describes the experience of being "cancelled" as akin to a lobster being slowly boiled to death, came under fire in May 2020 for comments in an interview about the inexplicable-to-her fame of Marie Kondo and Chrissy Teigen. Both women are Asian, and so many took those comments as selectively targeting the women based on race and a reflection of how today's food culture has long benefited from white women writing about cultures not their own. In the fallout, Roman parted ways with *The New York Times* in December 2020, and a year later, when interviewed by *The New Yorker*, she still had not recovered either her platform or her confidence. Roman explains to Lauren Collins that she hesitated to publish a recipe with lentils for fear that it would be received as cultural appropriation. When the recipe for "Gentle Lentils" got exactly the negative feedback she expected, Roman responded on Instagram in fatal all caps: "'Gentle Lentils' Was a Cheeky Name Meant to Describe the Contents / Story Given in the Newsletter, Not Meant to Rebrand the Centuries Old Food Some of You Know As Daal, [. . .] I Take No Ownership of This Food." Though Roman has recovered her audience enough to have a new show on CNN, the volume of ink (or megabytes) used on this conversation demonstrates the delicate rhetorical landscape cookbook writers can stumble into when accidentally invoking race. Traversing the path intentionally opens up writers to comments that they may not be equipped to handle without advanced degrees in cultural studies.

It's no wonder with so much at stake that cookbook writers (even professional co- and ghostwriters) exempt themselves from the sticky rhetorical wicket of talking about race and racism. However, many southern cookbook writers do choose to engage directly with the experience of enslavement, enslavers, and enslaved people. And some do choose to describe racism and discrimination as extending even into the present. Because this is an especially painful story and an especially optional rhetorical choice with high-stakes consequences, it seems especially significant to explore what happens when writers do make the decision to address slavery and racism.

I argue that at one level, these painful stories are used as certificates of traditional and historical authenticity, linking a recipe to a legible and distinctly southern past. While slavery was never practiced exclusively in the US South, and racism isn't exclusive to the region either, both have become essential to the metanarrative of southern identity. And for good reason. A region known as the South coalesced as an identity group around an armed defense of the use of enslaved laborers and the ownership of human beings. While this narrative marks the South as a special place for the suffering of people of color, Lost Cause rhetoric marks the South as a special place for the suffering of white southerners. The suffering caused by the end of slavery and by the consequences of a lost war to defend it has a unifying effect for bolstering myths of white supremacy. The particular meaning of the reference to slavery and racism may be wildly different based on the writer's identity, intention, and execution, but mentioning slavery at all has the effect of tying a recipe to an immediately recognizable southern past.

The very idea of a distinct geographic region within the United States called *The South* is a product of slavery. Where does the South begin? The Mason-Dixon line that starts by separating Pennsylvania from Maryland exists to create a dividing line above which slavery would be illegal in new states that could be admitted to the Union. Defining the geographic region of the South by the Confederate States is also placing slavery at the center of southern identity. Slavery is inescapable as a part of southern history and the process of forging regional distinction. Any attempt at traditional authenticity as an argument will have to place the origin of the recipe in time relative to the Civil War. If a writer wants to claim an ingredient's origin in Africa, that writer will somehow have to acknowledge how that African ingredient becomes part of the US southern diet through the capture, forced migration, and sale of human beings. Any attempt to credit an African American innovator will have to place that person in time relative to Emancipation, Reconstruction, Jim Crow, and the ongoing Civil Rights Struggle now represented by Black Lives Matter.

As Rafia Zafar argues in *Recipes for Respect*, a headnote explaining that a dish was invented by enslaved cooks or contains ingredients that enter the cuisine through African slave trade suggests that a historical origin in the practice of slavery is evidence of a distinctly southern dish (18). Having been invented by an enslaved cook is a connection to the Old South and all its attendant nostalgic nonsense but also a recognition of black knowledge, skills, and abilities (to borrow a phrase from Toni Tipton-Martin). Making a reference to enslaved innovations or innovators invokes both stories of pain and pride. Making the reference is not value-neutral nor immediately categorizable as insult or exultation, resistance or reification.

Certainly, invoking slavery and racism as authentic southern experiences may support narratives that naturalize white supremacy and black pain. There is always a danger of appealing to a racist white audience that looks to the antebellum South as "the good old days." However, the same action might also be an act of resistance by simply telling the truth. It may be a way to show the bodies in the rice fields (Romine qtd. in Severson par. 24) and acknowledge the real pain of the past. Narrating a recipe's origin in the pain caused by slavery may be one way that white writers show up as allies and Black writers tell truth to power.

If the story of pain ends in pleasure—and it must because of the cookbook genre's conventions—then that pleasure, too, has two sides: minimizing past pain or offering an alternative story of southern Black experience. One implication of the turn to pleasure after acknowledging pain is to suggest that the pain is over, complete, in the past. It denies the existence of very real and ongoing racism, as well as the exploitative labor practices that followed slavery and continue even now in the abuse of immigrant workers in agricultural industries everywhere. Or it may suggest that the suffering was necessary—worth the pain—for the good that it has brought in the form of culinary pleasure and cultural resilience. On the other hand, acknowledging how slavery, racism, and identity-based violence in all their complexities exist in our food systems may be an important first step in changing those systems. It also makes possible an open southern identity with space for the huge diversity of humans living in and identifying with the South.

"MORE RIFFING THAN CITING": PLEASURE AND PAIN AS RESISTANCE

What is thinking of the past with pleasure but *nostalgia*? Certainly *nostalgia* is the derogatory term given to white writers' sunny retellings of a past that is known to have pain. Sarah Trainer, Jessica Hardin, Cindi SturtzSreetharan, and Alexandra Brewis coin the term *worry nostalgia* to describe the particular anxiety around the perceived loss of local food practices (67). Their comparative study includes Atlanta, Georgia, where interviewees expressed memories of a better past and sadness at the "generational losses" of southern food traditions and even accents among younger southerners (73–74). Interviewees remembered an earlier time when food and lifestyles appeared to be healthier and more emotionally fulfilling (75). Looking back at that pleasant time made interviewees feel sad in the present or anxious about the future. That kind of worry nostalgia is familiar in the discourse of southern food which often predicts a dire future for regional distinction.

However, *Afro-Nostalgia: Feeling Good in Contemporary Black Culture* gave me an entirely new way of looking at historical narratives and their relationship to pleasure. I owe an enormous debt to Badia Ahad-Legardy for the ideas in this chapter. Ahad-Legardy bases her 2021 book on refuting the assumption that African-descended people have no past to look at with pleasure:

> Historical nostalgia, with respect to African American memory, is rarely (if ever) invoked, precisely because narratives of black subjugation and disenfranchisement do not easily mesh with the romantic wistfulness generally associated with nostalgia. The conventional idea of nostalgia as a longing to return or homesickness for any era in American history, for black people, is generally read as counterintuitive at best and traitorous at worst. (1)

However, Ahad-Legardy observes that contemporary Black artists, writers, and indeed, chefs engage in nostalgia with the purpose of generating good feelings in the present and imagining a future for "black redemption, triumph over white supremacy, and resistance to state-sanctioned violence and repression" (6). The assumption that people of color cannot access nostalgia is based upon racist pseudoscience of the nineteenth century that posited "African-descended people did not maintain the psychological capacity to experience nostalgia" (2). Conversely, the assumption also suggests that African-descended people have exceptionally long memories, but they are invariably traumatic, violent, and miserable—and centered on their interactions with white people and institutions (3). Ahad-Legardy argues that both views are the product of and in support of white supremacy (6). I assumed that Black writers were less inclined to discuss history and that Black audiences would be less motivated by arguments that used it because of the past's painful associations, but my assumption leaves no room for Black southerners to have any other relationship to the past that could be pleasurable.

Ahad-Legardy, by contrast, argues against the "dangerous suggestion" that "attempts to recall a more sublime past necessarily enacts historical revision or erasure" (4). Instead, Ahad-Legardy argues that "historical nostalgia is fully operative in contemporary black cultural life as a means of historical pleasure" (5) which is more important to the emotional well-being of African-descended people than most recognize (4). Where once nostalgia was pathologized as "malaise" brought on by mournful longing for a permanently lost African homeland (6), Ahad-Legardy suggests that contemporary artists engage in a "self-conscious solicitation of historical memory to foster good feelings in the present" (9). *Afro-nostalgia* represents a unique relationship with the past that negotiates between opposing impulses:

> Afro-nostalgia invokes such moments of joy and pleasure while reckoning with a history mired and memorialized in the traumatic. The realm of art creates space and time for the real and the imaginary, the past and the present, to collude to manifest a living memory that, in the case of black nostalgia, evokes sentiments of pain and pleasure, mourning and celebration. (7)

Not only is it possible for African American cookbook writers to look upon the past with pleasure, Ahad-Legardy suggests that nostalgia can be a way to resist metanarratives of suffering that limit the field of emotions available to people of color and a way to enact a "disruption of 'white nostalgia'" (21). Moreover, acts of nostalgia are productive in fostering feelings of solidarity with "the past and the present and a general sense of social connectedness and felicity" (20) as well as "a sense of community, continuity, and reparation for black futures" and "an emotional reprieve and, quite possibly, a way forward" (21).

Nostalgic memory, by definition, is selective and creative in its relationship to facts. Instead of reading inaccuracies or imagined pasts as erasure, Ahad-Legardy suggests that afro-nostalgia actually highlights ambivalence and contradiction (21). In art, nostalgia is "less about recovering lost pasts than about invoking ambient associations through food, clothes, and music. More riffing than citing, black nostalgia's suggestions, indeterminacies, flavors, and fleeting moments constitute a broader contemporary black aesthetic that works to break blackness out of a narrowly constructed frame of traumatic history" (5). The "vagueness" that I noted in *Inventing Authenticity* when Black writers invoke the past is not necessarily a strategy to appease white readers as I argued (reproducing a narrative that Black pain is always centered on white fragility)—though it may have that effect, too. Rather as Ahad-Legardy's argument suggests, the emotional appeal to Black readers to join in the pleasure of afro-nostalgia comes from "ambient associations" with a past that decenters trauma as the only possible experience of history, "motivated by a cultural want to be read as something other than 'victim'" (165).

Ahad-Legardy takes on stories of slavery in the first chapter and stories from cookbooks in the last chapter of *Afro-Nostalgia*, and while she does not examine stories of slavery in southern cookbooks, her critical approach and conclusions from each chapter are useful in considering the potential for resistance when Black cookbook writers imagine the past in service of pleasure in the present. Ahad-Legardy examines fictional representations of enslaved people that highlight moments of resistance or retribution against white enslavers, evoking what she calls "nostalgic retribution" (28). In imagining or reimagining Black subjectivity and agency in the history of slavery, the authors demonstrate "a desire for redemptive justice for the formerly enslaved" (28) by "radically reimagining slave rebellions [or] making visible the emotional lives of enslaved subjects" (30). Characters in these fictional stories get "retribution" and "reimagine the justice denied to the past's 'true victims'" (34) through "conversational rejoinders, ridicule, feigned madness. . . . 'clapbacks,' subversions, 'shade,' attitude and other displays of verbal and nonverbal contempt" (34–35) as well as "flippantness, craziness, anger, and bossiness" (59). "Affective resistance" is resistance mounted through the insistence on feeling good.

Ahad-Legardy addresses food and cookbooks in the final chapter of *Afro-Nostalgia* with an investigation of nostalgia in cookbooks and memoirs from chefs Marcus Samuelsson and Bryant Terry and "their nostalgic retreats to moments within the black historical past, specifically precolonial Africa, the Harlem Renaissance, and the Black Power movement" (119). She praises these chefs for continuing the legacies of Civil Rights era by "recovering a culinary history and heritage that is intimately tied to an emancipatory politic of black radicalism" (120). Ahad-Legardy reads Terry's *Afro-Vegan: Farm Fresh African, Caribbean, and Southern Flavors Remixed* as offering a deceptively simple message of pleasure—if you only read the text. Terry provides with each recipe a soundtrack and suggested readings. If the reader chooses to perform the recipe exactly to the chef's specifications with music and readings, Terry would put them in touch with both a delicious dish and acknowledgement of a painful past that extends into the present. For example, Ahad-Legardy cooks Terry's recipe for Corn Grits with Swiss Chard and Roasted Cherry Tomatoes. The headnote indicates that the dish was inspired by Juneteenth—a celebration of the end of slavery, and the dish should be served at a brunch gathering to observe the holiday with pleasure. However, Terry also recommends pairing this recipe with reading *The New Jim Crow: Mass Incarceration in the Age of Colorblindness* by Michelle Alexander, which argues that slavery is not ended at all; rather, plantations have been reinvented as prisons. The soundtrack recommendation is "Solace" by Scott Joplin, an African American composer and ragtime pianist most famous for "The Entertainer." If the cookbook reader experiences all this, they get a picture of "ambivalence" (138) that belies the celebration we might expect from a cookbook or that the reader only gets from the headnote without the full context Terry provides. Ahad-Legardy concludes that the nostalgic Juneteenth celebration meal of grits and greens is balanced by the critical historical work that Alexander takes on and the art that Joplin created—but only if the reader makes the intertextual connections. Talk about subtle rebellions in a tightly conventional genre.

Ahad-Legardy describes herself using Terry's cookbook exactly as he must have intended. She is positioned squarely in the center of Terry's ideal audience and is fully engaged with the intertextuality of the book. She describes serving Terry's grits to her children not only "to globalize their palates but also to introduce them to the food of their ancestors, as well as a past and a politics that become hazier with each successive generation." Ahad-Legardy has internalized and embodied both the nostalgic pleasure and the reflective critical engagement that Terry seems to intend:

> I am aware that the simple act of eating yams will not magically transport me or my children to the memory of an African (or even Southern) homeland, but the act of purchasing sweet potatoes from black farmers at the Healthy Food Hub and jamming out to Erykah Badu's "Back in the Day" while preparing sweet potato granola provides its own nostalgic possibilities for the future. (156)

In other words, Ahad-Legardy argues that acts of afro-nostalgia make a pleasant present which will become a moment in the past that future generations will find "worth being nostalgic for" (165). Noticing and practicing pleasure *now*, even if that means using the imagination to find it in the past, allows future generations to look back on this time without needing to change or rearrange the facts. It works best as resistance when it is combined with action, like buying from black-owned businesses and sharing both information and emotion with children. Afro-nostalgia is a form of resistance that may open space for social change and reparation through pleasure.

PAIN AND PLEASURE IN REMEMBERING SLAVERY: CASE STUDIES

This chapter examines stories from writers of color who address slavery or racism in cookbook narratives. I begin with Michael Twitty, whose James Beard Award Winning memoir with recipes, *The Cooking Gene*, is devoted to tracing the genealogy of his enslaved ancestors and exploring Twitty's professional career interpreting enslaved cooking at historical plantation sites like Colonial Williamsburg. *The Cooking Gene* offers a good example of the complexities of emotions that can arise when African American writers meditate on slavery and food. *The Cooking Gene* is, of course, not exactly a cookbook, even though it does have recipes. Since it doesn't quite follow the rules of the cookbook genre, there's more space for Twitty to explore pain without breaking genre expectations. In that way, Twitty offers a kind of benchmark to compare the more traditional cookbooks against to reveal the limitations of the genre.

I chose the cookbooks for this analysis to demonstrate a range of rhetorical approaches that authors could take to engage with the story of slavery in the South. They all also happen to be geographically located in Georgia, and in varying degrees, connect with the story of Gullah Geechee people and cuisine of coastal Georgia. As Matthew Raiford explains in *Bress 'n' Nyam: Gullah Geechee Recipes from a Sixth Generation Farmer*, Gullah people are "the descendants of enslaved people left there to die on the barrier islands along the coast after white landowners abandoned their cotton, indigo, and rice plantations. Instead of dying, the Geechee thrived in collectives that shared their bountiful resources as well as their own language, music, art, and spiritual traditions" (15). The story of Gullah Geechee culture is a direct result of slave trade, making slavery almost impossible to ignore when describing their culture or traditions.

The oldest books in the sample are both from 2015: Dora Charles's *A Real Southern Cook in Her Savannah Kitchen* and Nicole A. Taylor's *Up South: Chasing Dixie in a Brooklyn Kitchen*. I wrote about Charles's cookbook in *Inventing Authenticity*, especially her relationship with former employer Paula Deen and how Charles claims authority in the headnote for her recipe for Brunswick Stew. I also examined Charles's training with her grandmother as superseding her employment with Deen as a source of authentic knowledge ("Citation Narratives"). Though I mentioned in that project some of the same evidence of pain and enslavement, I didn't actually interrogate those stories of pain as a rhetorical act in themselves. I was only interested in them as parts of an appeal to ethos. This current analysis focuses more broadly on her references to her ancestors' experiences of enslavement and racism throughout the book.

Taylor's *Up South* is the first of her three cookbooks, and Taylor is a prolific James Beard Award–nominated food writer whose work has appeared in top-tier popular food writing spaces like *the New York Times*, *Bon Appétit*, and *Food & Wine*. In addition to food writing, Taylor started as host of the podcast *Hot Grease* for Heritage Radio Network. According to her website biography, Taylor is also a producer of a documentary about restaurant desegregation called *If We So Choose* and cofounder of "The Maroon, a marketplace and retreat house focused on radical rest for Black creatives." Taylor's work in and around food clearly shows her engagement with racial justice and food activism, with a strong connection to the history of Black Southerners. I look at *Up South* first to provide some background for comparing the book to her newest cookbook, *Watermelon and Red Birds: A Cookbook for Juneteenth and Black Celebrations* (2022).

The final book in this sample is Matthew Raiford's *Bress 'n' Nyam* from 2021. I first learned about Matthew Raiford in a profile written by Virginia Willis in her 2018 book *Secrets of the Southern Table: A Food Lover's Tour of the Global South*, where Raiford spoke candidly to Willis about his experiences of racism as a Black southerner and farmer on land owned by his family since Reconstruction, first purchased by Jupiter Gilliard who was born into slavery in South Carolina (11). I will look at Willis's decision to repeat and react to these stories in her cookbook at the end of this chapter, but first, I want to examine how Raiford writes his family story of eight-generation landowners in Georgia and their relationship to the Gullah Geechee story.

Together, these contemporary cookbooks by African American chefs and writers demonstrate the complexities of Black southerners' relationships with the past. They remember the pain of their ancestors as they celebrate their contributions. They express pain in their own life stories, but they also describe the good feelings that come from cooking and eating and remembering. They break the conventions of the cookbook genre by invoking these stories of pain to connect with an authentic southern history and navigate the reader toward pleasure in the present through acts of afro-nostalgia.

Twitty foregrounds pain in *The Cooking Gene*, opening the memoir by embarking on what he calls "The Southern Discomfort Tour," a purposeful exploration of his own complicated relationship with the South and his ancestors' roots in Africa and "the Old South." In the final lines of the first chapter, just before the first recipes in the book, Twitty writes about his experiences as a historical interpreter, acting in the role of an enslaved cook for tourists at plantations like Colonial Williamsburg in Virginia: "I'm in the clothes that call to mind what the enslaved wore, making food like the enslaved made for themselves and their slaveholders. I am in the plantation kitchens that are haunted to the rafters in places that few African Americans dare to tread. I watch ghosts walk by and among them is me." These lines hardly prepare a reader for a pleasant experience, instead highlighting that the project of exploring the realities of slavery that Twitty has taken on has high personal costs that few would pay.

I proposed earlier that a reader would not enjoy imagining themselves in the role of an enslaved cook when they are cooking in their home kitchens or ingesting food symbolic of slavery that would literally become part of their bodies. But Twitty makes a career in recovering and embodying the role of an enslaved cook. Twitty explains the physical pain of cooking in this way, as well as the emotional pain of embodying that experience: "I am the man in the waistcoat and trousers, the billowy shirt, surrounded by complicated and ugly produce and foul smells and spices that cut through rain on red clay. I am the new still life—a black man standing on the brick floor feeling the flames lick and the smoke choke surrounded by the plantation larder." Twitty's body is marked by the injuries of cooking, "scalded and branded, burned and seared," but he feels connection through them: "These are the marks of my tribe." Taking the experience of pain into and onto his body strengthens his emotional connection to the past.

Similarly, Twitty revisits a conversation with chef Therese Nelson who, like Twitty, sought out the stories of enslaved cooks in her own past and in the story of southern cooking to connect with a history of food innovators. Nelson's southern family refused to talk about "segregation" or "slavery time" among themselves, suggesting that these stories of pain were best kept silent. But this left Nelson feeling "fraudulent because I didn't know my roots, I didn't know where to start." Twitty and Nelson seem to agree that part of the process of learning to celebrate and feel at comfortable in African American food culture includes embracing discomfort and learning about the painful parts of history.

Twitty describes at length a particularly humiliating and infuriating encounter at an event at a plantation where he was cooking in character:

> The pots are extremely heavy when filled with water. One event involved cooking at a kitchen until darkness settled, with one modern light and a few candles, I struggled to move the massive pot, filled with water, to the fire. Then I tripped over something near the fire, sending a bit of the water spilling into it. The large group of visitors for the plantation Christmas event, almost completely white, thought this was rather funny. Nobody asked me if I was all right, and most shook their heads in amusement. I have never been so angry at one of these events. I wanted to tell them that if a slaveholder saw fit, an enslaved person in a house could be sold, beaten, or in a few extremely rare but gruesome cases, like an incident in Martinique, cooked alive in an oven for an imperfect cake.

This story highlights the layers of pain that come from Twitty's work: the physical pain of using nineteenth-century tools and techniques in the twenty-first century, the pain inflicted on his nineteenth-century ancestors, the emotional pain of being dismissed without empathy in the present, and the mourning for past victims of cruelty. Twitty recognizes that his presence in these spaces challenges white visitors to face the uncomfortable realities of enslaved labor—"a labor camp system for exiled prisoners of war and victims of kidnapping"—and he describes feeling pleasantly connected to the creativity of generations, but the personal cost is high.

Like Twitty, Dora Charles details the intense physical pain and suffering of being enslaved. Unlike Nelson's family, Charles's family discussed these painful stories frequently: "We grew up hearing the stories of slave times, and the tales of the cotton harvest, when my great-grandfather's hands got so tender they'd bleed, stick in my head today—but there was no stopping for pain or blood; you had to keep working until there was no more sun in the sky" (12). Charles's grandmother Hattie told her of the hardships and the fear that came with enslaved labor, even fear of thunder and lightning and the wrath of God (15). Charles reports that the women in her family were "house slaves," spared "the cruel work in the fields," but Charles makes clear that they earned this relative reprieve only through their superior skills in the kitchen (12). After Emancipation, Charles explains, the family became sharecroppers, working hard but returning two-thirds of their profits and crops to the landowners in a clearly inequitable arrangement that kept them impoverished and prevented her father from staying in school long enough to learn to read and write (13). The indignities and pain of cotton harvesting in this exploitative labor system are detailed; men were expected to pick 1000 pounds a day, women 700, children at least 100 or they were not paid (14). Charles's grandmother Hattie went to work as a cook when she was 6 years old, after her mother died and "she was sent to live with a mean aunt." The cooking job was in a "kind of jail, where workers who'd displeased the boss man were kept until they were forgiven and sent back to work" (14), another holdover from the slave system and an arbitrary abuse of power by white landowners. More than any other cookbook examined here, Charles unflinchingly details the difficulty of labor and racism, but not quite to the extent that Twitty does in his memoir.

References to the history of slavery or the slave trade in Taylor's *Up South* are less frequent and less specific, but not absent. The first image in the cookbook, across from the title page, is a photograph of a pie on a vintage-looking tablecloth surrounded by cotton plants, complete with dried bolls and stems. The picture is framed with a white border that is made to look like a vintage photograph: rounded corners, some discoloration, a suggestion of wear and age in a wrinkle from a fold in the top right corner. The image is repeated with the recipe for Buttermilk Pie later in the book without the vintage framing effect (154). The headnote for the recipe explains that Taylor made the pie for the Culinary Historians of New York and a special event celebrating food historian Andrew Smith's 2011 book *Starving the South* (subtitled *How the North Won the Civil War*) (155). Though the headnote itself does not reference slavery, the context of the event and the content of Smith's book suggest that Taylor chose the pie for the historians to connect with the story told in Smith's book. The cotton in the full-color photo also evokes an association between the pie and the crop grown and harvested by enslaved laborers (154). As in Ahad-Legardy's reading of Bryant Terry's subtler intertextual cues, Taylor's allusions suggest that there's more complicated subtext that might not reach audiences who only browse the pictures and read the headnotes.

Taylor is more direct in naming ingredients with connections to Africa and the Atlantic slave trade, but she still avoids the more explicit connections that we see in Twitty and Charles. In the chapter introduction to "Peas and Things," Taylor notes that "Field peas, sometimes called cowpeas or crowder peas) . . . journeyed from Africa to the Americas" (39). How the peas made that journey without human actors in the sentence is unclear. Taylor's recipe for "Purple Hull Pea Fritters" explains that "In West Africa, the golden fried nuggets are called Akkra" (40). The implication is that southerners picked up the tradition from West Africans who were enslaved, but this is not explicitly stated. Even though Taylor learned about the history of rice in a summer spent at Claflin College at Orangeburg, South Carolina, she only mentions that the experience "raised my awareness about the ingredient's history" (36). She does not tell the history itself which knowledgeable readers would connect to enslaved labor. Even benne, an ingredient of known African origin, is described as "a colonial-period version of sesame" with no discussion of its provenance (186). A certain kind of reader would know that Taylor is suggesting an association with slavery, but she is not making the connection explicit.

However, Taylor is much more specific about connections to slavery when invoking the Gullah from her home state of Georgia. In the recipe for "Sea Island Peas," Taylor directly links the red peas of Sapelo Island and the Gullah Geechee community to "a distinct culture connected to the slave trade." Taylor does not elaborate on the connection except to say that "The red pea is special to the island because it has been unaltered since it was brought over from West Africa during the slave trade" (46). Readers may or may not be aware of how the communities of enslaved Africans on isolated islands in coastal Georgia developed into "a distinct culture," but they are told that it has a history intersecting with slavery.

The most explicit reference to slavery in *Up South* can be found with a recipe for Fried Green Tomatoes:

> On June 19, 1865, two years after President Lincoln's Emancipation Proclamation became official, enslaved people in Galveston, Texas were told that they were free. Since the mid-nineteenth century, black communities across the nation have celebrated their culture, freedom, and accomplishments with a festive fete—Juneteenth. To keep up the tradition, I host an annual feast with green tomatoes on the menu. (190)

The most in-depth reference to slavery is to its end and to the ongoing celebration of the "culture, freedom, and accomplishments" of Black people. The story of Juneteenth here is an opportunity for *afro-nostalgia*. Taylor's annual ritual remembrance highlights the good and pleasant, but it does not ignore that the origin is in pain.

The roots of Taylor's 2022 cookbook *Watermelon and Red Birds: A Cookbook for Juneteenth and Black Celebrations* can be seen here. Knowing about Taylor's work since *Up South*, and even with the podcast *Hot Grease*, I conjecture that there is more that Taylor wanted to say about Juneteenth and the history of slavery than appears in *Up South*. Perhaps as a debut cookbook—even with the powerful endorsements of Bryant Terry and Jessica B. Harris—*Up South* is restrained by audience and genre expectations in ways that Taylor's later work is not. *Watermelon and Red Birds* opens with the story of Juneteenth's origins, similar to the story told in the headnote above. Taylor notes that "Unofficial" celebrations of the anniversary of the news of emancipation reaching Galveston began in 1866 and spread from Texas throughout the US (*Watermelon* 1). The holiday marks both the joy of freedom for African Americans and the cruelty of white enslavers who knowingly withheld information and defied the law of the land to continue exploiting Black labor for their own benefit. As Taylor explains, the official declaration of Juneteenth as a national holiday by President Joe Biden was attended by "jubilation ... mixed with trepidation" as it highlighted the incongruence of a celebration of freedom among crises of "the spread of COVID-19, new laws aimed at suppressing the Black vote, and the unrelenting community trauma resulting from the numerous killings of unarmed Black people, many at the hands of law enforcement officers" (1). Though Taylor does not chronicle the specific pains and indignities of slavery, she often reiterates the combination of pain and pleasure. Taylor concludes: "Black joy often emanates from Black sorrow, and so it has been with that small Texas tendril of freedom, which has continued to spread and strengthen" (1–2). Later in the introduction, Taylor defines "the Juneteenth theme of freedom delayed" by describing the long delays in securing the right to vote for people of color including Native Americans, Asian Americans, and Black Americans. Taylor follows this with the statement that "This book is intended to be light with the pleasures of good food and heavy with the weight of history" (4). Unlike in *Up South* where Taylor obscures some references to the painful past, here in *Watermelon and Red Birds*, Taylor invites the reader to hold these conflicting thoughts at once, to be prepared to celebrate without completely dropping the burden of history.

Raiford's title *Bress 'n' Nyam* is the Gullah phrase for "bless and eat," and identifying the book as representing Gullah Geechee recipes means centering the slave trade in the story of his life and cuisine. Raiford explains that the area of coastal Georgia where he grew up and where his family has been established as farmers for generations is home to "Saltwater Geechee" on the barrier islands (15) and "Freshwater Geechee" on the mainland (79). Raiford explains that his family "are descended from the Freshwater Geechee, the ones who reshaped the land to craft irrigation systems for rice fields from the brackish rivers and creeks" (79). Both groups share in the legacy of slavery, having been kidnapped and enslaved for their knowledge of irrigation and rice cultivation and then "left there to die on the barrier islands along the coast after white landowners abandoned" them (15). Though Raiford will praise the resilience and creativity of Geechee survivors, he does not spare audiences the story of how their isolation was exploited, and "they found their wealth stripped, parcel by parcel" (15). Raiford describes a landmark that is "sacred to [his] kinfolk" near his home in Glynn County, Georgia called Igbo Landing. As Raiford explains, this is "the place where once-free West African tribesmen, chained together during the Middle Passage, walked into the brackish waters and drowned together rather than live enslaved" (20). Though the reference is brief, it is powerful and graphic by comparison to the more vague allusions found elsewhere in this sample. Here, a mass death by suicide is a protest, a last act of agency. The next sentence describes another nearby "hallowed" landmark "where the last known slave ship, the *Wanderer*, landed more than 160 years ago" (20). These locations, tied intimately to the violence of the slave trade in Georgia, are "as sanctified" for Raiford "as the ancient sand-and-clay loam beneath Gilliard Farms, where Freshwater Geechee, experts in irrigation, cultivated rice" (20). Together, these painful stories of slavery mark his farm as intimately, geographically, and historically tied to pain: "This often unforgiving land is my home, and it has now fed my family for eight generations" (20).

Raiford locates the story of his family's farm within the larger history of the Georgia coast and Sea Islands. Raiford uses no euphemisms or equivocations to explain his family's ties to the history of slavery: "I'm the great-great-great-grandson of Jupiter Gilliard, a descendant of the Tikar people of what is now Cameroon.... Jupiter was born into slavery in South Carolina in 1812 and was sold or traded at some point before the Civil War to a landowner in Glynn County, Georgia" (11). Raiford's family story begins in Africa, but its recorded history starts with slavery in the US South. Their connection to the specific location in Georgia is a direct result of slave trade. Jupiter Gilliard is made free by the Emancipation Proclamation and the end of the Civil War, when he "began assembling property" (11) from former enslavers, land that was "most likely abandoned or sold off by white plantation owners afraid of slave revolt during the Reconstruction era" (12). Raiford describes Jupiter Gilliard and his wife Riner breaking and cultivating the swampy land and profiting from both farming and selling land, leaving an inheritance of about 40 acres for his sons in the late 1870s (12). The land passed through branches of Raiford's family until it was left to Ophelia (15), Raiford's great-aunt who raised his mother and whom he called Nana (13). Though Raiford left the farm at the age of 18, promising never to come back (11), Nana gifted the land to him and his sister Althea in 2011 (19). Raiford's final note of the introduction makes clear that he sees himself as the inheritor not just of the land but also of the story: "I am the prodigal son, the custodian of Jupiter Gilliard's legacy. This book is my origin story" (20).

As Raiford's promise never to return suggests, his relationship to the family story and to the ancestral land is complicated by pain, directly related to the history of slavery and racism in the South. "I knew it would be hard coming back," Raiford declares. "Not just the farming, but also as a Black man in the South who cooks in a kitchen and works the land. That's a lot of past to reckon with" (11). Raiford knew that past well through his childhood. He explains that his immediate family lived on the site of the Union School (15), a one-room schoolhouse that was "the only school for Black children in a 20-mile radius" (12). Raiford highlights both the unfairness of segregation that placed an undue burden on Black families to get their children to any school and the poor quality of the education they received there: "[Students] would walk through the woods or ride horses from all over just to study from history books that told them the Ku Klux Klan was simply a social fraternity that took on the role of keeping the Negro people in line from their 'excesses'" (12). Raiford slept, ate, and played in the rooms where Black children suffered. As he states with stoic understatement: "I grew up with this history as my inheritance" (12).

Raiford's life story is also marked by his parents' experiences of racism, especially his father's. Ophelia and Effie Belle (Raiford's mother) moved to Connecticut in the Great Migration where Effie Bell met Raiford's father, Ulious Raiford, who also left the South "seeking the promise of better schools, jobs, and less racism in the northeastern industrial cities. Those promises weren't always realized" (15). Though they went looking for better schools, Ulious "didn't learn to read and write until he was 25 years old;" and though they went looking for an escape from racism, Ulious saw that his opportunities to advance in his career as a baker were blocked by racism (15). When the family returned to the farm in the 1970s, Ulious could not find work "even though he was a pastry expert" who "could make the most delicate apple turnovers, tender-crumbed cakes, and [the most] shattering pie crust you ever ate" (15): "He was told flat out that he could not know more than his white bosses" (15–16). This experience led Ulious to believe that cooking professionally would never be a viable career option for his son, who showed interest in cooking from an early age: "'A lot of things you can do, boy, but cooking ain't one of them,' he said" (16). Raiford did eventually go to culinary school and become a professional chef, but these early painful experiences of racism affected the course of his life. Before Raiford can describe the pleasures of cooking or working his family's farm, he must first address the painful inheritance that comes with it.

Even as the writers in these cookbooks look back at their personal and cultural histories and see pain, they also look back with a kind of pleasant nostalgia. Though Twitty clearly wants to communicate to readers the intensity of pain experienced by enslaved cooks, he also engages in the kind of afro-nostalgia Ahad-Legardy calls nostalgic retribution. When he performs as an enslaved cook, he imagines that cook with an attitude: "I am the enslaved hearing the recipe or already knowing it and just humoring Big Missy." It's a glimmer of a rebellion in affect, *feeling* rebellious, and imagining people of the past with the agency to ignore their captors and rely on their own creative memories. Twitty's pleasures are few, but he does appear to take pleasure in feeling like he has had the last laugh. Twitty sounds almost gleeful declaring that "The Atlantic world has been an incredible experiment in how an enslaved population could get away with enslaving the palates of the people who enslaved them." The excellence of "the black cook—enslaved or free—was second to none," Twitty says, and looking at that excellence as a rebellion that enslaved the enslavers gives immense power to the people of the past and pride and pleasure to Twitty in the present. The cruelties of slavery never extinguished agency. As Twitty claims, "We Africans in the Americas have not just been adopters, we are border crossers and culture benders. We have always been at play with what was presented to us." Though Twitty's "Southern Discomfort Tour" will challenge him "to go beyond assumptions; to interrogate our pain," it also leads him to know his ancestors "intimately the way only I can know them after decades of memory loss." It is a resistance to and reversal of the intentions of enslavers for Twitty to restore the memories and agencies and pleasures of his ancestors and, by extension, the whole of the African diaspora.

Like Twitty, Charles finds moments pleasure and agency in the story of her family's past. Charles describes in detail the labors of her parents' and grandparents' generations as African American sharecroppers who endured both privation and plenty. In the midst of the story of suffering is also nostalgia. The turn from pain to pleasure can happen in a single sentence. For example, Charles writes of her sharecropping ancestors: "Although they could never get ahead, always owing the bosses rent or money for seeds or fertilizer or something else they had to get at the company store, it was a warm community that made its own fun—telling ghost stories, singing, and passing along tales from the old days" (13). The dependent clause outlines suffering, while the independent clause declares that suffering was productive, even fun. Whatever the cause of their suffering, the effect is a warm and vibrantly creative community. Further in the introduction, after Charles carefully documents the many difficult tasks of the farm—growing cotton, corn, tomatoes, peas, apples, peaches, pears, sweet potatoes, peanuts, cabbage, greens, carrots, and beans; foraging for berries and nuts; making cane syrup; raising cows and chickens; churning butter and rendering lard; curing bacon and hams; hunting duck, rabbits, squirrels, and possums; carrying water uphill from a spring; working before school or foregoing school to work—she claims that all of this work paid off in plenty:

> One year my grandmother canned more than a thousand quart jars from her own garden, so many that my grandfather had to add new wooden shelves up to the ceiling . . . . The family was really poor, but the food was so delicious that they often ate like kings. All the sharecroppers helped each other out, traded produce, and shared what they had. (13)

I will talk much more about this narrative of plenty through women's labor of canning and preserving in a later chapter. Charles's story of difficult farm work seems to bring about some of the best qualities or experiences of the family: resilience, creativity, generosity, loyalty. Ahad-Legardy might count this as an example of nostalgic retribution, granting agency to past generations who wrenched this abundance from the system that exploited their labor and kept them in debt. The act of growing, harvesting, preserving, and trading vegetables on rented land gave the family a chance to resist the landowners from whom they would otherwise have bought produce. When Charles remembers this time as a pleasant one of abundance and rebellion, she makes it possible to imagine a Black southern identity that can bring good feelings in the present existing outside of and irrelevant to the story of white violence.

Similarly, the fabulous cooking skills of all of Charles's family members were honed under difficult circumstances. The labors that degraded Charles's grandmother Hattie's health and precipitated her early death (18) were the same labors that brought Hattie pleasure and great distinction in the community. It was the same labor and suffering that taught Charles to cook and finally brought her personal satisfaction and professional success in restaurant kitchens. If Charles looks back at her past with nostalgia, it is because her elevated position in the present gives her the perspective of having seen the end of suffering.

After the introduction, Charles largely leaves stories of slavery and suffering behind. Recipes including ingredients typically associated with the slave trade (okra, black-eyed peas, yams, rice) make no mention of it. Even hoe cakes and collard greens, specifically linked to slave rations in the cookbook introduction, are not connected to slavery or suffering in the recipe narratives. Hoecakes remind Charles of her grandmother (84), and collards are "something you need to know if you're going to cook Southern" whomever you are (66). If the recipe headnote is an advertisement or an argument for using the recipe, then Charles emphasizes pleasure in those arguments, not suffering, by disconnecting from the history of slavery when it comes time to do the cooking and eating.

For example, in the introduction, Charles repeats a story told by her Aunt Laura about "a very old woman who had been a slave" who used to visit the family: "Little Laura would run and hide under the bed when she came because she looked like a witch and talked about very scary things, like the story of a child being traded for a pot of cane syrup" (13). That is a scary story, indeed, and not one you'd typically find in a cookbook. Though the cookbook does not give any evidence as to whether this is a true story or merely a family legend, there is plenty of evidence in the historical record that, among the many harrowing indignities of the American slave trade, a family might have a child taken away without explanation (Twitty remarks offhand that his ancestors might have been traded for cast-iron cooking pots from England). It does not stretch credibility to imagine an enslaved parent might even be offered the insult of a "treat" like cane syrup as a consolation for the kidnap and sale of their child. In the introduction, the cane syrup story adds to Charles's family story and to her deep connection to the South. If this story were in the headnote for a recipe, it would be called on to act as a recommendation for that recipe. It would hardly be appetizing to be reminded of kidnapping and the cruelties of slavery in the moments before heading into the kitchen.

In fact, Charles does include a recipe for a "Huffy-Puffy Oven Pancake" which includes instructions for serving with "100% real cane syrup." However, in the headnote, Charles writes about the goodness of "real" cane syrup, not the imitation "that comes in pretty bottles in the supermarket": "That real cane syrup is so good you won't believe the difference. Real cane syrup, fresh lemon juice, and melted butter take this pancake over the top" (44). Charles provides detailed information later in the book for how to purchase 100 percent real cane syrup from Charles Poirier who "is making the real thing now in Louisiana, using vintage equipment when he can" (263). Whatever associations cane syrup may have with the violence of slavery in the introduction, that connection is severed in the recipe headnotes in favor of connections with "authenticity" ("100% real"), superiority, deliciousness, and craftsmanship. The story of trading a human child for a relatively luxurious food does not reappear in connection with cane syrup in the recipes because the recipe pages, conforming fully to the conventions of the cookbook genre, are given over entirely to embodying pleasure. The contradiction seems to be both bending to the cookbook genre's demand for pleasure and contributing to a story of the South that is more ambivalent than it may appear at first glance.

Charles concludes the introduction with a grateful benediction that emphasizes a narrative of overcoming suffering and living in a pleasant present, making clear that this is the rhetorical purpose of the cookbook as a whole: "I love the moment when everyone comes to the table and their eyes are all lit up with anticipation. We always say a blessing then, because we *are* blessed and we ask for the food to be blessed too. I see this food as a tribute to those who came before me, who worked so incredibly hard for so little" (31). In Ahad-Legardy's formulation of afro-nostalgia, remembering suffering in the past is an important part of the process of present celebration. It's a marker of progress that highlights pleasure in the present by contrast with that painful past. Charles states explicitly that this kind of pleasure after pain is her purpose in writing:

> That's what I want to share with you in this book—especially the younger generations who are losing the connection with home-cooked food and why it's important. There really *is* joy in cooking. If

you don't cook real food, you have no idea of the great pleasure that is waiting for you when you do—the cooking itself, the tasting, the sharing, the passing along. (31)

Though Charles has highlighted the hard work, the physical pain, and the tragic loss that she has inherited from a family legacy connected to slavery in the US South, as well as her own personal emotional distress (including Charles's own introduction to the physical challenges of food labor at the age of six (16), a disastrous marriage at the age of thirteen characterized by "jealousy, violence, and abuse" from which she "was lucky to emerge in one piece" but "a little wiser" (18), and very public struggles with her former employer, Paula Deen, after years of inadequate compensation and racist discrimination (26–27), all lead directly to Charles's personal moment of triumph and a strong, creative community. Readers who engage with these stories and recipes are encouraged to nod along in agreement at the sadness of the suffering (for which no particular person is responsible; even Deen is treated gently and with dignity) and then to cheer alongside Charles as she narrates her success in the face of such unfavorable odds. The pleasures of the food are heightened by the turn from suffering to celebration; Charles's evident skill and success are heightened by the comparison to humble origins.

In her first cookbook, *Up South*, Taylor typically looks backward at her own childhood or stories within the living memory of her extended family for pleasant memories. Taylor uses ingredients in recipes that remind her of warm childhood memories including honeysuckle in cocktails (206) or the chocolate that reminds her of the "pure joy" of buying candy from the stores near her childhood home (166). Taylor attempts to "re-create the blackberry cobbler at Busy Bee Café in Atlanta" from her early college years (179). Part of Taylor's writing process included visiting family in her hometown in Georgia for "inspiration and to collect stories about my maternal family" (146). The family stories are of generosity, love, abundance, and skill. Taylor honors her "late grandfather Boley [who] had the biggest garden in the neighborhood and was unselfish with his entire harvest" (182). Taylor writes with the most affection of her cousins Tom and Bonnie Gartrell who taught her the importance of "a symbolic dish of stability" and family love: "Their home is where love overflowed. It's the place I first saw a pig roast and saw love in action. The abundance of memories influences my approach when catering to family and new friends" (109). In a gentle parody of "saying grace" before a meal, Taylor gives thanks for "the endless church functions that shaped my palate and the yearly repast of my family's first-cousin gathering. I'm beholden to you for the privilege to explore life outside the South and break bread with a 'new family.'" (119). These pleasant family memories are typical of most cookbooks.

However, Taylor occasionally engages in Ahad-Legardy's version of afro-nostalgia by looking at a few important moments and figures in African American history with pleasure including the Harlem Renaissance and the Great Migration and Hattie McDaniels and George Washington Carver. Taylor's connection to the Harlem Renaissance seems to be a short leap, being based in Brooklyn, New York. At the end of the Introduction, Taylor connects the joyful creativity of her own collection of southern expatriates in her home to those who once gathered in Harlem and urban areas of the North: "I'm reminded of the Harlem Renaissance and the great migrations, when thousands of creatives arrived in droves with musical instruments, pens, paper, and antebellum taste buds, all connected to their roots but focused on an elevated life" (13). In the headnote for the recipe for a "Savory Grits Waffle," Taylor references the invention of chicken and waffles in "the late 1930s at the now-defunct Wells restaurant in Harlem, NYC" (33). These references to the Harlem Renaissance demonstrate a nostalgia for the brightest and most pleasant moments in Black history.

Taylor's stories about the Great Migration also highlight pleasure. Taylor combines the historical with the personal in the headnote for "Yeast Rolls." The headnote begins by contextualizing the "the Great Migration (1900–1970)," as a time when "around 6 million African Americans left the South and journeyed, mostly, north." Taylor's ancestor and contributor of the recipe, her great-aunt Bessie Goolsby, "moved 'up nawth,'" as a part of this national historical moment. Taylor doesn't mention the specifics of her great-aunt's move north. Instead, she focuses on how Goolsby "solidified her name as the best roll-maker in Athens-Clarke County" as a beloved cook at a local middle school before leaving the South (129). As Taylor looks back on these moments of black creativity and community—much like Ahad-Legardy describes Marcus Samuelsson doing in *Afro-Nostalgia*—it seems clear that she is connecting herself as a modern-day echo of those moments. Like her great-aunt and the "thousands of creatives" who moved to Harlem, Taylor is also bringing the best of the South to the "Up South" of Brooklyn. There is pleasure both in the memory of those historical moments and in the re-creation of them in the present.

Taylor also notes connections to black innovators and important figures of the past with pride. Taylor describes being commissioned to create a recipe "centered on Hattie McDaniel's 1940 Oscar win." The first African American to win an Academy Award, and best known for her role in *Gone With the Wind*, McDaniels serves as an important figure in African American history.

Taylor honors the actress with "a knock out six-tier [cake] tribute.... This beauty is dedicated to Mrs. McDaniels's grand Californian lifestyle and love for floral" (160). Celebrating the icon with pleasure and excess recovers and reclaims McDaniels as a creator, not as the caricature she played in the film. Similarly, Taylor invokes Dr. George Washington Carver in the chapter introduction to "Fruits and Nuts." Carver is noted for his forty-four bulletins of recipes and instructions for farmers and his "generous" legacy of "a little less than a million dollars" upon his death "to further agricultural research" (165). Another figure of the past important to African American history is honored and remembered with pleasure.

Taylor includes contributions and headnotes written by and about contemporary African American food figures including Edna Lewis ("Pecan Cornbread Dressing" 132), Michael Twitty (on Chow Chow [189]), and historian Jessica B. Harris who writes the Foreword (10–11) and gave Taylor the gift of her own mother's punch bowl ("New Age Church Punch" 213). Bryant Terry provides an endorsement on the front flap and the back jacket. Taylor requests recipes and notes from other African American food bloggers Sanura Weathers ("Life Runs on Food" 56) and Heather Watkins Jones ("The Blacker the Berry Food" 42). The only extended profile in the book is a recipe and a "Q & A" with Charmaine Bee, owner of "Gullah Girl Tea" (208–9). Taylor asks Bee three questions, and all of them are about remembering southern roots and familial influence. Bee's answers highlight the abundance of produce and the "organic and rich relationship" her grandmother had with local farmers. Bee answers that "the stories, the connectedness that happens over a cup of tea" that she witnessed in her childhood are the inspiration for Gullah Girl Tea (209). Together, the celebration of other Black creators, past and present, is part of the pleasure of *Up South*.

This strategy of celebrating Black creators is even more pronounced in *Watermelon and Red Birds*. In the headnote for the recipe "Beer-Battered Shrimp," Taylor cites Gus Allen, "an African-American entrepreneur who owned a hotel, café, and several other businesses on Galveston's Church Street" as the inspiration for the recipe. Since the Juneteenth celebration originates from Galveston, Allen is a particularly effective authority to cite. Though she explains that the recipe is "in remembrance" of Allen and not directly his contribution, she nonetheless invites readers to connect the pleasures of the present celebration with remembering a "once-bustling strip of Black-owned commerce" that unfortunately "no longer exists" (96). A painful experience of loss is held between moments of pleasurable nostalgia.

Raiford, too, recognizes with pride other Black creators who inspire him. Raiford's father discouraged him from professional cooking for fear that his son's path for advancement would be as blocked by racism as his own path had been. However, Raiford describes a formative experience in culinary school when he assisted eminent Black chef and teacher Joe Randall with his "annual Taste of Heritage dinner." The dinner not only taught Raiford about the "rich heritage of African foodways as they sprang from the American South" but he also learned about "the alchemy of Native American fires, Spanish conquest, Caribbean inflection, and West African ingenuity." More importantly, the dining room and the kitchen alike were filled with chefs, cookbook writers, and historians of color: "[F]or the first time in my life I looked around a room and saw the representation I didn't know I craved—Leah Chase, Edna Lewis, Jessica B. Harris, Patrick Clark, all black chefs and cookbook authors who spoke with pride" (16). Unlike Raiford's father who "had never seen someone who liked like me or him as the head of a kitchen" (15), Raiford sees a room full of potential and pride: "These chefs, who looked like me, were doing some amazing work, and I knew that if I put in the effort, I could be there beside them" (16). Raiford takes pleasure both in the success of his predecessors and in the knowledge that his own success can be commensurate with his effort and agency, not based on limitations set by others. In a heartbreaking final note, Raiford wishes his father might have had an experience like this (16), suggesting that he, too, might have found the joy of professional satisfaction in cooking if only he had seen other Black chefs working with pride.

Still, when Raiford discusses the past, he is direct about the pain, even as it turns to pleasure in the present. Looking at his archive of family photos and documents reminds Raiford of "how those who came before me withstood the legal and social assaults of racism and discrimination by building self-sufficient communities" (20). The end result of self-sufficiency is good, but Raiford does not attempt to downplay or obfuscate the painful reasons that made self-sufficiency necessary. In the sentence immediately after this, Raiford goes further by declaring "that restaking our claim to these lands might help us heal, to reconcile, to create a healthier way forward. Good food and good community go hand in hand. Maybe it's the key to resilience, and maybe now, we know our worth" (20). The pleasures that Raiford and his family are experiencing in the present are also key to a pleasant—and more just—future. It isn't explicitly clear what Raiford means by "reconciling," though readers may assume that Raiford means reconciliation between the white southerners who are responsible for the "legal and social assaults of racism and discrimination" and the Black southerners like Raiford and his ancestors who resisted them by withdrawing into "self-sufficient communities" in the previous sentence. The possibility for this reconciliation comes from following Raiford's good example for building "good community" with "good food."

Even with that future of reconciliation and good community still in the distance, Raiford expresses pleasure in the present, first through gratitude and appreciation for other producers of color like himself and later through appreciation for the land itself. Raiford organizes his cookbook around the elements of "earth, water, fire, wind, nectar, and spirits" and their Gullah Geechee names, representing "the wisdom of the ancestors, our source." He also notes that he lives by the principles of Kwanzaa: "unity, self-determination, collective work and responsibility, cooperative economics, purpose, creativity, and faith." As organizing principles and underlying values, these lead Raiford to "lift up and honor the good work of people in our region who work hard daily to harvest wholesome, organic food, who honor animals through humane practices, and who nourish not just our bodies but our minds and spirits." Practically, that means that Raiford has identified specific suppliers of "peas, syrups, rice, and grits" so that readers can "seek out these purveyors and handmake a dish that is as authentic to the vision of this book as possible" (25). Through this argument of authenticity, Raiford also celebrates and shares gratitude with his community.

Raiford also shows a tender and emotional connection to the land that his ancestors worked, owned, and bequeathed. In the headnote for the recipe for "Za'atar Roasted Chicken," quoted entirely below, Raiford's love for the land blends the pain of the past with a deep appreciation for the present:

> The Middle Eastern spice blend of za'atar speaks to my soul. The benne seed, carried to this country by my ancestors, forms its foundation. They planted these seeds in secret to provide sustenance and flavor. The sumac grows wild among the woods of Gilliard Farms. The heavy laden stems bend with beadlike, crimson fruits in a kind of gratitude. The sweet fragrance reaches deep inside of me and conjures a memory that I cannot name. (155)

Within this poetic tribute to za'atar, Raiford links the "secret" rebellious planting of benne by people who were enslaved to the wild fertility of his land in the present. The "sweet fragrance" of sumac seems to awaken a memory that is so deep it might be what Michael Twitty calls "a blood memory." It doesn't belong to Raiford alone but comes to him through his ancestors. In this moment of communion with past through the sensory pleasures of the present, Raiford performs nostalgic retribution, seeking justice for his ancestors by recognizing their agency and acts of rebellion. Furthermore, Raiford gives readers the opportunity to share in this moment by offering the recipe so that they may literally embody the same sensations. If they choose not to cook the recipe, Raiford still provides three full-page, full-color photographs to share in the sensory experience: the cooked chicken coated in za'atar (154), a hand that appears to be Raiford's sprinkling the seasoning over a bowl (156), and arms picking a cluster of sumac berries, presumably Raiford's partner, Javon Sage (157). The reader is invited to share intimately in Raiford's pleasure, though it is edged with pain.

As Ahad-Legardy concludes in *Afro-nostalgia*, ambivalence—a mixture of pleasure and pain—and contradiction are the end result and rhetorical purpose of moments of nostalgia (21). Twitty's presentation of this experience is particularly complex and ambivalent. Like Ahad-Legardy, Twitty recognizes that the past he is exploring is "traumatic" and that trying to "participat[e] in the praise fest for rediscovering and sustaining America's food roots" may seem "trivial," especially in the context of the present: "The early and antebellum South is not where most African Americans want to let their minds and feet visit. It is a painful place, and the modern South is just beginning to engage the relationship between the racial divide, class divisions, and cultural fissures that have tainted the journey to contemporary Southern cuisine" (6). Twitty frequently forms paradoxes of conflicting emotions. The Old South is "a place caught up in a weird braid of nostalgia, lament, romance, horror, and fear" (xvi) but as a youth, Twitty "loved that Old South with all its funkiness and dread" (xii). Twitty acknowledges that "we are unwitting inheritors of a story with many sins;" however, he argues that the story "bears the fruit of the possibility of ten times the redemption" (xvii). Put briefly: "There is a lot of beautiful and a lot of ugly mashed together" (xiv). Twitty's memoir offers insight into what pain and pleasure African American cookbook writers and readers might have to contend with when considering how to write or perform the history of slavery in the US South. While the potential for pain is right at the surface, Twitty reveals that there can be pleasure and a powerful reclamation of identity when writers and cooks take the risk. Finding the balance might be the purpose of the work.

As Charles emphasizes throughout the introduction, the stories of suffering in the past are not stories to be silenced or forgotten. To the contrary, the stories and the foods that appear in those stories are important identity-making stories and performances. Even the painful parts are to be remembered and reenacted. Once again, Charles carefully details the privations of enslavement and suggests that telling the story of suffering and eating the foods symbolic of suffering times are powerful experiences that satisfy a craving:

> I don't have to tell you that the original make-do cooks in the South were slaves. I've been told that a field worker's rations for a week on a

cotton plantation like the one where my great-grandfather harvested cotton were just a few ears of dried corn and three pounds of fatback or sidemeat. They grated the corn and mixed it with water to make a meal of cornmeal mush, or they made hoecakes right off the flat part of the hoe over a fire, greasing it with a little fat from the fatback. That and whatever green things they could grow would be it for the week. There might be some eggs or a peach found growing off by the river, but mostly it was the same all the time. Yet those tastes are still what we crave: cornbread, bacon, greens. They speak to us, black and white alike. Cooked right, they sing a powerful song. (27–30)

In this lengthy passage, Charles begins with a familiar story of the privations of meager rations for enslaved workers: hog and hominy. However, Charles explains that cooks used creativity and resourcefulness, a combination of knowledge and effort, to stretch those rations into a cuisine that even today "speak[s]" and "sing[s]" and satisfies with pleasure. Moreover, Charles invites white audiences to access this story personally, too. The taste for cornbread, bacon, and greens may have begun with the suffering of slavery, but that story and those flavors are accessible to *all* southerners, "black and white alike." Though the pain and the creativity belong to enslaved people, all southerners may share in the pleasures of this inheritance.

Even though the stories in Charles's introduction are about Black slaves and Black suffering, they leave open just enough room for white readers to identify as well, subtly not naming them as aggressors while explicitly inviting them to share in a common cuisine. It is important to point out that while the suffering of Black southerners through slavery and sharecropping is made clear here, the white agents responsible for that suffering are absent from the narrative. The work of slavery is cruel; there is no mention of enslavers. And though there is a brief mention of bosses and landowners, they are in passive sentence constructions: two-thirds of the crop and profits "went back to the landowners," Charles's family was "always owing the bosses rent or money," the jail was a place where workers "were kept." None of these moments make the bosses or landowners subjects of sentences who create or inflict this suffering. On one hand, Charles may be performing a strategic rhetorical act by not explicitly naming or blaming a particular villain, instead allowing the reader to come to their own conclusion about who is to blame. White readers are not directly implicated in the crime; they can share in the pleasure without feeling attacked if they choose not to read between the lines. The erasure of the agents of suffering does not minimize the suffering of Charles's family, but it does leave space for white readers to empathize with Charles and the painful experience of slavery. On the other hand, while Charles is able to rhetorically appeal to readers of multiple backgrounds who will hear the truth about the suffering of slavery, the resistance is limited if white readers fail to recognize their complicity. In negotiating the cookbook conventions for pleasure, Charles seems to be making a bargain with readers that allows her to describe the pain of slavery in detail but limits her ability to be directly critical.

On balance, Charles's stories of slavery are multivalent and complicated, calling different audiences to different actions. First, they act as evidence of the "Real Southern Cook" Charles claims to be in the title of her cookbook. Charles gives evidence of her family's long history for traditional authenticity. She connects that long history to the geographically specific location of the Lowcountry and later to Savannah, Georgia. Lots of white southern cookbook writers can make the same arguments, but by narrating her connection to fabulous enslaved cooks, Charles uses an element of authenticity no white southern writer has access to. She can claim a direct link from the real, unsung founders of the cuisine right to her own kitchen. She leverages this connection to establish her ethos as a "Real Southern Cook" and to persuade audiences to spend their money on her book.

The effect of the stories of suffering may be vastly different depending on the identity of the audience. If Ahad-Legardy is right, then African American readers may be able to engage with Charles's stories as afro-nostalgia, feeling good about the little victories of Charles's ancestors and proud of Charles's success—which is itself a kind of retribution over Deen who infamously asked Charles and her coworker on multiple occasions to "dress up in an Aunt Jemima get up" (26). That good feeling and the invitation to join in a celebration of the pleasures of cooking and eating works by first linking the present to a past that is both painful and pleasant. The pain is expected; the pleasant defies expectations.

White readers may not be able to access the resistance that Charles is mounting without significant critical engagement with the text. It may be that Charles appeases some racist white audiences by keeping the bad actors off-stage and confirming fantasies that African Americans are "over" racism. What I see is more complicated. Instead of appealing to white guilt, Charles asks white readers to give their empathy and sympathy to the suffering of Black southerners who share a common cuisine and culture with them. If white readers are able to access the good feelings of community and connectedness that Charles invites all to share, what might they do with those good feelings? How might they reimagine the story of southern food and culture with the information they now have? Charles uses pleasure to invite Black and white southerners to a common table and unified community.

Raiford, too, reaches a state of ambivalence by narrating the origins of southern foodways as neither wholly traumatic nor wholly pleasant. In a side note titled "Rice as the Foundation," Raiford eschews euphemism or obfuscation when he explicitly states "enslaved West Africans from rice cultivation areas along the Niger River watershed and the coastline of equatorial Africa were brought to the Americas through ports in Sullivan's Island, Savanna, and New Orleans" (31). Though he doesn't mention this as a particularly painful moment, nor does he make white enslavers a subject of the sentence, he does not leave space for readers to misunderstand how or why rice "came" to the South except through slave trade. Raiford goes further by suggesting that rice was first cultivated in the South explicitly for feeding enslaved people, only later becoming "a valuable commodity for plantation owners" (31). This is the part of the story of the introduction of African ingredients into the southern diet that most writers skip over, but as with the benne seeds that Raiford describes as a "secret" rebellion, many ingredients were introduced first as "feed" for the "stock" of enslaved people. However, Raiford sprinkles this narrative with praise for the enslaved ancestors who "brought with them grains and seeds, plus the know-how to level land and create irrigation ditches with systems of gates to manage water flow through saltwater marshes and freshwater swamps" (31). Knowledge, skill, and rebellion transformed rice into a valuable commodity that "reflected the strength of the people who, when abandoned and left to die on the Sea Islands after the Civil War, instead thrived" and came to be known as Gullah Geechee. Raiford again praises their unique "language and other cultural traditions like call-and-response shout singing, oral storytelling, and intricate arts like crab net tying and sweetgrass basket making," but he also notes that these creations "also had the practical purpose of easing the brutal work" (31). That pattern of ambivalence is recognizable across the sample, but Raiford ends this passage with a rare second-person pronoun: "These dishes speak to where you came up, who your people are—from the mainland or the ocean, near the city or in the country" (31). Nowhere else in the note does he invoke a personal pronoun; even in the headnote on the opposite page, Raiford implies "you" only in one sentence. Who is being invited into the "you" of "where you came up, who your people are?" Raiford opens "you" geographically to include urban, rural, coastal, and inland. Does it also include the rest of the Lowcountry residents for whom rice is "the foundation" of cuisine, regardless of race? The ambivalence expressed here—even in the ambiguity of the pronoun—opens up possibilities for audiences to share in a common story and cuisine.

Raiford's personal ambivalence is perhaps best expressed in the introduction to the "Sweet'n/Nectar" chapter of desserts and baked goods.

Because of his father's profession as a baker and pastry expert, the topic readily lends itself to reflection on that part of the family story. Raiford explains how his success has changed his father's mind about the fears he had for Raiford's future in professional cooking based on his own painful experiences of racism. "If he knew what he knows now," Raiford explains, "he would have encouraged me to go to culinary school right out of high school" (187). Instead of expressing regret or anger, Raiford responds with ambivalence: "But we all got our journeys, right? And maybe this one wouldn't be as sweet had it been so easy" (187). Sweetness may, in fact, be the result of struggle, but the overarching feeling of this statement is the ambivalent shrug suggested in the question. What can he do about it now? What would be the purpose of probing the "what if?" The journey is both sweetness and suffering.

TOWARDS A CONCLUSION: TRUTH AND RECONCILIATION

Cookbooks as a genre are expected to be pleasant which may make them seem like the wrong time and place to look directly at pain, and yet the discourse of southern food tells us that the kitchen and the table are exactly the right places to "unlock the rusty gates of race and class, age and sex" as John Egerton famously has written, and to enact reconciliation and social justice at the common table (4). But this, too, is a suspect narrative of pleasure that seems too simple. When speakers in the discourse make food itself the actor with agency to affect change, this can distract from the necessary work that individuals must do in order to restore relationships and shake up institutions. While cornbread and collard greens may "sing" to all southerners, as Dora Charles writes, eating these foods with pleasure in our own homes (in historically segregated neighborhoods and gerrymandered voting districts) is not evidence of completed reconciliation. The private and domestic action of cooking and eating southern food from a cookbook may be a performance of southern identity open to all, but its democratic effect is minimal and temporary. Only relationships conducted in honesty and self-awareness can enact the reconciliation called for at the common table. Writers of color like Michael Twitty, Dora Charles, Nicole Taylor, and Matthew Raiford are grappling with the stories of slavery and racism in their personal histories and in the very public venues of their work. They offer a gracious model for meeting the conventions of the cookbook genre and appealing to diverse audiences while still telling honest stories about the past and present. What readers do with that model is beyond their control.

When southern cookbooks and other popular food media are criticized for not taking slavery and racism head on in writing, I always want to ask, "Well, how do you want them to do it? How will they do this and still pass the eye of an editor? Still connect with an audience? Still do what cookbooks are meant to do and bring pleasure?" The writers in this sample show that it is possible to be clear, direct, and honest about the pain of slavery while also helping readers to find a place for themselves as a joint heir of the same painful story *and* the same delicious cuisine. Writers of color lead the way in vulnerability, linking their personal stories and experiences with the metanarrative of the South, adding complexity and texture to what has been monolithic and homogenizing.

What can white writers learn from the example of writers of color? Perhaps white writers can meet them at the table by also leading with personal vulnerability, historical honesty, and unresolved ambivalence. I think the best example I've seen among white cookbook writers (not academics, but professional food writers) comes from Virginia Willis's 2018 cookbook *Secrets of the Southern Table: A Food Lover's Tour of the Global South*. Unlike Willis's earlier cookbooks—*Bon Appetit, Y'all* and *Basic to Brilliant, Y'all*—this one is less of a memoir for Willis than a journalistic experience. *Bon Appetit, Y'all* focuses on the intersection between Willis' formal French training and the southern recipes she learned from her mother and grandmothers. *Basic to Brilliant, Y'all* similarly presents recipes that are "basic" for cooking at home (with family stories) or "brilliantly" French-inspired for showing off. But *Secrets of the Southern Table* mostly leaves Willis's family story and explores the story of the region at large, especially the presence of non-Euro-American people and their influence on southern cuisine. Each chapter opens with two short feature stories of Willis's experiences traveling in the South and interviewing farmers, chefs, activists, and business owners who represent the wide diversity of southern food culture. The recipes are Willis's, but the stories focus on other characters through the lens of Willis's experience.

Willis signals her intention to open a conversation about race and racism with a dedication that reads: "In hope of nation where, in the words of Dr. Martin Luther King, Jr., people will be judged not by the color of their skin, but by the content of their character" (v). This invocation and quotation of Dr. King is risky, perhaps appearing to a cynical reader as lip service to the most well-known and easiest-to-access speech of the civil rights era. It doesn't show a deep reading knowledge of antiracist literature, for sure. But for a moment, imagine white audiences opening a southern cookbook from a well-known white writer whose face is on the cover, making her race obvious, and finding that the first words of the book are a call for suspending judgment based on race. It's an important signal of her intentions and hails her ideal audience as one who shares in this hope for the future.

The first two and a half pages of Willis's introduction review her southern bona fides from the "two strong Southern women" after whom she is named (xii) to the various southern cities and states where she has lived (xiv) and the foods she grew up eating (xv). In the middle of those first two pages is a full-page full-color photograph of an African American person's hands digging up a root vegetable that looks to me like a sweet potato. Below these hands is a pull quote from the introduction: "Southern cuisine is a living, breathing, growing thing" (xiii). While Willis is offering her personal story as evidence of her southern authenticity, she is also making a claim that resists defining southern cuisine as "authentic" at any particular moment. As a "living, breathing, growing thing," southern cuisine cannot easily be pinned down into one thing. Maybe the disembodied Black hands could be interpreted as tokenism, but in the context of the rest of the book's stated purpose, the image and the caption both suggest that Willis is interested in presenting an expansive southern cuisine beyond her own family and race.

Willis signals a turn in the narrative when she admits that while "growing up for me in the Deep South was somewhat idyllic," she "could not ignore the economic disparity between the classes and races." She goes on to acknowledge that much of her "idyllic" childhood was the result of systemic racism starting with "the enslaved Africans who once toiled on the plantations" of the Black Belt and continuing with the "quite significant" poverty of their descendants. Willis notes that she "attended an all-white private school that had been born out of the court-mandated public school desegregation in the mid-1960s," admitting that her privilege is the result of racist policies and decisions that created all-white spaces at the expense of Black and poor children. Willis narrates her personal experiences living in the segregated South, witnessing racism and poverty firsthand, and feeling that "This imbalance of money and power is and has been for a long time a simmering pot seeming ready to boil over" (xv). Rather than sticking with the "idyllic" personal story that Willis has told many times in her other cookbooks, she leads readers into the more painful and complicated story of the South and in the process, implicates herself in the South's problems with race.

Willis is also honest about her limitations as a white woman to speak for the wide variety of experiences in the South. "I don't know what it feels like to grow up as a person of color or someone of the Jewish, Muslim, or Hindu faith in the Deep South," Willis claims, but she is perfectly aware that "while the South is primarily built on a black-white narrative, it is actually not as homogenous as it seems" (xix). She can only speak about racism from her own experience. Willis specifically remembers a moment when she saw her friend's mother lock the car doors at the sight of a Black man walking by their car on the sidewalk. Insulted, the man "became outraged and yelled at the car, 'I don't want nothing in your damn car'" (xvi). Willis provides this story as evidence of her claim that tension over race and class in South is like "a simmering pot ready to boil over," but she also tells the story to demonstrate her own unenlightened state and an instinctive feeling that the man's outrage was deserved: "It shook me. I remember feeling embarrassed and conflicted" (xvi). Willis isn't claiming to have never been racist or to have ever been "colorblind;" to the contrary, she is opening herself up to criticism by honestly admitting how she participated (in this case passively as a child and passenger) in a racist act. She offers another version of the same kind of personal vulnerability that writers of color have used to speak about racism.

Willis is critical of other white people in the essays that precede the recipes. In the first chapter, Willis opens with two stories of two farmers, one white and one Black. The white family farm is founded by a Confederate veteran returning home from the Civil War. But the story of the farm is one of dwindling success and a broken system of federal subsidies that make food artificially cheap and perpetuate monoculture. The farmer, Will Harris of Blufton, Georgia, is unequivocal in his judgment of his implication in the harm done to the land:

> We didn't mean to turn our soil into a dead mineral medium, but we did. We didn't mean to implement a confinement system that deprived our animals of the ability to express their instinctive behavior, but we did. We didn't mean to contribute to the economic and social decline of our rural village, but we did. (Harris qtd. in Willis 7)

Other cookbook writers, like Sean Brock (who writes a foreword to Willis's book), are critical of industrial farming in the South, but none take responsibility for causing harm as Willis allows Harris to do in *Secrets of the Southern Table*. Willis ends the narrative by emphasizing how Harris and his farm are working to reverse this trend, but admitting fault is a vulnerable and honest decision that is a compelling step toward justice and unexpected in the pleasure-centered genre of the cookbook.

The second profile in Willis's cookbook is of Matthew Raiford, the same author of *Bress 'n' Nyam* discussed at length above. In contrast to Harris's story of environmental degradation, Willis describes Raiford and Sage's farm—as old as Harris's—as a place where "chemicals have never been used" (11). Not only is Willis impressed at the stewardship of Gilliard Farms, but she is also struck by Raiford's family's resilience in the face of racism. Raiford tells Willis about a neighboring white landowner who would charge Black people a toll for using the public road that went through his property (notably, Raiford does not tell this story in his own cookbook). Raiford explains that "As a result, as a young kid I learned to walk along this creek and in the woods instead" (12). Unstated is that this change in behavior is likely "a result" of fear of potentially violent conflict. Willis' reaction to the story is intense and emotional:

> We turn to walk back to the main part of the farm, and his words weigh heavily on me. Damn. Seriously, damn! I realize all at once that I have no real idea about this South . . . Matthew's family once toiled on nearby land as slaves. It all seems untenable and irrevocable at the same time. I'm stung by the juxtaposition of the breathtaking beauty of this veritable Georgia jungle against the bigotry and hatred that also can grow in this fertile soil" (12).

Willis's admission of her own ignorance and righteous outrage on Raiford's behalf goes beyond the mere celebration of African American culinary contributions that has become familiar in today's cookbooks by white writers to something like a recognition of wrong-doing. The feelings that Willis expresses are painful, heavy, "untenable," "irrevocable," stinging. The suggestion is of a story too big and too painful to fully comprehend, and yet, Willis holds this discomfort and shares it with her audience. Throughout the scenes with Raiford, Willis contrasts the beauty and peace of the farm in the present with its painful history, and she feels the contradiction as pain.

The contrast and contradiction between the two farms in the first chapter set a tone and expectation for how readers should see the rest of the book. Willis writes, "It was very intentional that I started this book with [two contrasting stories] . . . . So much of what defines the South starts with the complex and intertwined story of black and white. I know that the secret of the Southern table was birthed in this story" (11). But the recipes that follow go beyond Black and white. The first recipe (after thirty pages of narrative introduction), "Brussels Sprout and Benne Seed Coleslaw," describes benne as seeds from Africa, grown in the South, familiar in Chinese restaurants and on fast food hamburger buns. The second, "Southern Stir-Fry with Turnips and Greens" (19) references Chinese men working in Mississippi Delta cotton fields after emancipation: "When they arrived they found hard labor and low pay. To achieve economic independence, these new immigrants opened grocery stores, selling to black freedmen who had formerly used the plantation stores . . . incorporating their cooking into the local cuisine" (19). Willis invites ambivalence and complication into the story of southern cooking when she notes with some understatement that "The South is a complicated place, especially when it comes to race, and Southern food is a complicated cuisine" (xvi). Again, she links the complications to race: "the questions of ownership of Southern cooking are some of the most provocative points in our ongoing struggles over race" (xvi). Rather than attempting to adjudicate those questions or attempt to assign ownership, Willis lets the complications stand while also acknowledging the "tangled and compelling web of race, politics, and social history that is served up alongside our beloved biscuits and gravy" (xvi). The difficulty of the southern past and present are allowed to remain difficult.

The essays in *Secrets of the Southern Table* are problem-centric, bringing up conflicts and painful stories, even though they always end celebratory. The recipe narratives recognize the presence of diverse bodies in the South at all eras and the contributions of many races, ethnicities, and nationalities to the southern economy and culture—food and otherwise. The picture of the South is diverse but flawed. Its racist past is not far behind it, not even past, but southerners can recognize a path forward if they follow the example of nonwhite southerners like Raiford and Sage of Gilliard Farms. Willis's cookbook takes a risk by inviting pain and difficulty into the story of the South, but she does so with personal vulnerability and an eye toward justice. As she explains in the introduction, this is all intentional:

> All I know now is that I feel I need to do what I need to do to bridge that gap [between experiences], make that wrong right, and unlock the barriers that I can. I am not alone. There are many Southerners like me uncomfortable with the status quo. Division is the truth in the South, like in much of the U.S., but it's not the only truth and it's not my truth." (xix)

Willis qualifies the claim with phrases like "what I need to do" and what "I can," but the sentiment is an admirable one that is rarely stated with such candor by white writers and in the genre. She wants readers to see her gestures—like quoting Dr. Martin Luther King, Jr. and taking pictures of Black hands in the dirt—as part of an "authentic" expression of her true feelings and as expressions of solidarity and appreciation taken in good faith. Willis demonstrates that white southern writers can, indeed, wade into the complexities of race in the South, get it approved by their editors, and still sell their cookbook.

It seems clear that the turn from the suffering of enslaved people in the past to the pleasure of food in the present has a dramatically different valence depending on the positionality of the speaker and intended audience. Pleasure or suffering on its own does not determine the presence of resistance or protest. However, the books in this sample also make clear that there is room to play in the cookbook genre's rigid conventions, and cookbook writers may choose to use that room to speak honestly about pain or pleasure, adding complication and ambivalence to what has long been a too-simple story in Black and white.

As Charles makes so clear, there *is* joy in cooking. Of course narratives that invoke suffering in the past will eventually end with a celebration of a nonsuffering present to conform to the expectations of the cookbook genre. They emphasize joy, pleasure, flavor, and celebration of culture and family. This is not at all surprising given the rhetorical situation of the cookbook as a guide to pleasure and the conventions of the genre: the pleasures of cooking, the pleasures of hosting and entertaining, the pleasures of eating, even the pleasure of imagining that you are cooking, hosting, or eating.

The more interesting question to me is not whether the genre can tolerate pain, but whether reconciliation is best accomplished over narratives of shared suffering or shared pleasure. Southern cookbook writers work in a highly choreographed genre with deeply entrenched conventions including a commitment to pleasure and celebration of culture and cuisine. But as the contemporary cookbooks in this study show, the moments of resistance to these conventions are significant subversions that demonstrate the creativity and rhetorical skill of cookbook writers while also showing the potential for new ways to understand a shared past and look forward to a more just future.

WORKS CITED

Ahad-Legardy, Badia. *Afro-Nostalgia: Feeling Good in Contemporary Black Culture*. U of Illinois P, 2021.

Charles, Dora. *A Real Southern Cook in Her Savannah Kitchen*. Houghton Mifflin Harcourt, 2015.

Collins, Lauren. "Alison Roman Just Can't Help Herself." *The New Yorker*, 13 Dec. 2021, https://www.newyorker.com/magazine/2021/12/20/alison-roman-just-cant-help-herself.

Egerton, John. *Southern Food: At Home, on the Road, and in History*. Knopf, 1987.

Raiford, Matthew. *Bress 'n' Nyam: Gullah Geechee Recipes from a Sixth Generation Farmer*. Countryman Press, 2021.

Severson, Kim. "A Powerful, and Provocative, Voice for Southern Food." *The New York Times*, 9 May 2017, https://www.nytimes.com/2017/05/09/dining/southern-food-john-t-edge-profile.html.

Taylor, Nicole A. "About." *Nicole A. Taylor*. http://www.nicoleataylor.com/about.html

Taylor, Nicole A. *Up South: Chasing Dixie in a Brooklyn Kitchen*. Countryman Press, 2015.

Taylor, Nicole A. *Watermelon and Red Birds: A Cookbook for Juneteenth and Black Celebrations*. Simon and Schuster, 2022.
Tippen, Carrie Helms. *Inventing Authenticity: How Cookbook Writers Redefine Southern Identity*. U of Arkansas P, 2018.
Trainer, Sarah, Jessica Hardin, Cindi SturtzSreetharan, and Alexandra Brewis. "Worry-Nostalgia: Anxieties around the Fading of Local Cuisines and Foodways." *Gastronomica*, vol. 20, no. 2, Summer 2020, pp. 67–78.
Twitty, Michael. *The Cooking Gene: A Journey Through African-American Culinary History in the Old South*. Amistad, 2017.
Willis, Virginia. *Secrets of the Southern Table: A Food Lover's Journey Through the Global South*. Houghton Mifflin Harcourt, 2018.
Zafar, Rafia. *Recipes for Respect: African American Meals and Meaning*. U of Georgia P, 2018.

MAKING DO
Pain of Poverty and Pleasure of Resilience

I had this friend in grad school, Terry Peterman, and one of our favorite games was a "poor off," a competition in one-upping to see who could come up the best evidence of their childhood poverty. Maybe joking about poverty was in bad taste, but it was *our* poverty, and it made us laugh. The "poor off" was mostly a conversation about food. Ground beef was in and on everything. I didn't eat a fish that wasn't out of a can or in the shape of a stick until I was twenty-two. We weren't always complaining. Some of my favorites were the government grilled cheese sampled from my great-grandparents' "commodities" that we collected from the courthouse and delivered to their home, canned tamales with ketchup over a box of Rice-a-Roni, the leftover-catch-all-casserole my family called "El Toro," or my favorite: Beanie Burgers. A Beanie Burger was a half a hamburger bun, spread with Frito's bean dip or some other canned refried beans, a slice of Velveeta or Kraft Singles or that commodity cheese, and a couple of green olives, toasted under the broiler on a cast iron griddle pan. It was cheap and delicious and made use of the tail ends of things, the kind of dinner my sister Melinda calls "nasty good."

This competition was, like all measuring contests, a gross exaggeration (on my part at least). No doubt, my farming family was often cash-strapped, relying on big loans from the bank to operate between harvests and my mother's mostly adequate salary as a public school teacher. I learned about postdated checks and overdrafts before I learned how to count change. Across the street from the bank was The Grocery Store—that was its official name—where we could still charge our groceries to an in-house credit account that was kept on handwritten receipts. (Fun fact: one year my whole class lost points on our state standardized test in writing because we all capitalized Grocery Store as a proper noun.) But I had braces when I needed them, money for cheerleading uniforms every year, and a hand-me-down car when I turned sixteen. My wages from working at the local newspaper and the Dairy Queen were mine to spend as I pleased on CDs and ordering from the *dELiA*s* catalog. There were families in my rural hometown better off than mine, but many, many more getting by with less. I *liked* beanie burgers and El Toro. If the pantry was empty, it was likely because we were too busy hustling between basketball practice and church and the twenty-mile commute from the farm to town to restock. Though I remember conversations about waiting for pay day or the refinancing of the farm loan to get something not absolutely necessary, we had a closet full of Ball jars of home-grown black-eyed peas and pinto beans. If I ate a Beanie Burger instead of actual garden-grown beans, that was on me.

Terry and I had these competitions in the cubicle-filled common workspace for English and Rhetoric graduate instructors at Texas Christian University. We were working on our dissertations, making $24,000 a year in teaching fellowship stipends. Our students dressed better in their pajamas than we could have on our best days. Maybe we were living our parents' and grandparents' wildest dreams, but we were still poor kids surrounded by wealth. We still scavenged leftovers from catered lunches and ate greedily from the free happy-hour buffet that came with the purchase of a half-price drink at a Mexican restaurant down the street.

I shouldn't speak for my friend Terry here, but I think I was feeling something like the bends, rising quickly but not yet surfacing in something like the middle class. I hoped, but didn't dare believe, that when I finished my degree I'd see my income double and triple, and if I was very lucky, I'd be able to pay off the trips to conferences I'd just charged to my credit card sooner rather than later. Beanie Burgers and three-day-old turkey wraps kept my head attached to my neck. We were proud of the progress we were making, but the ritual of the "poor off" kept us hungry for what was next.

The "poor off" game was about reminding ourselves that even though our lives constantly made us feel like imposters, we weren't phonies. How could we be accused of putting on airs? Here we were, publicly proclaiming our poverty in the hearing of our peers, though later we might have an argument about French philosophers. In *Foodies: Democracy and Distinction*, Josee Johnston and Shyon Baumann describe the kind of authenticity we sought to perform as "individual sincerity, or being 'true to oneself'" (76). Sincerity is at the root of "simplicity," one definition of authenticity that Johnston and Baumann identify as emerging from food discourse. Simplicity refers to the qualities of "honesty and effortlessness" (76); in conversations about food, it also connotes "small-scale and non-industrial production techniques" and "the purity of 'simple' high quality ingredients" (77). The ironies abound. My tall tales of poverty were embroidered with fiction, and the foods of our poor pasts were mostly mass-produced convenience foods from the industrial food complex. And yet, stories of these "simple" delights of bread, beans, and cheese toasted until bubbly and golden brown are the evidence of my own authenticity. I didn't have to try to be poor the way I had to study to acquire middle-class distinction. There was a pleasure and relief that came from slipping out of my neutral accent and sophisticated palate to drawl and twang about processed cheese.

Johnston and Baumann explain that food discourse does not automatically exclude so-called poverty foods but may in fact contribute to a valorization of "simple" foods with humble origins. The authors describe the tension that modern consumers feel between competing priorities of aesthetic taste and political identity. While the self-identified "foodies" that they interviewed maintain an interest in the "distinction" they receive from seeking out the rarest and most capitalized food experiences, they are also attracted to the illusion of "democracy," the promise that anyone from any social identity can learn to participate in food culture and that their food choices can affect social and environmental change (38–42). To counteract the charges of snobbery and pretension, and to bring in a little "simple" authenticity, diners and food writers may valorize the foods of poverty like beanie burgers or foraged greens or government grilled cheese (83). Omnivorousness is democratic rather than snobbish. My friend and I relished our underprivileged pasts because they gave us license to recognize, reject, and someday wreck the systems of power we found ourselves improbably succeeding in.

DEMOCRACY AND SIMPLICITY: POVERTY FOODS AND SOUTHERN CHARACTER

Southern food writing lives in the same tension that Johnston and Baumann describe, feeling that pull between the simple, democratic "authenticity" of foods with their origins in poverty and the distinction promised by highly capitalized, chef-centric cuisine. One way that cookbook writers can bring fine-dining restaurant recipes to home cooks is to emphasize the origin of those recipes in the experiences of poverty while also demonstrating how those recipes have been "upgraded" in ingredients or techniques. Readers and cooks can feel opposing forces in balance: this will taste good and give me social capital without risking the charge of elitism. This, too, is a way to avoid pain and emphasize pleasure.

For self-identified southern writers, the strategy of connecting humble origins to haute cuisine has the added rhetorical benefit of linking to the stereotypical southern experience of rural poverty. From the Lost Cause rhetoric that pitted the agricultural South against the industrial North as incompatible economic, political, and cultural systems to the Nashville Agrarians who enshrined those differences as essential to the southern character bound to be crushed under the homogenizing weight of modernism in *I'll Take My Stand*, rurality and subsistence farming have long been associated with the essence of southern identity. Many scholars—including Sarah Robertson and David Davis—credit photography of the 1930s and 1960s for cementing the metanarrative of poverty as essential to the character of the South. According to Robertson, the iconic images from the Depression such as Dorothea Lange's "Migrant Mother" and photo essays such as *Let Us Now Praise Famous Men* (reissued in 1960), "are largely responsible for generating the popular conceptions of the southern poor white that continue to shape how the nation views those living on or beneath the poverty line" (27). These photographs tend to paint the South as an exotic "Third World" outside of the United States and its geopolitical influence; "surreal," "macabre," and "grotesque" (43); dirty, gritty, rough.

Today's cookbook writers have coopted some of the same set dressings of poverty from these influential photographers as a signal of authenticity and distinction. From the "ruin porn" of degrading barns and distressed wood to the nostalgia of mason jars and homespun fabric, visual cues connect the recipe on offer to a recognizable history of southern poverty, even in cookbooks that represent fine dining restaurants and haute cuisine. These visual cues are supported by textual evidence that describes southern food traditions born of poverty (like hoe cakes, moonshine, or foraged greens), now "upgraded" for fine dining. The connection to poverty might suggest the pain of deprivation or elicit pity or disgust, but in the cookbooks examined in this chapter, markers of poverty have been repurposed for communicating a pleasant form of "down home" and democratic authenticity that rejects the pretensions of contemporary gourmet food culture that have led to distaste for the term "foodie" and its connotations of exclusion. Simultaneously, stories and images of poverty link the writer to an "authentic" southern experience of pain that they can narrate into the pleasures of simplicity, historical tradition, nostalgia, pride in resourcefulness, and gratitude for relative privilege in the present. In this chapter, I'm looking at the arguments for authenticity in contemporary southern cookbooks that rely on poverty as a marker of both democratic omnivorousness and essential southern character. Cookbook writers draw on stories of past poverty (their own and their ancestors') as evidence of their own connection to "authentic" southernness.

The painful parts of poverty in these instances are in the past, and pleasure often comes from upward mobility; looking back is safe because the present is comfortable and privileged by comparison. I start my analysis with Matthew Mickler's notorious *White Trash Cooking* (originally published 1986, twenty-fifth-anniversary edition reissued with a foreword by John T. Edge in 2011) as a particularly influential and long-lasting representation of white southern poverty. The pleasure here comes from voyeurism and humor, laughing at and with the poor. By contrast, I examine Vivian Howard's *Deep Run Roots* (2016) as a contemporary text that represents poverty as a painful experience intimately tied to the pleasures of place and community. Howard narrates her ethos as a chef and authenticity as a local insider by telling the story of her family's past in poverty. However, Howard's cookbook and restaurant approach poverty with an intentional eye toward social justice. Howard acknowledges that her privilege gives her a responsibility to improve the conditions of the community where she lives. While the pleasure in the narrative comes from a sense of pride at having "made do," Howard is quick to emphasize the painful labor associated with poverty and the luxury of choosing to prepare food in labor-intensive ways.

Whether the cookbook successfully critiques systems of economic oppression or reinforces them depends largely on how writers negotiate the turn from past pain to promised pleasure. Despite the deep and lasting influence of stories of southern poverty, Robertson suggests that more contemporary photography collections, may "offer counternarratives, or countervisualities, that destabilize the gaze" (28). In Robertson's examples, the images are accompanied by text that acknowledges the "complex personhood" of people in poverty, by "conferring the respect on others that comes from presuming that life and people's lives are simultaneously straightforward and full of enormously subtle meaning" (Gordon qtd. in Robertson xvii). My goal is to seek out texts that provide an example for cookbook writers which might be able to provide a more honest and complex picture of how poverty has affected traditional southern foodways and how the poor people of the South have contributed to the creation of southern culture. Rather than using poverty as a symbol of personal authenticity that perpetuates harmful stereotypes and ignores systemic economic neglect, stories of poverty might then be used as opportunities to discuss potential solutions to poverty and its comorbidities.

POVERTY AS ESSENTIAL SOUTHERN EXPERIENCE

In the entry for "Poverty" in *The New Encyclopedia of Southern Culture* (Volume 20: Social Class), Robert A. Margo begins with the simple declaration that "poverty and deprivation are persistent themes in southern society and culture" (201). While Margo concludes that the South today is "no longer a synonym for poverty" and is as likely to have "pockets of poverty" as any other region (208), much of Margo's essay is devoted to arguing against the common explanations that the South's distinct poverty is a legacy of the region's unique commitment to slavery and sharecropping. Margo argues that the South's antebellum economic growth was on par with the rest of the nation, but "the depth of the hole the southern economy had to dig itself out of after the Civil War" set back the region's economic progress well into the 1960s (202).

Margo's arguments seem to be semantic. Slavery didn't cause poverty, Margo argues, because while slavery was institutionally viable, "labor productivity of slave farms in the South—the value of agricultural output per worker—was actually higher than labor productivity on free farms" (204), meaning more profit per worker. The "gang system" that strictly divided enslaved labor—where "force was applied, and few workers, including children or women, were underutilized"—was "highly productive" and highly profitable (205). Surprisingly, "free labor was unwilling to work in the gang system" (205). What really caused southern poverty, according to Margo, was the decline in "labor productivity in agriculture" attributed to the decision of formerly enslaved people, especially women and children, "to work less intensively than under slavery," and a decline in demand for American cotton (205). Margo summarizes that "most scholars believe that the decline in labor productivity was the chief culprit" (206).

It is difficult for this reader to see a difference between the argument that "slavery caused poverty" and the argument that Margo seems to be making, which appears to be twofold: slavery caused poverty for Black people and the end of the forced labor of enslaved Black people caused white people to earn less income. Certainly, Margo is aware that the system of slavery systematically prevented Black people from earning capital that would help them to establish wealth by denying literacy, ownership of property, and the basic human needs of adequate food and shelter. Margo puts it mildly: "These deficits in physical capital and human capital adversely affected the economic mobility of generations of African Americans well into the 20th century" (205). The practice of sharecropping was "(relatively) attractive" to "farmers with limited experience or other skills (e.g., literacy) and a lack of capital to draw upon ... African Americans farmers were frequently in this position and were, in fact, disproportionately sharecroppers" (205). Sharecropping didn't cause poverty, Margo argues, but the economic efficiencies of the gang system were superior to the diffusion of laborers onto small, individually-owned farms. Sharecroppers on small plots were less economically productive than forced laborers on large plantations (209).

Margo seems surprised that sharecropper relationships between tenants and owners were not more efficient; both the tenant and the owner should have been equally incentivized to be as productive as possible. He notes that Black sharecroppers "could face horrendous consequences" such as "a beating or, worse, a noose" if they were not "mindful of their economic status and their place in the social order" (206). It is not shocking to learn that this antagonistic relationship did not yield better economic outcomes; it is much more shocking that Margo does not seem to see the direct line from slavery to sharecropping to perpetual poverty in his own evidence.

The idea that the South is a unique place of poverty—or that the South's poverty has unique origins or markers—has plagued many a southern apologist. In *The Mind of the South* (1941), W. J. Cash describes the Old South paradoxically as a classless system that was obsessed with aristocracy. It seems impossible to have an aristocracy and no sense of class, but Cash later clarifies it not as a lack of class consciousness but "an absence of class antagonism" (79). While there were obviously widely varying levels of wealth in the South, Cash suggests that even poor whites fabricated genealogies and family legends in which every grandfather was a colonial aristocrat, and so all white southerners fancied themselves essentially a part of the same class (75). Cash also credits the Civil War with perpetuating the classless "unity" by causing "common whites" to take pride and part ownership in the aristocratic genealogies of their wealthier neighbors in order to make sense of the conflict and their role in it (79). Cash describes this fantasy of unity as evidence of a "naive capacity for unreality" that permeated southern culture (70). No matter how poor the poor whites were, they saw their lives through this fantasy as "tol'able" and could manage subsistence somehow (60). This led to "a tragic descent into unreality on the part of the masses;" the failure of the poor to judge their position accurately and defend their own interests encouraged their further economic "degradation" (61). In Cash's estimation, poverty was a painful consequence of attempting to hold up a pleasant fiction: "This Old South, in short, was a society beset by the specters of defeat, of shame, of guilt—a society driven by the need to bolster its morale, to nerve its arm against waxing odds, to justify itself in its own eyes and those of the world" (61). Cash does not suggest that poverty is a particularly southern experience, but he does suggest that poor white southerners experienced poverty uniquely by denying it, tolerating it, and eventually succumbing to it by inaction.

By 1975, it seems, this legacy of a unique experience of poverty in the South had taken hold nationally. In *The Enduring South: Subcultural Persistence in Mass Society*, John Shelton Reed sought to quantify southern distinctiveness through surveys and poll data, comparing responses from northerners and southerners over time to discover what, if anything, distinguished southerners as a cultural group. In the final chapter on the future of southern distinction, Reed concluded that, at the time, to be southern is to be viewed as "more rural, less educated, and less middle class than one is" (83). In an ironic reversal of Cash's accusation that southerners pretended to have more wealth than they had, Reed discovered that now the assumption was that all southerners were poorer than they really were. The dominant image of the South according to Reed was one of economic depression. Reed attributes much of this perception to southerners themselves for some of the same reasons Cash identified; southerners demonstrated a stubborn resistance to "mass culture" through "efficient" maintenance and transmission of regional beliefs between generations (84–85).

While Cash (a historian) and Reed (a sociologist) attribute the perception of southern poverty to the southern character or distinctly southern habits, Sarah Robertson looks for the genealogy of this idea in media, namely literature and photography. In *Poverty Politics: Poor Whites in Contemporary Southern Writing*, Robertson describes the long tradition "from colonial days to the present" of travel writers going to the South in search of the "Other," looking for evidence to support their view of the South's essential "strangeness" (3). "Under the auspices of localism," Robertson argues, "the US South remains a place of interest, with travel writers continuing to seek out encounters with 'distinctive' or 'authentic' figures" (4). Poor whites, especially, have long been a subject of fascination, alternately being represented as tragically "unfit" for modernity and heroically standing as "the last stalwart against the increasing pressures of capital, which continue to erode free will" (6). Cash, Reed, and Robertson all seem to agree that the story of southern poverty is a wild mixture of fact and fiction; however, while Cash and Reed tend to hold southerners responsible for perpetuating fictions, Robertson focuses attention on those representations made by relative "outsiders" (both geographic and class outsiders) to serve their own purposes—chiefly to isolate white poverty as a uniquely southern experience caused by the South's unique moral and political failings. Robertson's conclusion echoes C. Van Woodard's famous thesis in *The Burden of Southern History*, which similarly paints the South as an aberrant moral exception to America's exceptional character. The South, in short, is a place for America to store the painful, the pitiful, and the poor.

Robertson focuses on two moments of economic crisis in the US that drew special media attention to the pain of southern poverty: The Great Depression of the 1930s, and the so-called War on Poverty of the 1960s. Cash (1941) and Reed (1975) are each writing about a decade after each crisis; little wonder that their investigations reveal that the South is represented as uniquely poor. In each of these crises, art photography played an outsized role in communicating the pain of these experiences to the larger public. While photography as a medium of art seems to capture the "truth" of a moment, Susan Sontag reminds us that photography is rhetorical: "In deciding how a picture should look, in preferring one exposure to another, photographers are always imposing standards on their subjects" (qtd. in Robertson 31). Robertson concludes that many of these photographic images were purposefully selected by their artists, and by the writers who contextualized them, to emphasize the miserable Otherness of poor white southerners, solidifying the pain of poverty in the American imagination as a recognizable marker of essential southern identity.

Robertson argues that in the 1930s it was the photographs of the Farm Security Administration and other Works Progress Administration artists like Eudora Welty, Walker Evans, and Dorothea Lange that gave Americans the iconic images of the Great Depression, stubbornly associated with the South (29–31). In his essay on James Agee and Walker Evans's "Cotton Tenants: Three Families," later published as *Let Us Now Praise Famous Men*, David Davis highlights the representation of food in the photography and narrative which "juxtapose[es] rapidly modernizing systems of corporate agriculture, infrastructure, and technology with comparatively simple means of subsistence farming" (167). More importantly, Davis interrogates the rhetorical situation of the article as originally composed as an assignment for *Fortune* magazine, a luxury publication targeted at an audience of middle-class readers who aspired to even higher class standing (168). The article ran in the "Life and Circumstances" section of the magazine which featured stories of struggling workers for the purpose of counterbalancing the stories of successful industrialists and to drive home the magazine's message that "free markets were but one means, and not necessarily the best means, to achieving a more democratic, more fair, more just society" (169). The message of the article would be that the poor were morally deserving of assistance from their economic superiors, but Davis concludes that the article ended up being more of a critique of "the intrinsic inequality of consumer capitalism" (178). Still, the imagery emphasized the dignified suffering of poor southern whites.

This is the message that Davis identifies in "Cotton Tenants," but as Robertson observes, the "haunting legacy" of *Let Us Now Praise Famous Men* is recognized by many to have overdetermined the perception of the South as a place of poverty (31–32). The book's reissue in 1960 coincided with a renewed interest in southern poverty, coalescing into Lyndon B. Johnson's plan to create the Great Society through social welfare programs, nicknamed the War on Poverty. Robertson credits the reissue of *Let Us Now Praise Famous Men* for setting off a wave of similar projects returning to the South to document poverty (32), many of which "perpetuat[ed] a one-dimensional view of the region and its people" (37) and followed many of the same conventions as the 1930s photographers, even revisiting the human subjects of the earlier era. Dale Maharidge and Michael Williamson photograph and interview the Ricketts family, featured in *Let Us Now Praise Famous Men*, in their 1986 book *And Their Children After Them*. Robertson identifies in the 1986 book a pattern that I see in the cookbooks of today: a story of overcoming poverty that praises individual determination and resilience as the way to upward mobility (32–33). The influence of *Let Us Now Praise Famous Men* on the story of poverty in the US South is remarkable and traced far better by these scholars than I can capture here. This single photographic collection affected not just how we think about southern poverty, but how we think about southern poor people.

To suggest as Margo does that the South does not have unique economic institutions that perpetuate poverty through purposeful decisions is simply unsupportable. It is difficult to separate the metanarrative of white southern poverty from white supremacy. While Margo acknowledges African American poverty as an inevitable outcome of slavery and racism, the rest of this literature review focuses on white southern poverty as an aberration in need of explanation. A common explanation is that the racism of white southerners solidified into stubborn political resistance to efforts that would alleviate poverty for anyone. In *The War on Poverty in Mississippi: From Massive Resistance to New Conservatism*, Emma J. Folwell explains that Johnson's Great Society programs like Head Start "marked the start of a new phase of white resistance to black advancement," leading poor white families to reject aid to which they were eligible (3) and starting "a war against the war on poverty" (4) that ultimately perpetuated white poverty and solidified Mississippi's Republican party into what Folwell calls "a new conservatism" (5). Kent Germany's chapter in *The War on Poverty: A New Grassroots History* makes much the same claim for the success of the "war on the War on Poverty" in the Louisiana Delta: "In the late 1960s, the War on Poverty was little match for the Delta's poverty and traditions, which engendered extreme white resistance to black advancement and racial inclusion, an economy too dependent on the land and on low wages, and an education system designed to perpetuate white privilege" (232). Both scholars argue that racial discrimination and an almost pathological commitment to white supremacy kept even the most innocuous antipoverty programs from making any lasting improvements for anyone of any race (Folwell 4; Germany 233).

These two regions, the Louisiana and Mississippi Deltas, make up what James C. Cobb famously dubbed "the most Southern place on Earth," regions that are famously, perpetually, and it may seem, incurably poor. Cobb details the failure of even economic growth through industrialization to make a dent in southern poverty in "Why the New South Never Became the North: A Summary." Cobb argues that the fear of losing regional distinctiveness—the kind bemoaned by John Egerton in *The Americanization of Dixie: The Southernization of America* in 1973 and called "a cultural lobotomy" that would make the South indistinguishable from California by Marshall Frady—undercut the economic growth that might have come from the "open for business" New South mentality (Cobb 142). Cobb notes that "Economic gains often require cultural sacrifices, and nostalgic references to the good old days when times were bad increase in proportion to the pace of economic change" (143). If poverty and rurality are viewed as essential to southern identity, then programs that promote economic development and urbanization must be read as a threat to distinction and resisted by those invested in maintaining the "authenticity" of the status quo.

Robertson makes a related argument in *Poverty Politics*. The problem with making poverty a *characteristic* of a culture and not a *consequence* of a political-economic system, Robertson explains, is that it makes it somewhat rude to attempt to alleviate poverty. To take away poverty means to take away a distinct identity and source of pride from people already suffering. Walter Benn Michaels also notes that this framing distracts from the real sources of poverty: "it's our attitude toward the poor, not their poverty that becomes the problem to be solved, and we can focus our efforts of reform not on getting rid of classes but in getting rid of what we call classism" (qtd. in Robertson xii). The danger of narratives that turn the pain of poverty into the pleasure of authenticity is that they may fall into the trap of making poverty appear as a tradition and an essential characteristic with such positive outcomes that it undercuts the urgency of disrupting the systems that perpetuate it. And if the storytellers fail to name those political-economic systems and offer a path toward resisting or reversing those systems, then the narratives only serve to reify the rigid boundaries of class. Making poverty food fashionable will likely do little to eliminate poverty, and it may instead place the traditions of poverty out of the price range of those who innovated with them in the first place.

Because the metanarrative of southern poverty focuses on poor whites, this chapter also focuses on texts by white authors. This is not an intentional oversight of Black southerners and their experiences of poverty, nor a suggestion that white southerners experience poverty differently or in any way more or less intensely. In some ways, I covered Black southern poverty and resilience in the previous chapter, noting that Black southern writers like Dora Charles make sense of the pain of enslavement and ongoing racism by making very similar rhetorical moves as poor white southerners in this chapter: emphasizing community, generosity, self-sacrifice, resilience, and pride in overcoming. Many of the same foods associated with slave trade and enslaved people will be described in this chapter as "poverty" foods. Both "slave foods" and "poverty foods" arise from meeting a nutritional need with limited resources. Therefore, in some ways, simply acknowledging that a food tradition is born of a lack created by the political system of slavery, segregation, and racism is doing exactly what I hope these stories of white southern poverty will do: name the causes of poverty in order to point out how they might be undone.

The discourse of soul food offers a pattern for using foods associated with poverty and pain as a means of political resistance. Though many have been critical of soul food's mythologizing power, the cuisine as we know it was solidified in the 1950s as a form of collective Black resistance to mainstream "American" foodways. As Adrian Miller argues in *Soul Food*, the creation of a distinct cuisine called "soul food" reinforced a cultural distinction between Black Americans and all other categories of American, all based in making pleasure in food and taking pleasure in identity and community (7). At its heart, soul food is a cuisine of protest, pointing to systems of oppression that necessitated its creation and offering an alternate view of African Americans as contributors to a distinct culture. Soul food is political. Could poverty food—whatever that is—be similarly mobilized into political action on behalf of a multiracial "underclass"? The language of soul food may offer a pattern for the valorization of white poverty food that does not merely profit from suffering but codifies its own history and points toward unified political action. The food itself is incapable of political action, but writers may harness the potential of poverty foods to serve as an energizing rallying point for intervention, disruption, and subversion.

PAIN AND PLEASURE OF POVERTY: CASE STUDIES

In this chapter, we see again a tension between the cookbook genre's pull toward pleasure and the narrative of southern authenticity pulling toward pain. When cookbooks invoke poverty as a unique southern experience of pain, they are breaking a convention of the genre in order to examine a darker side of southern identity. However, as I will argue, many cookbooks resolve this dissonance by highlighting individual resilience, self-reliance, resourcefulness, generosity, and respect for material culture to reorient the narrative toward pleasure. As I've noted, there is danger in that rhetorical move that can undercut the urgency of restorative justice, but it is possible to accomplish both a praise for the grit and grace of the self-reliant while also grappling honestly with the systems that perpetuate poverty.

LAUGHING AT POVERTY: WHITE TRASH COOKING

According to John T. Edge's foreword to the twenty-fifth-anniversary edition published in 2011, Ernest Matthew Mickler's *White Trash Cooking* was originally published in 1986 by a small literary press, Jargon Society. Within six months, Ten Speed Press bought the rights to the little spiral-bound book. In the eighties, Ten Speed was known for the self-help classic *What Color is Your Parachute?* (Edge, xi). Today, Ten Speed publishes some of the most famous chefs and award-winning cookbooks around: Yotam Ottolenghi's *Jerusalem*, Aaron Franklin's *Franklin BBQ*, Heidi Swanson's *Near and Far*, Mollie Katzen's *Moosewood Cookbook*, among others. Ten Speed has a large catalog of southern cookbooks including Virginia Willis's first cookbook, *Bon Appetit, Yall*; John Currence's most recent cookbooks, *Big Bad Breakfast* and *Tailgreat: How to Crush it at Tailgating*; Lisa Fain's *Homesick Texan* series; Ashley Christensen's *Poole's*, and *Southern Living* contributor Rebecca Lang's *Fried Chicken*, to name a few ("Ten Speed Press"). In 2021, Ten Speed named James Beard award-winning author and Ten Speed alum Bryant Terry as editor in chief of a new BIPOC-focused imprint, called 4 Color Books, to publish three to four nonfiction books by writers of color each year (Maher). Ten Speed Press's reputation today is as a high-quality producer of best-selling cookbooks.

The twenty-fifth anniversary of *White Trash Cooking* in 2011 comes just a couple of years after Willis's *Bon Appetit, Y'all* (2008) and forms a fascinating foil to that book. Willis is a classically trained chef bringing French cooking techniques to her grandmothers' southern recipes. Mickler's collection of convenience-ingredient-centric home recipes are as unpolished as the speech of his contributors and collaborators.

Mickler presents white poverty as not merely a matter of money, but an attitude: "the first thing you've got to understand is that there's white trash and there's White Trash. Manners and pride separate the two. Common white trash has very little in the way of pride, and no manners to speak of, and hardly any respect for anybody or anything" (1). Mickler's idea of White Trash centers on pleasure: having pleasant manners and focusing on the pleasant feeling of pride and mutual respect. Edge quotes a review from Harper Lee that also highlights pride: "*White Trash Cooking* is a beautiful testament to stubborn and proud people" (Edge x). Mickler expounds on this pride, explaining that White Trash is "in love" with itself, both its pleasures and its pains:

> [O]ur good times are the best, our bad times are the worst, our tragedies the most extraordinary, our characters the strongest and the weakest, and our humblest meals the most delicious.... And what really makes us different from others is that we are 'in love' with our bad times and weakest characters, we laugh at our worst tragedies, and with a gourmet's delight [we] enjoy our simplest meals. We might tell stories that others think are vulgar or sad, but we make them tales to entertain ourselves and anyone who will listen.... Cooking food, laughing and storytelling—that's what we're made of and that's what we enjoy the most. (1)

The pleasure of storytelling, in Mickler's depiction here, requires finding or manufacturing humor, even—or maybe especially—in painful stories. This introduction sets the expectation that what is to come will be stories to laugh at *with* the White Trash characters who are making jokes for their own benefit. It's not a great recipe for social change to be "in love" with bad times and to laugh at tragedies, inviting others to laugh, too, and not to assist or change. Mickler's cookbook glosses over any pain that might extend from poverty, making no attempt to identify the causes of poverty or even acknowledge that a person in poverty might want to get out.

Instead, *White Trash Cooking* focuses on the charming characters, delightful accents, and clever wordplay of the folks that make up the contributors to this collection. Are they real people? They all seem to have the most stereotypical names and come from the most absurdly named places, and they speak in the most charming sound bites. "Corn Beef and Hash" comes with Edna Rae Mills's endorsement: "So good it'll make your tongue slap your jaw teeth out," (35). Mills is identified as Mickler's mother (1) and contributor of Edna Rae's Smothered Potatoes (22). Mickler does not provide headnotes for the recipes, but most of them bear the name of a contributor in the recipe title and end with a quotation from the contributor, adding color and humor to the recipe instructions.

The humor of *White Trash Cooking* is associated with "camp," which may simply be a way to describe Mickler as a gay man and *White Trash* as funny. Edge writes in the Foreword that Mickler first imagined *White Trash Cooking* as "a campy television show, a drag queen riff on *The Galloping Gourmet*" (xi).

Michael Adno's biography of Mickler in *The Bitter Southerner* describes the book as "an eloquent medley of camp and honesty" (Adno). Edge obliquely refers to Mickler's sexuality by noting that Mickler died of AIDS in 1988 (xii), but Adno is more direct in describing Mickler's romantic relationships with men and noting that *White Trash* editor Jonathan Williams identified himself as "artisto-dixie-queer." Certainly camp has its roots in gay male culture (Shugart and Waggoner 22), but the authors of *Making Camp: Rhetorics of Transgression in U.S. Popular Culture* define camp "at the most basic level as over-the-top, playful, and parodic" (4). Specifically, they focus on women's expressions of camp as a critique of gender and sexuality through aesthetics of excess and irony. Shugart and Waggoner argue that camp is by nature a balance of "play and critique" (2), and camp performances are "infused with critical promise" (3). The pleasures of *White Trash Cooking* come in part from Mickler's parody of the community cookbook form, inserting himself as a gay male observer in a feminine genre.

Even without this layer of gender critique, Mickler's genre play extends from another description of camp provided by Shugart and Waggoner. They describe pop music icons Macy Gray and Gwen Stefani as embodying camp by borrowing "highly recognizable icons and aesthetics from the past and incorporating them, in excessive and ironic ways, into [their] public persona[s]" (4). The community cookbook genre, I would argue, is an aesthetic from the past that Mickler parodies with excess and irony from the spiral binding to the jokey attributions.

One of the subtler but longest running jokes in the book is an ongoing war between Betty Sue Swilley and her sister in-law Raenelle. Mickler dedicates the book to "Betty Mae Swilley, the best cook in Rolling Fork, Mississippi," and to Robert "who found her on a tombstone" (ix). The tombstone is pictured in the folio of color photographs in the center of the book, clearly marking Betty Mae's death in 1952 (page sixteen of the unpaginated photo insert). Betty *Sue* Swilley is named in the introduction as a paragon of White Trash cooking, the kind of cook the reader will become once they have internalized the "true spirit" of the book (5). Betty Sue is always written of in the present tense, and often with her sister-in-law Raenelle close by. Betty Sue says the best way to learn is to "go straight to the kitchen and 'get it did'" (3). Raenelle is introduced on the next page as Betty Sue's sister-in-law who complains that Betty Sue is always trying to one-up her in the kitchen by improvising with recipes she has given Betty Sue: "If I fry down three onions, she's gonna fry down four. If I put in one pack of Jello, she's gonna tump in two" (4). This antagonism keeps up throughout the book. Mickler provides "Betty Sue's Fried Okra" on one page and "Betty Sue's Sister in Law's Fried

Eggplant" the next (18–19). Raenelle has already complained of Betty Sue taking her recipes, and in this one, Betty Sue has even supplanted Raenelle's name and identity. These two pages have four recipes for fried vegetables: okra, eggplant, cucumber, and squash. Only the okra is attributed to Betty Sue, but the preparation for the cucumbers is the same as the okra, and the squash recipe's only instruction is to "cook the same as fried okra and cucumbers" (19). Raenelle is left out again.

Another example of this war—and the device of placing their recipes side by side for a joke—can be found between "Plain Ole Potato Pone" (99) and "Fancy Sweet Potato Pone" (100). The "Plain Ole" pone is noted as "another one of Betty Sue's Favorites" (99). But on the next page, Raenelle claims to be both the originator of a simpler version and the owner of the Fancy Pone: "This is my recipe but Betty Sue added all the extras, so it's hard to tell it's the one I gave her. She's always changing things" (100). By attempting to take credit for both, Raenelle ends up not getting credit for either, really. Betty Sue added the fancy things that make the pone fancy, and Mickler has already established that Betty Sue gets credit for the plain pone. It's easy to imagine Raenelle's fury at the way Mickler is clearly taking Betty's side.

One last time, Betty Sue and Raenelle face off over consecutive recipes. The "Low Calorie Pick-Me-Up" of frothed skim milk and a pack of Sweet'N Low seems credited to Betty Sue who says, "This is a life-saver before Sunday dinner and just after church, when it's so hot you caint' hardly stand it." The "High Calorie Pick-Me-Up" that follows is a pack of salty peanuts poured into a Pepsi, also credited to Betty Sue through Raenelle: "Raenelle told me this was one of Betty Sue's concoctions. She said: 'But it's so trashy she won't own up to it!'" (131). Raenelle takes the low road again by accusing Betty Sue of trashiness, but it ends up, as before, giving Betty Sue the credit for new recipes and making Raenelle look petty. Betty Sue is sipping a low-calorie glass of milk on a Sunday, and Raenelle is outside shouting insults.

The plot of this humorous rivalry is dispersed, but it appears that Betty Sue may be winning. Betty Sue contributes more recipes, all of them undisputed. Raenelle's accusations show some of the prejudices of White Trash by eschewing "the fancy" in favor of the humble. Raenelle insists that she is the inventor of the plain and it is Betty Sue who is pretentiously putting on airs with complications and additions. Betty Sue uses this device, too, claiming that Raenelle got her recipe for "Superior Shrimp (Mississippi)" from "some fancy book." Raenelle's rejoinder doesn't help her case much: "she still swears she got it at a high-priced restaurant while she was on vacation in Shell Beach, Miss" (58). Whether Raenelle is a reader of fancy cookbooks, a patron of high-priced restaurants, or a taker of vacations to the beach, Betty

Sue, once again, emerges as the salt-of-the-earth type and Raenelle is the unknowing butt of the joke.

Mickler invokes Betty Sue and Raenelle in the final words of "About the Author" in one final joke, this time at his own expense: "I can just hear Raenelle and Betty Sue at every Tupperware party in Rolling Fork saying, 'Ernie went from white trash to WHITE TRASH overnight.'" Now it is the author, "Ernie," who has gone from plain white trash ("Common white trash has very little in the way of pride, and no manners to speak of, and hardly any respect for anybody or anything" 1) to that higher class of White Trash—no richer, likely, but suddenly possessed of a pretense to pride and manners. Are Betty Sue and Raenelle real contributors or convenient characters for Mickler to play with as he laughs through *White Trash Cooking*? Betty *Mae* Swilley's real tombstone gives Betty *Sue* Swilley a thin sheen of verisimilitude, but the set-ups and punchlines are awfully convenient additions to the camp aesthetic of the book. Though certainly Mickler is playing with gender expectations as he inserts himself into the squabbles of women, he is also playing with the cookbook genre by seemingly creating two fictional characters who fight out their domestic dramas in the polite pages of a domestic document. While something is being critiqued through this humor and play, it isn't poverty. The pleasure of camp obscures the pain of poverty.

Since photography is partially to blame for the stereotype of southern poverty, the photography of *White Trash Cooking* bears scrutiny. Edge claims that Mickler's photography is responding to Agee and Evans's *Let Us Now Praise Famous Men*. The photographs are Mickler's, but Edge quotes Mickler's first publisher, Jonathan Williams, who compared Mickler to William Christenberry. Christenberry was directly influenced by Agee and Evans (x). Though the photographs feature some of those hallmarks of poverty like tall grasses and distressed wood buildings with rusted tin roofs, they also depict a humor and an abundance not evident in Agee and Evans. The cover photo is of a woman in an unusual layering of a tank top or sports bra under a tube top, no makeup, and unstyled curly hair. But she's in front of a load of watermelons stacked as high as her head. Even sitting down, that's an impressive plenty. The collage of convenience ingredient labels and brands surrounding the image, interspersed with bright piles of beans and greens with potatoes (presumably from these convenient cans), paints a picture of plenty, an artistic abundance of food.

The first of the photographs in the folio is an open refrigerator, full to bursting with cans and bottles of supermarket items like Tab cola, canned "Thrifty Maid" grapefruit juice, Vitamin D Milk in a carton, and something that looks like it might be prepared mayonnaise. The next two images are a full skillet of something frying and a pantry shelf of industrially canned vegetables, dried beans, and a can of Steen's cane syrup. Though the interiors of the homes are not out of the pages of *Southern Living*, they are stocked with comfortable-looking, well-used furniture. There are images of rust (an old-fashioned iron and a rusty washtub), decay (a faded 7UP advertisement and a boarded-up well), and a lot of furniture out of place (an iron bedstead functioning as a gate in a fence and many couches, chairs, and recliners on porches instead of in living rooms), but interspersed are bushels full of peaches, stuffed baskets of tomatoes and squash, a full plate of food ready to eat, and a nearly empty plate of boiled shrimp surrounded by the shells and tails that prove a bounty has already been eaten.

I don't see the suffering of poverty here or any argument that the people in these images need assistance. The images do suggest a bygone age that 1986 hasn't touched: a room lighted by oil lamps, wooden wheelbarrows, an antique wringer for laundry, a washstand and mirror by the front door, so much peeling paint, rust, and untrimmed windows. But against this backdrop of well-used items, there is a suggestion of plenty. It's not new or nice, but it is sufficient. The photographs associate poverty with poor taste but plenty to eat.

If Shugart and Waggoner are correct, then critique is "inherent" in the camp aesthetic that privileges pleasure in excessive proportions (4). Perhaps the critique of *White Trash Cooking* is against the metanarrative of southern suffering. If the overarching story of southern poverty is unending misery, then there is something of a resistance in allowing poor white folks to be depicted as happy and creative with an abundance of resources—both the seasonal produce that appears to be grown in gardens and on farms and in the convenience ingredients available for purchase.

Mickler also invites poor white women into the hallowed genre of the community cookbook, reserved for the most respected and exceptional women of a respectable and exclusive community. Betty Sue and Raenelle bring to the surface the kind of petty squabbles that rarely make it into the pages of community cookbooks but are easy to imagine bubbling under the surface.

While Mickler does invite readers to share in these recipes and consubstantiate with the poor people who have produced them, the journey is temporary and entertaining, unlikely to move a reader to action to solve any problem. The poor are spared the indignities of performing their sorrows on a public stage again; however, focusing on pleasure spares readers from sympathizing with the poor, identifying their culpability for the pain of the poor, or recognizing a responsibility for justice. Mickler makes no call for action at all except to listen and laugh and play.

POVERTY SHAME AND SOCIAL ENTREPRENEURSHIP: DEEP RUN ROOTS

Vivian Howard's *Deep Run Roots* offers an example of how the suffering and pleasures of white southern poverty are employed in chef-centric contemporary southern cookbooks. Howard offers evidence of her own experience and knowledge of southern poverty both in narrative and photography to suggest honest intentions and remaining "true" to local and regional roots in order to convince readers that her recipes are appropriate for performing a distinct but responsibly democratic southern identity. While acknowledging her own privilege as someone whose class status has improved through her parents' economic success and her entrepreneurship, Howard intentionally seeks out opportunities to share the wealth. Howard describes how the business model of her restaurants and decisions that she makes as an employer and wholesale buyer are intentionally designed to improve the economic condition of her local community through social entrepreneurship. Howard's example isn't without flaws, but it may serve as a potential model for taking the suffering of poverty seriously in narrative and in action while also meeting the conventions of the genre and expectations of the audience that pull toward pleasure.

Howard is chef and owner of Chef and the Farmer and The Boiler Room in Kinston, North Carolina. She is maybe best known for the PBS docuseries *A Chef's Life*, which had five seasons and ended in 2018. The show won a Peabody award and some Daytime Emmys, and *Deep Run Roots* was winner of the IACP Cookbook of the Year. Howard has been a semifinalist for the James Beard Best Chef Southeast a handful of times, and she won Outstanding Food Personality or Host in 2016. What is unique about Vivian Howard is her choice to establish her fine-dining restaurant not in an urban center like Raleigh or Charlotte or even New York where her career began, but near her birthplace in Kinston, population 21,677 (as of 2010 census). As the restaurant website states, Howard's goal in establishing the restaurant was to effect economic and environmental change in her hometown: "Naive but determined, I opened Chef & the Farmer with the hope that our restaurant might light a spark in our little town and help transition some of eastern Carolina's displaced tobacco farmers into food farmers" ("About"). With her restaurants, Howard sought to create a stable demand for locally grown foods, opportunities for employment, a point of interest for tourism, and a boost of local morale that might result in relief for an economically depressed community.

In the cookbook, Howard describes the origin of the restaurant after a visit back home to North Carolina from New York. In 2006, Howard had been selling soup by subscription from her Harlem apartment and thinking of opening her own Manhattan storefront (13) when her family suggested she open a restaurant there in North Carolina. The idea starts to sound better to Howard when she and her husband return to NYC in the "dirty, stinky" snow after a forty-dollar cab ride from the airport, only to climb four floors to their apartment and find the heat was out (14). Howard's initial resistance to the idea was a feeling that "fine dining" would never work in eastern North Carolina which had "shrunk into one of the poorest regions in the country" (14). Back home, she writes, "*fine dining* meant steaks, baked potatoes, and salad bars, not tasting menus with wine pairings . . . our kind of restaurant could never be lucrative there" (14). The "ambitious, high-end dining experience" they had planned (14) was built on buying from local farmers, but the farmers resisted growing the unfamiliar ingredients Howard requested. Howard realized she was imitating her New York mentors and "forcing someone else's style on folks who didn't like it" without her own personality. Eventually, Howard began to find a balance between New York fine dining and the foodways of eastern North Carolina by investigating the local food products and traditions, including her own family's recipes, based largely on subsistence farming born of rural poverty (15).

Howard's description of the restaurant's origins rhetorically locates the sweet spot between distinction and democracy that Johnston and Baumann describe in *Foodies*. Diners may be attracted both by the opportunity to sample the cuisine of a celebrity chef and to "vote with their forks" in support of a business with a social justice mission. Diners may taste food that is "authentic" by being geographically specific while practicing "good citizenship." They can conspicuously consume an expensive meal, but since it is based in humble traditions of poverty, they can avoid the charge of being a snobbish foodie. Howard uses the opportunity of celebrity to ask the readers of her cookbook to confront the difficult parts of the story of southern poverty while they indulge in the pleasures of haute cuisine.

Howard's most common method for acknowledging poverty is to narrate her family's three-generation journey from relative poverty as tobacco and pig farmers to her own success as a chef and business owner. Howard acknowledges regional poverty through stories of her family's changing economics, of the city's economic condition, and of her restaurant's role in changing the fortunes of both.

Howard describes her childhood as more privileged than that of her parents and grandparents. Even her older siblings grew up with less economic security. Howard grew up in Deep Run, North Carolina which she describes as "a tiny farming community about halfway between Raleigh and the Atlantic Ocean" and "a nondescript dot" (3). Howard's parents and grandparents "made their living in tobacco, and when that industry faded, [they] farmed hogs instead"

(11). In many of the chapter introductions, Howard notes that her forebears did considerably more labor in growing, procuring, and preserving their own food because of their lack of capital. She defines her parents' poverty this way:

> Did you grow most of your own food? From the day you could dress yourself, did you contribute to the household income? Did you get up before dawn and go out on the road to pick up the pecans that had fallen overnight before a car or truck could crush them so your mom could sell those pecans in town and accumulate what she called your Christmas money? Today, we call that poor. (127)

Howard describes her maternal grandmother, called Grandma Hill, as a product of the deprivations of the Great Depression who "lived everyday like she was going to have less tomorrow" (310) and "moved and loved like a woman whose work was never done and rarely noticed by anyone" (309). Howard's family has an "inability to understand waste" that comes from generations of making the most of limited resources (359–60). She narrates in detail how her father's parents and extended family worked together to provide meat for the families in annual hog killings. Howard is careful not to romanticize this activity, noting that is "Part celebration," but also "part hard-as-hell physical labor" (357). She spares few details in describing the hot, dirty, bloody, disgusting, but vital work made necessary by poverty (358–59).

Howard herself does not have to experience most of these hardships because at the age of four or five, she reports, "family economics changed." Though it isn't clear precisely what precipitated this increase in income, the text suggests it had something to do with the family's move from tobacco farming to raising pigs. Evidence of their relative wealth is described in terms of foods available to the family: "Mom and Dad went from rarely spending money on anything other than the farm to going out to eat on weekends" (103). The change in fortune meant that they could skip some of the more difficult labors of a subsistence garden and depend on the conveniences of industrial food systems, "dabbl[ing] in processed food, and, for the most part, [buying] their meat instead of slaughtering it" (128). She guesses that her parents were happy to give up some of this work for the relative luxury of grocery shopping: "Mom saw the Piggly Wiggly as a promised land of peas she didn't have to shell, chickens whose necks she didn't have to wring, and tomatoes she didn't have to can" (21). While Howard does look back to these poorer times as having more meaningful, healthy, and delicious foodways, she is not nostalgic for some vague simpler time; she acknowledges that her own distance from this labor was hard won by the labor of others.

While the increase in discretionary spending described by Howard is hardly a windfall in most people's estimation, the change in circumstance means that Howard lives with more privilege than her parents or even her older siblings. She was able to attend a boarding school in the more cosmopolitan Winston-Salem (128), go to college, experience prestigious internships, and live in New York City. When the restaurant opens in 2006, Howard remarks that her detractors assume "her daddy will foot the bill" for her extravagance and catch her financially when the place inevitably failed (193). Howard uses her family history as "working poor" to simultaneously acknowledge her relative privilege while also marking herself as a class insider, not just a geographic insider.

Rhetorically, these moves to declare her insider status are necessary in response to criticisms from the Kinston community. Even though Howard grew up in the area, some of the locals still saw her and her husband and business partner Ben Knight as "interlopers from New York City who didn't go to church and owned the fancy restaurant in Kinston" (417). Not only does Howard need to prove her local authenticity, she must also demonstrate to detractors that she is a class insider—not one of those snobbish foodies but a democratic chef who can relate "authentically" to the community around her.

One of the ways that Howard demonstrates her local and working-class citizenship is to get in touch with her family's poorer roots by voluntarily taking on some of those labors of poverty that are no longer necessary, but more "authentic." In the introduction to the chapter "Sweet Corn," Howard describes how in her lower-income childhood her family processed corn for freezing in an all-day community event that resulted in putting up a year's worth of corn to eat on holidays and Sunday dinners. The tradition paused when the family no longer needed to garden and "put-up" because they could easily afford grocery store corn (217). After Howard establishes her restaurant, she gathers "three generations of Howard women and children" to "put up four hundred ears of corn," just for the experience of connecting to her family's poorer roots: "I wanted to relive some of the food rituals I had read about or remembered, and even though putting up corn is a bit of a production, it's less involved than slaughtering a hog or putting up tomatoes" (218). Even though Howard herself has not experienced what might be called poverty, her family's subsistence farm work and the foods associated with poverty are rituals to be celebrated and enacted as evidence of a traditional, "simple," personal authenticity. Howard even mourns the loss of these traditions in the intervening years and the loss of family connection through cooperation: "It made me more than a little sad that we don't do it, or things like it, anymore, and it raised the question of what kind of family-building exercises we've replaced these experiences with" (219). Howard intentionally seeks out experiences of poverty as a kind of exercise in nostalgia, but she presents the experience as a family tradition—last practiced in her living memory—in order to emphasize the personal authenticity of her insider knowledge of poverty.

In the example of putting up corn, poverty is painful in terms of physical labor, but the most common story Howard tells about the pain of poverty is to relate it as a source of shame or painful embarrassment in her younger days. She turns the story to pleasure by seeing it now as a source of pride in creative resourcefulness. In the "Ground Corn" chapter, Howard describes making a dish of instant grits, slices of Velveeta cheese, and link sausage. Even though she thinks it is delicious and comforting and "the gold-standard" for a weekend breakfast, she "knew even [as a child] that there had to be something unwholesome about grits that swallowed up water in a mere minute . . . there would be more highbrow food in my future once I made it out of Deep Run" (22). The story is told with a kind of humorous disgust and embarrassment at the tastes of a child. When Howard begins working in chef Scott Barton's New York restaurant Voyage, she doesn't even recognize her "South" in his "storied and sophisticated" take on grits (22–23). Seeing this upscale way of cooking made her feel the way "a woman who never went to college looks at a sister with a PhD," comparing her mother's canned biscuits to the "tall and fluffy and made from scratch" biscuits of Voyage. "Once again," Howard writes, "I was ashamed of where I came from" (23). In this example, Howard's processed, convenient, instant cuisine is revealed as inauthentic in the shadow cast by the artisan authenticity of Barton's southern cuisine. However, Howard clarifies that the source of her shame and poor taste is not related to her poverty, but to her relative privilege: "Our grits had not always been instant. After all, I grew up on a road named after a gristmill! Instead, my *generation's* grits were instant." Her region is not "worse" than other parts of the South, but her parents' relief at "not having to grow, pick, and pickle everything" led them sometimes to choose "not to grow, pick, preserve, or cook anything" (23). Apparently, her parents experienced the same kind of painful shame at the physical labor that poverty brought them and relief at the chance to skip that pain. In the end of the narrative, Howard recognizes that the poorer generations of her family hold a "gold mine of history, wisdom, and tradition" that would make her cuisine just as authentic, "storied and sophisticated" as her mentor's.

When Howard begins to investigate her local cuisine to find her own culinary style, she faces her prejudices and abandons that earlier sense of shame: "We started eating at the buffets and barbecue haunts I had once avoided, thinking that nothing good could sit on a steam table or be slung into a Styrofoam bowl. Now I saw that these places represented years of recipe development shaped by our common place and ingredients" (15). A paragraph later, Howard repeats the same formula: "With my eyes open to the realities of country living and sustenance farming, I realized my parents, grandparents, and neighbors owned a wealth of practical knowledge that in no way proved embarrassing. Instead, they were cool and smart. They had not, in fact, 'just fallen off a turnip truck'" (15). Similarly, when Howard witnesses the process of making collard kraut for *A Chef's Life*, she recognizes that "maybe all the older people around me were planets of wisdom orbiting around a bunch of young people who didn't even know enough to ask the right questions" (422). Howard's parents' example suggests that part of upward mobility means hoping that the next generation doesn't have to endure the same suffering, but there's also pain in losing the resourcefulness that is born of surviving poverty and the feeling of "authenticity" those experience provide.

Though she chastises herself in narrative each time she brings up her childish shame, one of the ways that Howard's family expresses a similar shame is in a kind of linguistic denial of poverty. They do not accept that they are poor, but they insist on being "frugal." Her parents would "call themselves, their parents, and their grandparents all frugal farmers—people who lived a ways from town, worked the land, and wasted nothing" (127). Howard also notes her family's discomfort with the class connotations of cornbread. Under the heading "What Cornbread Means," Howard notes, "Cornbread started out as poor-people food, a way to stretch a meal, and it evolved into soul food, a way to celebrate it" (27). She titles one recipe in this section "Mom's Cornpone," but clarifies in the headnote that her mother would never have called it that, suggesting that "pone" signified something inferior to cornbread (28). Similarly, Grandma Hill's Hoecakes on the facing page were never called hoecakes: "Grandma Hill probably never heard the term *hoecake*... we called them little cornbreads." Hill kept the method for making hoecakes a secret, and as Howard reports, she "never took them outside her own kitchen" (29). The motivation for such secrecy is not explicit, but the family's determination to be "frugal" and not "poor," might suggest that publicly eating something called "pone" or "hoecakes" would be to admit to eating "poor people food" and worse, to admit to being poor.

The sense of shame in her family's poverty is clearest in the chapter introduction for Pecans. This is the chapter where Howard is most specific about her family's "frugal" background. Howard is moved to anger in the eighth grade when she receives a gift of a bag of pecans from her grandmother for Christmas:

Didn't my redneck family understand there was more to the world than turnip greens, pecans, and *Hee Haw*? Weren't they curious about these highly populated places called cities? Places where you could order Chinese food and have a Chinese person bring it to your door? ... That's what I thought cosmopolitan life meant at the time and I knew my family was not cosmopolitan. (128)

Though her new life at boarding school in Winston-Salem gave her access to the wonders of cabs, malls, and national chain restaurants, Howard still felt the need to hide her "shameful and backward" farming history (128). She begins to understand a difference in class within southernness: Her wealthier classmates "were *Southern*. I was *country*. I was ashamed." She hid her accent and let friends at boarding school believe her people were "affluent landowners," not pig farmers (129–31). However, as in the examples above, Howard finds a way by the end of the chapter to find the pleasure of having roots in poverty. At this point in the narrative, she stops being ashamed of being poor and starts being ashamed of pretending to be someone else, someone "inauthentic." Howard catalogs the strength of character that she inherited from her grandparents' and parents' experiences in poverty: "Thankfully I just covered up the values, work ethic, and principles my parents gave me; I didn't lose them. I'm a hard worker. I'm honest, kind, resourceful, and compassionate" (131). Howard's narratives highlight the painful feelings of shame associated with poverty, but ultimately, poverty yields both the most authentic foodways and the most superior qualities of character. Howard invites her readers to see poverty as something that can ultimately give pleasure through pride.

Howard recovered from those feelings of shame after starting the first restaurant in 2006: "Today I wear my pride in my place and my people like a badge" (131). Throughout the book, that pride is connected to resourcefulness, wisdom, and creativity that come from making more with less. At the end of the pecan essay, after detailing her feelings of shame, Howard espouses pride in her place and cuisine: "I believe my parents, with all their country ways, are some of the smartest people I've met anywhere" (131). Throughout the book, she praises the "culture of resourceful cooks who prepared year-round to feed their families" and who innovated southern cooking (4). Many of the traditional recipes, Howard notes, arise from "stretching" limited supplies: cornbread is "a way to stretch a meal" (27), North Carolina fish stew is loaded with eggs as a way to "stretch a weekend's catch and to feed more people" (41), watermelon rind pickles "highlight the home cook's need to waste nothing" (86). Using "seasoning meat" like ham as a condiment comes from having meat only a few times in a week and using all the parts of the animal left over from a hog killing. This preserved meat was stored "till a cook imitated Jesus with His loaves and fishes and called on a hunk of cartilage and bone to turn a bunch of nothing into supper" (8). Canning and preserving, especially, are a refrain that speaks to the foresighted wisdom of poor white southern cooks, as well as their skill, creativity, and hard physical labor. All of these elements make Howard proud not only to have a background in poverty but to return to those practices born of poverty, even in times of plenty, to get in touch with her "authentic" roots.

This narrative of "return" to her family's past communicates "authenticity" in the sense of being "true to oneself," delighting in "simplicity," and connecting with a personal history. Howard is aware that this backward looking might earn her criticism for nostalgia. She addresses these concerns directly in her essay for the okra chapter by making the divisive but distinctive vegetable a metaphor for the South. "Parts of our region's history are incredibly shameful," Howard admits, "and some people who call themselves Southerners make me want to stick a pencil in my eye" (399). She is openly critical of the "Confederate flag-toting Rebels" who espouse an uncritical love for the South and its "nicer, slower paced people" who do not exist except in myth. She is equally critical of the observers from the outside who "look at the South from their couches and see racism, fried food, slow talkers, and Honey Boo Boo" without getting to know the place directly (399). Later, Howard admits that her "penchant for nostalgia is not unique," but she emphasizes, "nor is it blind" (508). Her narratives are careful to acknowledge that there is a danger in being too romantic about the past or about the experience of poverty.

Not only does Howard acknowledge her family's personal experience of poverty, she describes the pain of the region's economic depression. Howard's decision to establish a restaurant in her hometown is presented both as a response to and a solution for the town's economic condition. As Howard explains in the introduction, Kinston is used to cheap restaurants and cheap tastes (15). While her family's fortunes had increased, the nearby town's fortunes had decreased in part because of two major industries leaving the area: tobacco farming and textile mills (173). As Howard explains it, "As a kid, a trip to town from rural Deep Run meant getting dressed up. In 2005, it meant getting depressed" (174). In a now familiar tale, Howard describes the downtown strip of abandoned storefronts, closed businesses, empty homes: "If you made Eastern North Carolina its own state, it would have been the poorest state in the country" (174). The sandwich shop that would become Chef and the Farmer was located in the center of "Kinston's ruins" where it "was adjacent to the only business still open."

Howard's motivation in the beginning emerged from a sense of superiority. Howard and her partner would "*change the town, leave the town, do more than run a restaurant*—whatever *more* meant" (174). As the restaurant website states and the cookbook suggests, that something "more" included patronizing local farmers and artisan businesses. In 2006, Howard writes, "the pickings were slim in terms of farmers and artisans doing things in small, quality-driven scale. So when a farmer from a place called In the Red showed up with an unusually creamy goat cheese, I vowed to help In the Red get in the black" (186). Over time, the attitude of doing a favor for the town with inferior tastes and skills turned to a matter of pride. In the chapter on tomatoes, Howard tells a story of hosting the Southern Foodways Alliance as a stop on a barbecue tour in 2013. The restaurant "appeared to be a raging success" but Howard and her husband/business partner continued to struggle with attracting, hiring, and keeping staff:

> Kinston didn't have a restaurant community flush with aspiring chefs and managers looking for the next step up. Instead, Kinston housed a lot of folks in need of jobs but with no relevant experiences . . . I wasn't looking for cooks with finesse, technique, or creative ability. I was looking them in the eye to see if they had crack habits. (258)

Howard's depiction of the workforce as unemployed, unskilled, and drug addicted is a reflection of the town's economic depression, but it also highlights the story of democratic upward mobility Howard is invested in. If the restaurant is successful, it will be a story of overcoming odds with scarce resources now familiar to this genre.

While Howard begins with low expectations, through the trial-by-fire that was the SFA luncheon and the subsequent excellent press for the restaurant (Howard's tomato sandwich was featured as one of John T. Edge's top ten things he'd eaten all year in *Garden & Gun*), Howard and her staff come to recognize their own value: "The story sent a ripple of pride through our staff. Locals had always said our restaurant was good . . . for Kinston. John T. said it was good for anywhere" (260). These stories of the town's poverty show Howard as a good citizen of her community, doing her best to use her privilege to share the success of the restaurant to increase the quality of life for the workers, suppliers, and diners connected to it. Investing in this town is evidence of Howard's "honest intentions" to produce good food in a self-denying and disinterested way.

Because the story of southern poverty is so deeply entwined with photography, it seems appropriate to analyze the ways that the images in *Deep Run Roots* contribute to the associations with poverty and serve as evidence of authenticity. In the final chapter of *Inventing Authenticity*, I describe some paratextual elements, including photography and design, as "badges of authenticity." These nondiscursive objects in the text signal the same kinds of authenticity that are present in text: geographic specificity, a personal connection, historical tradition, and simplicity (160–62). Taken together, the images and the text suggest a link between humble images of poverty and personal sincerity.

Photography in the cookbook suggests a preference for heirloom-type items and a general distaste for the new. I argued in *Inventing Authenticity* that historical authenticity is often signaled through antique flatware or rustic wooden tables, signaling a kind of "timelessness" (161). The images and photography in *Deep Run Roots* reinforce the narratives that link poverty to authenticity. The images suggest the kind of authenticity linked to tradition and age through old-looking dishes and utensils, rustic linens, and distressed wood. They suggest "simplicity" through handcrafted details like drawings and handwriting, mismatched vessels, and plain white dishes. They suggest a personal connection through images of the author and her family, as well as items that appear to be second-hand or heirloom objects. Alone, these objects don't necessarily have to connote poverty, but they clearly aren't new or typical of fine dining. They suggest age and things collected secondhand or by inheritance rather than commercial acquisition. They may have been costly at one point, but now it seems clear that their sentimental value exceeds their collateral value. The narratives which focus on Howard's family's background in rural southern poverty suggests that inherited objects would not have been expensive, and keeping those objects is evidence of their resourcefulness and care.

Even the photographs of the author-chef signal "down home" authenticity, even if they don't signal "poverty." Howard is mostly depicted in T-shirts with her hair down and naturally wavy. These representations of the chef's body are a way to suggest the chef-author's authenticity and personal connection to the food on offer. Howard's casual appearance makes her approachable and seem "true" to herself, not to a carefully crafted image. Her children are represented frequently, another suggestion of intimacy with the audience, inviting them into the family circle. Though these are not pictures of poverty, they are also very purposefully not pictures of wealth. They depict the image of "simplicity" that Howard's book has cultivated throughout the book from cover to cover, image to text.

The jacket cover art highlights the rural setting of Deep Run. In the background, a red barn is just out of focus. Howard is pictured seated on a weathered wooden picnic table with a bench seat. She sits on the table with her feet (wearing a weathered-looking pair of boots) on the seat in a casual slouch. This posture and placement—compared to a more formal headshot in chef's whites, standing in a kitchen, or even seated conventionally on the bench—conveys a sense of familiarity and accessibility, "authenticity" in the sense of being true to oneself. Beside Howard on the table is an uprooted collard plant, the broad leaves yellowed at the edges, dirt still on the roots. Besides the visual link to the metaphorical "roots" in the title, the greens are in their most "natural" state and refer to one of the most widely recognized foods in the southern culinary canon. The image is carefully composed to signal the opposite of pretension with multiple visual badges of authenticity.

Similarly, the back cover and spine, set against a distressed wood background, continue in the same vein. A bone-in porkchop is laid out on a plain white dish with a salad garnish of peanuts and celery. The recipe for "Big Bone-In Pork Chops with Pickled Peanut Salad" is included in the peanut chapter, but this plated image is not included in the book itself. Within the chapter, the pork chops are on a tarnished metal baking sheet and the pickled peanut salad is in a ceramic dish with a rough-hewn wooden spoon. All are against a wooden background. The image on the back cover, by contrast, has a hint of the fine dining experience in the plain white plate and the artful smear of sweet potato puree under the meat. However, the plain wood background and the tumble of the salad also hint at the relaxed cuisine mirrored in the chef's casual posture on the cover. Within the book, the wooden background and utensils and the unfinished presentation of the dish further indicate the "simple" authenticity communicated by the text.

Throughout the book there are a few recurring artistic layouts and motifs that reinforce these messages of "simple" authenticity linked to poverty. Each chapter, organized around a single ingredient, opens with a colorful two-page spread. On the left is the name of the ingredient in Council font; the color-fill effect on the letters hints at wood-grain. On the right side is a graphic representation of the item. Some of the foods appear to be against a wood-grain backdrop, too, like peaches and tomatoes. The hand drawn effect and the repetition of the wood grain motif suggest artisan simplicity. Like the collards on the cover, these graphic images are typically of the whole, raw ingredient with some, like the summer squash, still pictured on the vine.

The next page is usually a full-color photo either of the individual ingredient or of several varieties of the ingredient. For example, various pickles are pictured on one page, followed by another full-page photo of varieties of cured pork products. In these variety photos, the items are arranged on a concrete background, each with a handwritten label on tape attached to the table. Items are in a variety of mismatched vessels with some ingredients spilling from their packages, marked with splashes of juice or crumbs (7, 9,

20, 148, 380). These pages again suggest artisan simplicity, a sense that the reader is looking into the chef's personal pantry and looking at the chef's personal handwriting. That access to the chef is not necessarily an indication of poverty, but Howard's appreciation for the unsophisticated is linked in text to embracing her family's poorer past. In the case of the cured pork varieties page, it directly follows "An Ode to Seasoning Meat" that explains how cured pork meats were used as a condiment in the absence of more substantial meat which was scarce (8). The images provide more evidence of "authenticity" to echo and amplify the stories of poverty in text.

Notably absent in these narratives of southern poverty, though, are any bad actors responsible for the depressed conditions of the town of Kinston or any real pain experienced by the citizens. The kind of poverty described is largely an inconvenience. While her chapters on sweet corn and ground corn both acknowledge millwork and some of the challenges of being poor, neither touch on the devastating effects of the food insecurity characteristic of mill towns. The association of corn with pellagra and severe poverty probably accounts for Howard's mother's rejection of "cornpone" and Grandma Hill's "little cornbreads" instead of hoecakes, though Howard makes no reference to the disease or its link to malnutrition. Even the family's insistence on being "frugal" and not "poor" signals an intentional distancing from these tragic consequences of poverty and exploitation of labor. These signals may be too subtle for the average cookbook reader to absorb as a critique.

A focus on one family's or one town's poverty overcome may also be a distraction from the longer history of southern class issues, deeply imbricated in racial inequality and hate and violence, exploitative industrial extraction, environmental degradation, neglect of infrastructure and education, epidemics of substance abuse, and agricultural subsidies. Howard's stories give enough evidence of poverty to make a gentle emotional appeal and highlight the outcomes of upward mobility without engaging critically with the systemic issues that might cause other families to have a much harder time being so resilient.

TOWARDS A CONCLUSION: RESISTANCE AND RESILIENCE

Why talk about poverty and economic depression in a cookbook at all? Even *White Trash Cooking*, a cookbook explicitly dedicated to representing poor white southerners, makes no mention of the problems or pains of poverty. Neither the genre conventions of the contemporary cookbook nor the influential forerunner of *White Trash Cooking* requires Vivian Howard to address poverty in *Deep Run Roots*. Does Howard's background in rural poverty help readers to understand the procedures in the recipes better? Do the stories help us to imagine the flavor or texture of a dish? Of course not. But they do help us to put the dish in a context of social meaning. Howard and Mickler both use an origin in poverty to frame a recipe's meaning in the community where it comes from and what it will mean to the reader if they decide to prepare the dish. If the South at large is associated with rural poverty, then stories and images of poverty are representative of the South. The stories are there to give evidence of an authentic southern experience.

But Howard's narratives demonstrate how these stories of deprivation and limited opportunity are carefully crafted so that they do not bring down the cookbook's rhetorical aim of pleasure. Poverty in the past is a chance to talk about the South's most desirable qualities: resilience, resourcefulness, work ethic, family and community cooperation, humble antimaterialism, preindustrial small-scale agriculture, seasonality and harmony with nature, and delicious snacks. Mickler's campy contributors highlight humor and self-deprecating humility. Howard's family story demonstrates the pleasure and promise of upward mobility, each generation doing a little better than the one before. All these are linked to that "simple" category of authenticity, broader even than southern authenticity. The story of poverty that results in creativity fits into the discourse of "foodies" who are reacting to the reputation of snobbishness of gourmet foods by valorizing "simple" foods with humble origins. *Deep Run Roots* offers readers a chance to have the best of both worlds: to taste the simple traditions of eastern North Carolina and to experience the fine dining versions of those created responsibly by an authorized chef. Howard's direct statements of purpose for her restaurant—to sustainably revitalize the economy of Kinston—offers readers another way to "vote with their forks" and partake in a democratizing food culture. Howard's stories and images of poverty tell readers that they are buying the "right" experiences in order to demonstrate good citizenship through their consumer practices. They will *feel good* about *doing good* while they make food that *tastes good*.

Howard and so many other chef-authors like her have helped to valorize the "poverty foods" of my own rural past into highly capitalized food experiences. I used to tell people of my childhood, "If we hadn't been so poor, it would have been a very hip upbringing." If not for the attention to these foods as valuable in the popular discourse of food, I would not be able to value them as I do. Our simple meals of fifty-cent cornbread mix, black eyed peas from the garden dosed with Chow Chow that was canned by our neighbor, cucumber and tomato slices in white vinegar, hamburger steaks with ketchup, and salted chunks of cantaloupe for dessert start to look like something to aspire to, like evidence of deep roots in southern soil. For readers wishing to perform a southern identity, Howard's story may be a bridge that connects the script of a recipe to the physical performance of an identity that is cleared of all its shame.

I end this chapter in the same way that I end most everything, with a better sense of the complications, but not a definitive value judgment or solution. If cookbooks use stories or images to link their cuisine to the experience of poor people in the South in order to sell more cookbooks, this sounds pretty bad. It might even be a reification of a "bootstraps" mythology and blaming the poor for remaining poor instead of being lucky enough to hitch their fortunes to a famous chef and going along for the ride. However, the visual and textual cues related to southern poverty might also serve as evidence of democracy and distinction in balance. The recipe (and the author's success, by extension) are accessible to all, regardless of class, and yet the recipe also promises the aesthetic pleasures of gourmet cuisine. It could be a resistance to capitalism by offering a business model that places people above profits. When invoking stories of poverty and pain seems to be in service of a democratic aim, writers may share credit for innovations in southern cuisine with the least capitalized but most highly authorized cultural creators.

What separates the "good" from the "bad"—the subversive from the status quo—is whether they address poverty as a consequence of political decisions (good) or personal character (bad). Neither Mickler nor Howard are explicit in laying blame for poverty at the feet of any particular actor. Mickler enshrines poverty as a category of identity that has such positive outcomes in humor and charm that it would be a shame to disrupt it with anything like political action. Howard gently implicates the tobacco and textile industries in the economic downturn of Kinston, and she offers social entrepreneurship as a potential solution. There is a hint that poverty is political, but Howard's response is largely based on individual responsibility. Both break genre conventions and expectations of food writing by making poverty visible, but neither mount a particularly successful resistance to systems of power.

The best and most just kind of narrative of poverty would be the one that makes clear the systemic origins of this poverty and offers a critique of systems, if not systemic solutions. The personal experiences of deprivation and making do, then, are framed as resilience and self-reliance that subverts and disrupts the system on a personal level, leaving an open door for imagining large-scale disruptions. If the character of the poor white southerner is resilient, it is only because the systems of oppression that thrive there are relentless.

WORKS CITED

"About." *Vivian Howard*. https://www.vivianhoward.com/chef-the-farmer.

Adno, Michael. "The Short and Brilliant Life of Matthew Mickler." *The Bitter Southerner*, https://bittersoutherner.com/the-short-and-brilliant-life-of-ernest-matthew-mickler.

Cash, Wilbur, J. *The Mind of the South*. Doubleday and Co., Inc., 1941.

Cobb, James C. *The Most Southern Place on Earth: The Mississippi Delta and the Roots of Regional Identity*. Oxford UP, 1992.

Davis, David. "Modernism, Primitivism, and Food in James Agee's Cotton Tenants." *Modernism and Food Studies: Politics, Aesthetics, and the Avant-Garde*, edited by Phillip Geheber, Adam Farjado, and Jessica Martell, UP of Florida, 2019, pp. 166–81.

Egerton, John. *The Americanization of Dixie: The Southernization of America*. Harper's Magazine Press, 1973.

Folwell, Emma J. *The War on Poverty in Mississippi: From Massive Resistance to New Conservatism*. UP of Mississippi, 2020.

Germany, Kent. "Poverty Wars in the Louisiana Delta: White Resistance, Black Power, and the Poorest Place in America." *The War on Poverty: A New Grassroots History*, edited by Annelise Orleck and Lisa Gayle Hazirjian, U of Georgia P, 2011, 231–55.

Howard, Vivian. *Deep Run Roots: Stories and Recipes from My Corner of the South*. Little Brown, 2016.

Johnston, Josee and Shyon Baumann. *Foodies: Democracy and Distinction in the Gourmet Foodscape*. Routledge, 2010.

Maher, John. "Ten Speed, Chef Bryant Terry Launch 4 Color Books." *Publisher's Weekly*, 3 May 2021, https://www.publishersweekly.com/pw/by-topic/industry-news/publisher-news/article/86237-ten-speed-chef-bryant-terry-launch-4-color-books.html.

Margo, Robert A. "Poverty." *Social Class*, edited by Larry J. Griffin, Peggy G. Hargis, and Charles Reagan Wilson, vol. 20 of *The New Encyclopedia of Southern Culture*. U of North Carolina P, 2012, 201–9.

Mickler, Ernest. *White Trash Cooking: 25th Anniversary Edition*. Ten Speed Press, 2011.

Miller, Adrian. *Soul Food: The Surprising Story of an American Cuisine One Plate at a Time*. U of North Carolina P, 2013.

Reed, John Shelton. *The Enduring South: Subcultural Persistence in Mass Society*. U of North Carolina P, 1975.

Robertson, Sarah. *Poverty Politics: Poor Whites in Contemporary Southern Writing*. UP of Mississippi, 2014.

Shugart, Helene A. and Catherine Egley Waggoner. *Making Camp : Rhetorics of Transgression in U.S. Popular Culture*. U of Alabama P, 2008.

Talde, Dale. *Asian-American: Proudly Inauthentic Recipes from the Philippines to Brooklyn*. Grand Central Life & Style, 2015.

"Ten Speed Press." *The Crown Publishing Group*, https://crownpublishing.com/archives/imprint/ten-speed-press

Tippen, Carrie Helms. *Inventing Authenticity: How Cookbook Writers Redefine Southern Identity*. U of Arkansas P, 2018.

Woodard, C. Van. *The Burden of Southern History*. Louisiana State UP, 2008.

A SEASON OF SWEETNESS
Gardening, Canning, and Women's Labor on Farms

Didn't I tell you in the last chapter about growing up on a cotton farm with a big vegetable garden? Do you also remember me telling you that I hated it? Summers were the worst. Instead of going to town for school every day, and gymnastics and errands on Saturday, and church twice on Sunday, we mostly stayed on the farm during the summer. Except Sundays, obviously. I had hours to myself to lay in the sun and work on my tan, bounce on the trampoline with the radio blaring, read Jane Austen, write terrible poems, walk the caliche dirt roads, and think big thoughts. But we also had the damn garden.

My poor, sainted mother. I can't imagine that the garden was her idea. Our two closest neighbors were our landlady, Bernice Anderson, for whom we were essentially sharecroppers, and my father's mother, Dorothy Boswell Helms. It had to be they who inducted my mother into the garden. She grew up in Amarillo—The City in my imagination—and couldn't have had much experience with gardening anything more than a geranium or two before settling on the farm with my dad. All three women worked in and benefited from the garden, for sure, but I suspect the older women set the expectation for what it should be like. It was my mother who had to reach for that expectation to prove her fitness as wife, mother, and farm woman without much assistance or sympathy.

We're not talking about a backyard hobby garden with a stand of fussed over tomatoes and coddled prize roses. "The Garden" was twelve rows, a quarter mile each in length, running alongside the roaring irrigation well and pump, in the cotton field up the hill from the house. If you're counting, that's three miles of garden: black-eyed peas, Contender and Kentucky Wonder green beans, pinto beans picked early for flat green beans and late for speckled red beans, tomatoes, cantaloupe, watermelon, okra. My mother set up some experiments each year like zipper cream peas and long asparagus beans. Nearer to the house in a far more manageably sized plot were the zucchini and squash, cucumbers, peppers, radishes, and cherry tomatoes. It was a huge undertaking.

From the time we were old enough to not eat the dirt, my sisters and I were on garden duty with my mother. It sucked. The work was always early morning in the summer to beat the heat and be home to make lunch. We dragged and played possum and feigned illness to be allowed to sleep in under the window A/C unit that spit chunks of ice. We whined as we loaded the five-gallon buckets into the back of our old GMC Jimmy. We piddled in the rows picking our nail polish and fighting among ourselves, groaning and irritated and hot with short fuses. My mother brought a wooden paddle into the field to spank us when we were too annoying and to kill snakes that sometimes curled up under the vines.

When it was breezy and cool, we sang songs from church in four-part harmony and played a game where the next person had to come up with a new song that used a word from the song we were singing. When it was good, it was like being a troupe of living Earth goddesses, walking the rows of plenty, perfectly in tune. When it was bad, and it usually was, we stuffed the bottom of the buckets with shoes and jackets to make them look fuller so we could leave faster. We pinched and punched and kicked and screamed. We were bitten by mosquitos and stung by wasps and volunteered for every other possible chore so we could get out of there. My older sister didn't mind too much because she liked the tan and the lean muscles of work, and anyway, she usually got to leave early to cook lunch for the family. My baby sister got a pass for, well, being a baby. As a middle child born on the cusp between Taurus and Gemini, I was a full-on brat and an unbearable horse's ass from minute one. No one had fun when I was around, and sometimes I was banished from sight just for being the ever-loving worst. Again, I say, my poor sainted mother, who did not look forward to the fights and bugs and bending and squatting any more than we did.

There were often guests in the garden, which necessitated better behavior. Relatives and women from church and friends from school would come and pick a bucket or two for themselves. We would load up the car with cantaloupes and watermelons in August and bring them to school to give away to our teachers. We donated watermelons to the church picnic. My grandmothers on both sides and our landlady/babysitter/honorary grandma Mrs. Anderson would clean, snap, shell, and sack up what we picked. I didn't mind the shelling part, especially after we bought our own electric pea sheller and I could run the long peas through the motorized wringer while watching *The West Wing* and *ER* on Bravo and drinking gallons of sweet iced tea in front of the air conditioner. I'd eat handfuls of raw peas. The mush left behind on the rollers was tasty, too, green and fresh. I lived in fear of catching my hair in the rollers like Samantha's poor friend Nelly in my favorite American Girl Doll book, so I kept a careful watch on my ponytail.

Then came the season of canning. We ate a lot of what came out of the garden immediately or shared it with friends and family to eat fresh. But eventually, the bounty would overwhelm us, and we looked forward to the hot bowls of cornbread and black-eyed peas on New Year's Day and red beans all winter. Canning was a multiday, all-hands-on-deck affair, and yet, I remember staying pretty far out of it. A kid's job might be gathering glass canning jars and metal lids and rings from Mrs. Anderson's cellar and from our closets and from around the house where they held pens and paintbrushes and hair ties so that they could be washed and boiled. The Ziploc bags of shelled peas and snapped beans were distributed into jars. Someone was taking jars out to cool while someone else was prepping jars to go in.

Maybe I was still in the living room snapping and shelling and bagging, or maybe I had made my escape outdoors while the adults were busy. After the peas or beans went in the jar, the details are fuzzy for me. There was heat and boiling water and a pressure cooker, and these delicate processes were for experienced adults, not bratty kids and sulky teens. My baby sister and I both remember the smell, metallic and sweaty. I often think weight rooms in gyms have the same kind of smell. The kitchen was hot, and the sound of the pressure cooker weight wiggling and steaming was a constant. I remember watching *Briscoe County, Jr.* or *Star Trek* and listening for the pop of the lids from the living room. My mom tapped each lid to listen for a good seal.

In my most nostalgic moments, I remember the singing and the community of women in our kitchen and the clean, bright green jars. I remember knowing that anytime we liked, we could grab a quart jar from the boxes kept under the pants and skirts in mother's closet to make a meal. I also remember forgoing all green beans for years so that I had a rhetorical leg to stand on when I refused to pick them in the field. I could shout, "I don't even eat them!" and not be contradicted. This garden of plenty that fed my whole world and represented the opposite of all my poetic ambition was a confusing site for painful labor and feminine strength, community and loneliness, play and drudgery. I suspect that fighting with children in the dry heat and scalding fingers on boiling glass jars was a necessary annoyance that any of the women in my family would gladly have skipped if they could. We depended on the food we grew; some of the families we fed depended on it even more. It was a site of family tension; it was a site of family bonding. It was a place of silliness and work. It was a place of danger and violence. It was a place of ingenuity and cleverness and resilience. It was hard work that made bodies ache and itch, turn red and peel, bleed and scar, and grow strong. It smelled bad and it tasted good.

PLEASURE AND PAIN OF WOMEN'S WORK IN THE GARDEN

The garden is yet another site for mixing pleasure with pain in cookbook stories. In stories about agricultural labor and food preservation, women's physical pain and exhaustion are presented alongside images of abundance and resilience. Women—especially mothers and grandmothers—are depicted as experiencing suffering for the pleasure and security of their families. While they are praised for strength and skill, their pleasure or need for relief from physical toil are not often centered in the narrative. This chapter examines the paradox of recognizing women's painful labor in a pleasure-centered genre. I argue that references to women's labor in growing and preserving food is another signal of southern "authenticity." Not only is canning and preserving tied to a narrative of an essentially rural southern practice, but canning and gardening also connect the cookbook writer to work that is antithetical to "inauthentic" mass-produced and industrial food. Gardening and preserving represent traditional and "simple" authenticity along with a suggestion of geographic specificity.

The subject of gardening and preserving is a signal of authenticity to readers, but cookbook writers also have choices in how to present women's labor in order to resist metanarratives of gender roles and identities. It may be that by naming women's pain in a genre that expects pleasure, writers present an alternative story that values women's work. But is the pain itself part of the authenticity narrative? If buying mass-produced, industrially canned food is painless and convenient, then painful toil by hand must be part of the narrative for the work of gardening and canning to be "authentic" as the opposite. When the stories inevitably turn to pleasure to meet the genre requirements of the cookbook, it matters who experiences the pleasure of this work. Perhaps women are able to access pleasure in the work, but often the pleasure in the narrative is focused on the beneficiaries of the work. This chapter asks, who hurts and who benefits when women's work is evidence of authenticity?

WOMEN'S PLEASURE AND RESISTANCE

Much of the scholarship on women's pleasure focuses on sexual pleasure as serious business. In the introduction to their 2006 collection *Women, Sexuality and the Political Power of Pleasure*, editors Susie Jolly, Andrea Cornwall, and Kate Hawkins argue that "sexual pleasure can be affirming and empowering for people not seen by their societies as deserving of this kind of enjoyment," but more importantly, "pleasure can also provide energy to fuel political mobilization" (3). Their collection focuses on political action and interventions based on pleasure. Where earlier formulations of pleasure as empowering stopped at an individual's intimate experience of pleasure, the editors and contributors explore public interventions that use pleasure as a tool for enacting social change. While they acknowledge that work on ending sexual violence is vital to women's empowerment and human rights, "This focus on the negative can be paralysing—both in terms of ease with one's own body, and in terms of mobilizing around women's wants and desires" (1). Pleasure plays an important role in finding appropriate solutions for ending suffering, but the editors are careful to point out that neither suffering nor pleasure are particularly useful on their own. Taken together, pain and pleasure can be catalysts for action.

Sexual pleasure is just a starting point for enacting policies and practices that support women's health, well-being, and happiness. Ana Francis Mor writes about using laughter and comedic performances to begin to unravel metanarratives about women's suffering in rural Mexico. As Mor explains, women see themselves represented in ubiquitous soap operas as essentially suffering beings: "In the farthest and most hidden corners of the country, where only misery visits, it arrives accompanied by soap operas and their Cinderella stories: where the female hero has a terrible life during a hundred chapters or so and then, when she gets to the final chapter, finds happiness by getting married" (287). In the absence of reliable information, Mor argues, these fictional narratives appear as reality, which has an insidious negative effect on real-life health outcomes. For example, Mor suggests that even though women may have plenty of information about prevention, early detection, and treatment of cervical cancer, a culture that reifies women's suffering and demonizes sexual pleasure may prevent them from using available gynecological services and resources, taking their pain as a natural consequence of their gender (288–89). Through a farcical play about a woman whose "circumstances were so hilariously ridiculous that no one wanted to be like her," Mor's theatrical company uses laughter and satire to dismantle oppressive narratives. Where logic, information, and even fear could not persuade women to change their behavior, pleasure and laughter had the desired rhetorical effect: "By making laughter a main character of our stories, we placed the pleasant choice above and before the painful one" (291).

Mor concludes that laughter and the pleasure that it brings to the body and to the mind are "a missing link to empowerment," revealing a capacity for change and growth that renarrating suffering cannot offer:

> Laughter gives us the opportunity to tell our stories not from the accumulation of our tragedies, but through our ability to reach a deeper understanding of these tragedies and transform them. Laughter allows us to place ourselves in positions far from solemnity and rigidity. It leads us to laugh at our fanaticism and question our structures, over and over again. With laughter we can complete the map of the body, the human anatomy, because if we try to understand people or communities without studying their ability to laugh, to feel pleasure, then our analysis remains incomplete. Because, as people, we are not only the sum of the situations that make us live in misery, violence, hunger and indignity. As people, it is necessary to add our laughter, our orgasms, what we dream of, what we love, what makes us explode with pleasure. We are also whatever we can imagine we are. (291)

Feeling pleasure can be an energizing experience that motivates change and electrifies resistance. "Misery, violence, hunger and indignity" are serious problems, and while serious people seek out solutions, they may get closer to their target by recognizing that people who are suffering are capable of and worthy of great happiness, too.

Mor's example from the Global South applies well to the cookbook and the US South, though it takes place in a different culture and genre of art. Like the soap operas that repeat and entrench a culture of suffering, narratives of southern women's suffering in the past and ongoing in the present have the potential to naturalize suffering as unassailable realities, flattening people who experience this suffering into caricatures of pain who cannot imagine their own pleasure. As writer Courtney Balestier remarked in an interview about stories of Appalachian foodways, there is a temptation to "focus on pain until the pain is the identity" (25:25–31), an inadequate representation of the fullness of the culture.

At some point, those stories of suffering lose their ability to meet their rhetorical aims; they no longer move audiences to action because they begin with defeat. But if the audience feels pleasure through art when they receive the message—through laughter and theatre in Mor's example and through gustatory delight and entertaining reading in cookbooks—the message is refreshed, and the possibility of moving from a feeling of empowerment to an empowered action seems more probable. The imagination, now envisioning a pleasurable future, is the engine of personal and social change. Cookbooks are not disqualified as a genre from being effective tools for resistance because of their focus on pleasure; on the contrary, pleasure remains a viable rhetorical strategy.

It is not difficult to extrapolate from this body of feminist literature a principle of pleasure more broadly as resistance to metanarratives of women's suffering. Food, eating, cooking, and cookbooks are key parts of this conversation as well as radical tools for pleasure. Anne Bower's 2004 article for *Gastronomica* titled "Romanced by Cookbooks" combines the idea of sexual pleasure and the pleasure of eating to argue that cookbook reading is an imaginative experience similar to the experience of reading Romance novels. Bower draws on Janice Radway's ground-breaking analysis of women's romance novel reading to suggest that women reading cookbooks may be experiencing the same kind of subversive commitment to their own pleasure through fantasy that can be interpreted as empowerment. Bower imagines the cookbook as akin to a romance novel, an imaginative experience that meets a reader's "own needs to escape out of the mundane or into idealized settings and self-images" (35). Like romance novels that recenter women's sexual pleasure as a convention of the genre, cookbooks are also generically focused on celebration: "Not only is [reading] a relaxing release from the tension produced by daily problems and responsibilities, but it creates a time or space within which a woman can be entirely on her own, preoccupied with her personal needs, desires, and pleasures" (36). While the actual process of cooking a recipe may be frustrating and fraught with the anxiety of seeking approval from others, the selfish pleasure of *reading* a cookbook and *imagining* perfect cooking is a form of resistance (albeit passive and private) that allows a reader to begin to imagine a future of bodily autonomy and agency.

What is a better form of resisting gender norms and compulsory heterosexuality? Is it unflinchingly naming women's pain or reveling in their capacity for pleasure? When the genre of the cookbook makes it so easy to do only the latter, why would cookbook writers choose the former? I argue that women's labor is connected to a metanarrative of southern suffering.

SOUTHERN WOMEN AND FARM WORK

Rebecca Sharpless and Melissa Walker have been leading scholars in southern and rural women's labor for nearly two decades. Their scholarship and oral histories—authored and edited alone and together—gives a picture of the complexities of women's work on farms in the South that must negotiate between strong, opposing economic and social forces. An activity like gardening or canning could have a wide range of valences in a farm family depending on their class status and racial identity.

As Walker explains in *Country Women Cope With Hard Times*, the farm women she interviewed viewed their labor "as an integral part of the family economy." Women were responsible for "stretching scarce resources as far as possible," and growing and preserving food was a key part of that responsibility (xxvii). Activities like raising chickens for eggs, milking cows for butter, and growing and canning vegetables fed families but also provided women with income and resources when surplus home-produced goods could be sold or bartered (xxvi). Products could also be shared in systems of "mutual aid": women shared the labor of canning and the fruits of that labor to "build and maintain [mutual aid] networks that were crucial for surviving hard times" (xxvii). The physical labor of women on the farm was valuable to an entire community's viability.

As economic conditions changed after World War II, the kinds of work socially appropriate for women and the meaning of women's work changed, too. When "cash crop" farms became more profitable, Walker argues, women's labor growing food and tending animals freed up cash to invest in the crop rather than in meeting the family's needs for subsistence: "Men's work came to be seen as the 'real work' of farming because it produced the cash income. Women's food production simply saved money" (xxviii). Walker explains that "Southern farm people, like all Americans, subscribed to the notion that men and women were suited for different kinds of work," and most agreed that the bulk of field work was more appropriate for men (xxvi). Women and children still "formed a vital pool of surplus labor to meet the demands of peak seasons" (xxvii). Don't I know it.

In *Work, Family, and Faith: Rural Southern Women in the Twentieth Century*, Walker and Sharpless further explore how the realities of farm labor intersected with culturally constructed ideas of gender and race in the early twentieth century. While the idea of "separate spheres" of labor for men and women reigned culturally, as Walker noted above, it rarely prevailed in lived experience. In the Depression era South, women's work on cash crops like cotton and tobacco and producing goods for sale in the market meant that they were "very much part of the national marketplace that women were supposed to avoid according to the cultural principles of the time" ("Pretty Near" 42). Walker and Sharpless explain that "all but the wealthiest farmers relied on family labor, including the work of women and children," ("Introduction" 9) and "most farms lived on razor-thin margins of sufficiency" (10).

Though the practice of women working in fields was widespread, the idea of women doing physical labor marked for men had a "great social and emotional significance for many rural people" depending on their race, class, and personal interests ("Pretty Near" 42). For some white women, the ability to abstain from the most difficult farm work was a sign of both class success and white supremacy. As Sharpless and Walker explain, after the transition from enslaved labor to a sharecropping system, Black and white southerners were more likely to find themselves in similar economic positions as tenant farmers and small landowners. Since Black women had been forced to share in field work as enslaved laborers, it was socially accepted and expected that they would continue field work under tenancy or as landowners. However, Sharpless and Walker argue that some Black women withdrew from farm labor as a signal of their control over their choice of labor and a nod to white notions of class status (45). Meanwhile, white women in similar farm situations withdrew from field labor as a way to reaffirm divisions of race: "the less whites were able to distinguish themselves from African Americans in economic terms, the more they sought to do so in cultural terms" (46). The authors summarize pithily: "the separation of gender roles carried much cultural weight, heavily laden with the notions of class and race that formed much of the foundation of white southerners' sense of self" (43). The decision for women to participate in the hard work of farming was and is imbricated in a system of values that connect southern identity with carefully policed divisions of gender, class, and race.

Walker and Sharpless are sympathetic for the complex feelings that farm work must have generated for the women they interviewed and researched who had labored on farms in the South in the first half of the twentieth century. Though their findings overall show "mixed feelings" about women and field work, they acknowledge that some "women also actively chose work in the fields, taking pleasure in the work itself and their ability to do it well" ("Pretty Near" 44). Some took pleasure and pride in hard physical labor, like the "Working Lass" who wrote to *Farm and Ranch* magazine in 1919 to offer pity for the women who do not take a share in farm work:

> Any work that is honorable is worth while and it gives me an indescribable feeling to hear someone boast 'I never had to work' . . . . Now that woman has unconsciously suffered a misfortune. She knows not work, nor life, for in real life we get a taste of work and it makes better boys and girls, men and women of us. (qtd in 53)

Similarly, "Happy Belle," who wrote to *Farm and Ranch* in 1910, defended her feminine identity, even as she took pleasure in her work: "I worked everywhere, and I am still a lady. If a girl is going to be anything, she will be it anywhere you put her" (54). In the cases where women filled in as farm managers for an "ill, dead, or ignorant husband or father," women proved to be strong and capable farmers despite stereotypes and cultural expectations (62).

Even as Walker and Sharpless listen to the stories women tell about themselves, they consider whether the speakers are comfortable admitting the whole truth of their working lives or the depth of ambivalence they might feel about their physical farm labor. One interviewee "admitted, seeming reluctant" that she worked in the fields, only after the interviewer pressed her, and she immediately changed the subject. Walker and Sharpless speculate that "her reluctance to talk about her field work suggests that she was uncomfortable with having worked in the fields. Perhaps she believed the interviewer wouldn't have approved. Or perhaps fieldwork violated her own notions about the work a prosperous farm woman of her status would do." The interviewee spoke more freely and enthusiastically about cooking for large groups of workers, "an important and more socially acceptable part of her life," perhaps, the authors speculate, as "a way of avoiding talking about her field work" that might have brought a sense of shame for breaking norms of gender, class, and race ("Pretty Near" 61). The authors are clear that there is not a single story of women and farm work that could be generalized across the South, and perhaps even the women who lived it cannot say all that it meant to them to do farm labor.

Furthermore, Walker and Sharpless admonish "twenty-first-century scholars" not "to dismiss these arguments [against doing field work] as women accepting too easily culturally dictated limitations" about gender roles ("Pretty Near" 50). Though the women who argued against doing field work may use cultural norms about feminine weakness or white supremacy to frame their choices, the authors remind us that field work was hard, physical labor for both men and women: "stories abound of women working a full day in the blazing sun and still cooking two hot meals, of babies left with siblings who were little more than babies themselves, of damaged uteruses and strained backs. One can scarcely blame a woman for electing not to go into the fields" (50). There's a bargain to be made with the patriarchy; in exchange for accepting some parts of the gender stereotype, women could keep some power over their choices about work and avoid physical pain.

Similarly, Walker and Sharpless argue that even though the arguments about "separate spheres" consign women to work in and around the home—including kitchen gardens—the line between "public" and "private" work on a farm is hard to parse since women's work contributed to the family's economy and sometimes took them into the marketplace. Whether through saving money on goods that would have been purchased without their work or preparing surplus goods for sale or barter, gardening and canning or tending animals could be seen as "market oriented work" ("Pretty Near" 43). Walker and Sharpless conclude: "The home was not a 'haven' from the public world or the world of production; it *was* the location of production" (44). Farm women who did not plow or pick cotton still performed difficult physical labor that blurred the lines between unpaid domestic work and valuable economic production for the public marketplace.

The authors conclude that the variety of work arrangements and opinions expressed by women about their own farm labor "reveals much about the complex interaction between autonomy and necessity. In the early twentieth century, southern farm women exercised the limited freedom of action available to them to choose their lives to the greatest extent possible" (63). Whether they chose the hard labor of field work, the hard labor of gardening and animal tending, the hard labor of preserving and canning, the hard labor of moving surplus goods to market, or the hard labor of child rearing and domestic work—farm women did make choices about their lives and labor.

Even farm girls earned distinction through canning and gardening labors. Elizabeth Engelhardt devotes a chapter of *A Mess of Greens: Southern Gender and Southern Food* to a cultural history of Tomato Clubs, social clubs for girls in the early twentieth century that, according to founder Maria Samuella Comer, focused on learning "how to grow better and more perfect tomatoes, and how to grow better and more perfect women" (qtd. in Engelhardt 83). Girls in tomato clubs grew tomatoes to can for their families and sell for independent income, which Engelhardt argues "pulled girls' economic earning abilities out of the illicit background and into the center of a national conversation about southern food and gender, valuing their abilities and intelligence in the process" (85). Though the tomato club movement had a brief "heyday from 1911 until the eve of World War I" (85), it grew quickly and garnered considerable national attention (88), and the girls who participated in these clubs left a significant archive of reports, poems, and songs that Engelhardt argues demonstrate changing norms of gender, economics, and industrial food. Engelhardt reiterates the earning potential of girls in tomato clubs who sold their goods and competed for prizes, and the organizers intentionally set parameters for participation that would move "beyond the home and domestic space and consumption into public, economic production" (99). The tomato clubs offered a unique and ambitious resistance to gender, race, and class, as Engelhardt explains (115), but they also sound kind of like fun with opportunities for creativity as well as the pleasure that a little economic freedom and self-efficacy can bring.

The foregoing work on oral histories is important to this study of cookbooks because most of the narratives written in cookbooks about women and farm work, especially gardening and canning, come second- and third-hand from the children and grandchildren of women who did this labor. As Walker and Sharpless admit, even when women tell their stories directly, they interpret their work through complex lenses of gender, race, and class, and sometimes they don't tell all, even to objective historians. Stories are filtered through families and across generational lines, and they are shaped again as they are presented for an outside audience through the genre of the cookbook. The representation of pain, pleasure, choice, and necessity may be subject to revision to suit various rhetorical purposes as women's stories of farm labor are told.

Still, remembering women's work, even through a game of telephone, can be an important act of recovery. As Letitzia Guglielmo argues in the introduction to *Remembering Women Differently: Refiguring Rhetorical Work*, feminist rhetoricians have long focused on "recover[ing] women's histories and their work as part of recorded history and public memory" (1). Because women's stories, especially those about mundane domestic work, often go unwritten, scholars of women's rhetoric like those represented in the collection, "bring to light or refocus the lens on women's stories that may have existed in the shadows of another's more convenient, accepted, or publicly sanctioned narrative" (1). Guglielmo defines this action of memory as *re-collecting*, implying "a feminist rhetorical act of gathering or assembling again what has been scattered" (2). "Remembering differently" from the title means using narrative to rewrite a story that may have been silenced or "misremembered" by other narrators. The re-collected story of women's work can "disrupt or destabilize established memories created by prior acts of recollection and public remembrance" (4). Walker emphasizes the importance of collecting oral histories from working women because "women whose lives were filled with an endless round of physical labor rarely enjoyed the leisure or, often, the education, to create written documents" (xvi). When today's cookbook writers re-collect the memories of women's labor, they have a choice between reinscribing established memories that follow the dominant metanarrative, or they may "remember differently" and tell a narrative which "consider[s] the deliberate and consequential ways in which women have been obscured from and remembered differently within public memory and the cultural and social norms—always evolving—that constrain and shape women's reputations and memories" (Guglielmo 15). In this chapter, I will be looking for writers who use the opportunity of describing women's often painful physical farm labor as an opportunity to destabilize overdetermined metanarratives and allow for the complexities of lived experience to show through.

Today, gardening and canning have a completely different valence for so-called "Gen X" and "Millennial" women like me than they did for the women Walker and Sharpless studied. Emily Matchar's 2013 book *Homeward Bound: Why Women are Embracing the New Domesticity* started with her investigation of a group of "young, educated women" who were canning enthusiasts. Though Matchar thought of canning as "a fun, nostalgic hobby," it was clear that the women she interviewed saw it as significant personal, social, and political action: "They spoke of self-sufficiency, of rescuing 'lost' domestic arts, of sustainable lifestyles, of reclaiming the concept of 'homemaker'" (13). These women prompted Matchar to ask, "Why are women (and more than a few men) of my generation, the children of post-Betty Friedan feminists, embracing the domestic tasks that our mothers and grandmothers so eagerly shrugged off?" (5).

Matchar's primary answer is that the "New Domesticity," as she calls it, is a pendulum swing reaction to the "'You can have it all'" feminism that today's young adults grew up with; young women are "wary" of these promises after "having watched our mothers struggle" to meet that unrealistic expectation (14). In the world after the "Great Recession," Matchar argues, anxieties about the future are high, and faith in capitalism to solve the world's problems is low. "We're taking shelter. We're learning to knit. We're embracing slow food," Matchar explains. "We're fantasizing about ditching the corporate world to run a Vermont goat farm" (11–12). "Educated, progressive Americans," (and women in particular) are disillusioned with American work culture and the "expectations of sixty-hour work weeks, lack of maternity leave, [and] massive 'mompenalties' on salary" (12). Domestic work like gardening and canning offers a kind of satisfaction that the workplace and careers often do not. As one interviewee with a PhD in English (not me, I swear) commented, "Canning is a confirmation that our generation hasn't forgotten how to do things.... There's a reality to that stuff that I don't feel about academic life" (100). Another (still not me) told Matcher that she discovered "home-making could be creatively fulfilling in a way she'd never imagined" (104). Some of the women that Matchar interviewed for her book are opting out of public workplaces "as not just a personal choice but an explicitly political act" (22). As one interviewee explains, "This is the new wave of feminism—women taking back the home" (22). In the twentieth century, gardening and canning might have been seen as a giving in to social pressure to accept narrow gender roles and "separate spheres," but the twenty-first-century women that Matchar interviewed see it as a political choice and a feminist rebellion against a different set of gendered expectations.

Matchar argues that much of the DIY food culture associated with New Domesticity—gardening, canning, backyard chicken farming (all things that I do as a hip, urban, elder Millennial)—is a response to anxiety about industrialized food systems and a romanticization of the past. Matchar quotes southern food scholar Marcie Cohen Ferris, who describes the movement as "a response to a broken food system . . . a response to an industrial model that's not working" (99). Matchar argues that it is also in response to a discourse about food "that places an immense amount of faith in the idea of food as a solution for a variety of social ills, from childhood obesity to global warming to broken families to corporate greed" (96). The problem with assigning so much power to food, Matchar argues, is that "our outsized expectations of what food can do leads to an outsized sense of guilt among a group traditionally responsible for food: women" (118). While Matchar recognizes that for some women, "the new cooking culture is incredibly empowering" (100), for many others, aligning kitchen work with saving the world "can drain all the fun out of cooking and turn dinnertime into a referendum on good global citizenship, good parenting, good morals" (115).

After hearing from women past and present who grow and preserve food in gardens and on farms, it isn't clear what any of this labor should mean to women. It isn't clear if it is painful or pleasant, if it is an expectation of gender or a rebellion against expectation, if it is private work or public work, if it is a feminist protest or a patriarchal bargain. Is making jam a withdrawal from capitalism or a vital part of a family economy? The meaning of work seems too tied up with race and class to be generalizable across gender. It seems too dependent on context to be summarized across time. Narratives about women's farm and kitchen work in southern cookbooks, then, are not likely to tell a single story about womanhood, southerness, pleasure, or pain. Drawing any conclusion about the rhetoric of women's suffering will require examining narratives closely.

WOMEN'S PAIN AND PLEASURE IN THE GARDEN: CASE STUDIES

In the previous chapter, I described an episode of gardening and canning in Vivian Howard's *Deep Run Roots* (216–19). In that cookbook, canning seems to be connected to poverty by the rural experience and the assumption that preservation is about reducing the cost of food or storing up against future food insecurity. Like the women in Matcher's investigation of DIY food culture, Howard is neither food insecure nor poor. Howard explains that her motivations for putting up hundreds of ears of corn are primarily nostalgia and curiosity (218). The goal was to experience something that was familiar to her ancestors but distant from her own life. Maybe Howard's insistence on embodying the painful work of her grandmothers is not too far removed from Michael Twitty's insistence on embodying the painful work of his enslaved ancestors. The conditions of the work are dramatically different, and so the intensity of the emotional pain brought on by the exercise are likely to be very different as well. Still, the motivations seem to me to come from the same place: a desire to strengthen the connection to the past through action in the present. Painful labor now might also bring the pleasure of feeling continuous with a past that is also geographically specific to a southern homeplace. Gardening and canning may be trendy for fourth-wave DIY feminists, but for the cookbook writers examined in this chapter, it is not *merely* a trend, but a way of "being true" to a recognizably southern historical tradition.

"LIKE I'M DOING SOMETHING 100 PERCENT HONEST": AN ESSENTIAL SOUTHERN EXPERIENCE

For readers wishing to perform a southern identity, the story of canning vegetables may be a bridge that connects an activity to an identity. To that end, many contemporary southern cookbooks have a section devoted to pickles and preserves, recipes that make use of garden produce in order to extend the life of that ingredient into another season. In Hugh Acheson's 2011 cookbook *A New Turn in the South*, that chapter is called "Pickles, Put-Ups and Pantry Items" (245–65). Acheson explains that his Atlanta restaurant Empire State South envisioned a table-side "sommelier-like preserve service" for pairing pickles and preserves for diners but abandoned the idea as "uber fine dining" and "not me" (247). However, the restaurant and the cookbook still feature many of "the pickle-based cultural icons of the southern table such as chowchow, dilly pickles, pickled green tomatoes, spiced tomatoes, and packed-up okra" (247). Acheson suggests that while southern preserves are "new to most diners [at Empire State South] but familiar to southern cooks," they are also unique among a global tradition of preserves, unlike "the sweet jams that are made everywhere and not the English or Indian chutneys" (247). Acheson names Pickled Green Tomatoes "one of the backbones of Southern food" (251), signaling that canning and preserving are "authentic" southern traditions.

Similarly, Sean Brock devotes a chapter to "Pantry" items in both of his cookbooks, *Heritage* (2014) and *South* (2019) with claims that these are essential to what makes southern cooking distinct. Brock writes in *Heritage* that "Pickling and preserving are two techniques that anchor Southern cooking" (206). Indeed, Brock states directly that "they are also essential to authentic Southern cooking" (206). In *South*, Brock links canning vegetables to saving southern cuisine and culture from the homogenizing influence of commercial farming and supermarkets:

> Preserving is not just a practical act of saving the year's crops; in many cases, it's also about protecting a practice that has been part of Southern culture and identity for centuries. To me, the continued tradition of conserving food for later use is an important one to keep alive at a time when almost everything we want is available year-round at the local supermarket. (245)

Brock's mission throughout *South* is to convince readers to follow his lead and approach cooking as "hyperseasonal and hyperlocal" with an emphasis on the "purity and authenticity of those ingredients" (15). Canning, again, is a practice that Brock identifies as part of his regional identity: "As a Southerner, I'm serious about preserving the things I love and am proud of. The history and traditions of these techniques are the roots of my idea of Southern cooking" (245).

Brock gives a specific example of how deeply connected one particular recipe is to his view of southern identity. When Brock reflects that "Picking, stringing, washing, and canning my family's haul of greasy beans each summer is one of [his] strongest food memories," he might be speaking only for his own personal "authenticity," in terms of being true to his earliest experiences. However, Brock specifically links the memory to a larger, regional identity: "Pole beans epitomize the food heritage of the South, from the effort to develop and preserve special bean varieties to the necessity of putting up food. My pantry is empty if it doesn't hold a few jars" (277). Both the ingredients and the practice of canning are presented as evidence of southern authenticity.

In *Victuals*, Ronni Lundy also connects canning and preserving with defining southern traditions. Lundy describes salt cured meat as "a defining ingredient in the foodways of the southern mountains." The salt used in this preserving process, Lundy explains, is naturally occurring and ancient, the residue of prehistoric oceans (72). Preserving in salt is responsible for all kinds of dishes and ingredients that define Appalachian foodways: "Lip-puckering country ham and salt-cured pork. Sour corn and pickle beans . . . Jerky, kraut, and pickles of all kinds" (72). Lundy summarizes: "Salt is the element that enabled life and nourishment through the harsh, stark winters of the mountains, winters that helped create a cuisine that was in one sense distinctly Southern and at the same time distinctly its own" (73). Later, in a chapter devoted to Preserving, Lundy again notes that "Preserving foods by means of drying, burying, curing, and fermenting was essential to the settlement of the mountain regions and a part of the foodways of both native peoples and the Europeans who began moving in during the 18th century" (205). Like Acheson and Brock, Lundy argues that canning and preserving are essential to the uniqueness of—and indeed, the creation and survival of—southern and Appalachian foodways.

Not only is canning associated with geographically specific and historical kinds of authenticity, but it also represents the kind of small-batch, artisan, homemade authenticity that Johnston and Baumann noted as appealing to "foodies." Sean Brock notes that making preserves "makes me feel like I'm doing something 100 percent honest" (Brock *Heritage* 206). At the core of his "hyperseasonal and hyperlocal" cooking (*South* 15), preserving is the most "honest" work that the chef can do to resist the dishonest work of commercial farming and cooking with industrially mass-produced convenience foods.

Even when chef-authors aren't specifically describing the act of canning and preserving, they often rely on the equipment of canning to signal "authenticity" visually. I'm talking about Mason jars, of course. In a 2015 article for *The Atlantic* entitled "The Mason Jar, Reborn," Ariana Kelly explains that the Mason jar was created by a bona fide nonsoutherner, New Jersey native John Landis Mason, in 1858 (par. 4). Mason's clear glass jar and screw-on, self-sealing metal lid revolutionized food preservation and made it easy enough to practice safely at home (par. 4). When wartime rationing and victory gardens of the early twentieth century generated an abundance of produce and anxiety about scarcity, Mason jars and home canning made a comeback on a national scale, only to recede again with the postwar innovations of inexpensive industrially canned vegetables, refrigeration and freezing, and indestructible plastic containers (par. 6). Later, countercultural "back-to-the-land DIY movements" of the 1960s and 1970s turned again to preserving food in Mason jars (par. 7). And in 2015, Mason jars were back again, not just as a way to abstain from processed food by preserving fresh and local produce (par. 8), but also as an aesthetic and utilitarian object. The Internet offers instructions on turning Mason jars into "oil lanterns, soap dispensers, terrariums, drinking glasses, speakers, vases, planters, and snow globes, in addition to food and drink storage" (par. 9). The Mason jar itself is not exclusively associated with the US South, but it is linked with the language of authenticity: "It's repeatedly praised for its reusability, its aesthetic appeal, and its purity: Mason jars aren't mixed up with some of the more nefarious chemicals used to produce plastic" (par. 9). Mason jars are associated with "resistance to the mass production of food and culture; they emphasize the values of self-sufficiency and community" (par. 12). In short, the Mason jar is recognized as a symbol of authenticity all on its own.

The Mason jar's specific relationship to the US South through the practice of canning makes it an efficient visual shorthand for southernness. Hugh Acheson uses this visual cue frequently in *A New Turn in the South*. Of course, the photographs of pickles in the "put-ups" chapter are in jars, but so are the images of salad dressings in the salad and soup chapter and many of the beverages in the cocktail chapter. For example, the first image in the "Libations" chapter (19–37) is the chef's hands pouring tea between large canning jars (20). In the recipe for "A-Team Waiter Sweet Tea" a few pages later, Acheson notes that "you will need two nice clean quart jars" to properly prepare the tea (26). The accompanying photo shows three jars (and the chef's distinctive radish tattoo) (27). "Watermelon Limeade" is photographed in a canning jar (24), and instructions suggest serving it in "6 pint glasses" (25). Similarly, the salads and soups chapter (94–140) opens with a two-page spread of salad dressings in a variety of glass vessels including canning jars (96–97). The instructions for "Shallot-Thyme Vinaigrette" (111), "Dill Pickle Vinaigrette" (122), "Serrano Chile Vinaigrette" (128–89), and "Caesar Dressing" (135) all instruct readers to store the dressings in a "Mason jar." In some of these recipes, the only signal that the dish is related to the South is through invoking the jar.

Acheson is certainly not alone in using the Mason jar as symbol. Lundy also notes that preserving in Appalachia began long before the Mason jar when food was preserved in "crocks and earthenware containers or in jars sealed with wax." The mass-produced glass jar "ensured the food's safety, extended the time for keeping food, and broadened the scope of what could be 'put by.'" Lundy explains that "Mountain women embraced this concept of canning food so enthusiastically that the mason jar became a symbol of mountain life, and a useful container for potables as well" (205–6). Implied at the end of that sentence is a reference to moonshine and other homemade liquors that could be stored in Mason jars just as easily as pickles or jam. Both the jar and the potables within them come to represent the region visually.

Ariana Kelly, the author of *The Atlantic* article on the history of the jar, is more than a little skeptical of the attraction to the canning jar as evidence of authenticity: "This current incarnation of the Mason jar has a lot to do with the hunger for greater legitimacy: How can I be more real, and more unique in my realness?" The ubiquitous glass jars "with their enticing aura of thrift, preservation, and personal labor—have become a potent signifier in this quest" (par. 18) for the paradox of authenticity: to conform to the expectations of a group while simultaneously standing out as distinct. The Mason jar may, in fact, have a strong connection to the South, but I tend to agree with Kelly that sometimes the jar can give the opposite signal of trying too hard to look effortless.

Canning and its material accouterments are employed as evidence of southern authenticity, along with gardening and farming that provide the produce for preserving. Though southerners certainly do not have a monopoly on growing vegetables and fruits, cookbook writers connect these activities with "a very distinct way of living" in Appalachia and the South, as Brock puts it in *Heritage* (13). Gardening is so ubiquitous that Brock comments, "If you don't have a kitchen garden, you're considered lazy." More importantly, if you aren't harvesting your own food—including hunting and fishing for proteins—"you're not upholding the traditions passed down from your dad and grandpa." Gardening and farming served as ways to fit into regional identity and simultaneously stand out in the local community: "When I was a kid, everyone had a garden, and I mean everyone. It denoted status. Who could grow the best beans and the best tomatoes? Who had fewer weeds in her garden? Who took better care of his tractor?" (*Heritage* 13). Brock encourages readers to do as he and his parents and grandparents have done and cultivate their own gardens for regional and traditional "authenticity." He states unequivocally: "I hope that a few folks will put this book down and plant a garden, even if it's just a little herb garden outside the back door. I also hope they choose plants that reflect the heritage of the place they live" (*Heritage* 19). The garden makes the canning necessary, and both are essential southern experiences that connect a current practice with an "authentic" past.

Lundy also remembers the centrality of gardening to her experience of Appalachian foodways. As she remembers, "Food was magical . . . because I got to be part of the making." This included both eating from the garden and helping with the activities of preservation. Lundy recalls with fondness "a handful of warm, sweet, tangy tommy-toes [tomatoes] all my own any time anyone went to the summer garden," alongside "tables teeming with summer squash, sliced cucumbers, simmered beans of many kinds, [and] corn cut straight from the cob only moments before it landed in the bacon-scented skillet" (19). She also refers often to the pleasures of slicing and drying apples in June to preserve and make pies in the fall, enjoying the summer work and the autumn pay-out equally (19, 75).

These pleasant personal memories are added to a historical narrative of gardening and preserving in the region at large. In the first chapter of the cookbook, Lundy explores the multiple "origins" of southern foodways through a survey of Indigenous and immigrant communities that populated Appalachia in the story of a tour of the Frontier Culture Museum in Staunton, Virginia. All the groups mentioned have a connection to growing and preserving food. Native Americans of Appalachia, represented in the museum by a simulated community of Ganatastwi, had a specific tradition of gardening and gathering including "a communal garden at the tribe's settlement" and another "far afield [at] the hunting grounds" (28). The Irish farmstead at the museum reminds Lundy that a vegetable-centric diet with little meat extended from the need to raise pigs for sale in Ireland, keeping little for themselves to eat; however, immigrants to Appalachia were more likely to keep the fruits of their labor: "It must have seemed a gift, then, to come to these far mountains and find you could slaughter your own hog, cure the ham and bacon, and eat off it for the whole of a year" (32). Lundy also recognizes the contributions of Scots and German gardeners to Appalachian foodways. The "Kale Garden" in the Scots settlement featured kale, dandelion greens, and herbs for food and medicine that were familiar to Lundy as a child (32). The dried green beans called Leather Britches and dried apples that Lundy thought of as indigenous turn out to be from German traditions of preservation (33). Lundy also gives credit to African American innovators like Malinda Russell (not featured in the museum, 34) for the canning traditions of "chowchow, green tomato preserves" and more (35). Lundy concludes that "Preserving foods by means of drying, burying, curing, and fermenting was essential to the settlement of the mountain regions and a part of the foodways of both native peoples and the Europeans who began moving in during the 18th century" (205). Though the specific contributions of each group are transplanted into what we now know as Appalachian foodways, all are linked by the common practices of gardening and preserving garden harvests as a means of survival. Lundy cites "environmental anthropologist Jim Veteto" who studied the "foodshed" of Appalachia with "ethnobotanist Gary Nabhan" in 2011, saying:

> People across southern and central Appalachia are crazy about plants and animals. In my lifetime of interacting with Appalachian farmers, gardeners, and wildcrafting enthusiasts, I have never ceased to be amazed by their knowledge and love for all things green and growing. Whether they save seeds, graft fruit trees, dig roots and bulbs, can foods, harvest wild plants, hunt game or raise heritage livestock breeds, it is a truism that older people and a smattering of younger people across the region have immense wildcrafting and agricultural skills. (qtd. in Lundy 22)

Lundy, through Veteto, reinforces the message that growing and preserving fruits, vegetables, and meats are all essential characteristics and skills of the region.

Since these cookbooks are traveling outside their regions of origin to general audiences who may not have access to their own southern farmland, the authors tend to give readers a second option for accessing material for preserving without losing authenticity. If you can't garden or farm yourself to make your own preserves, then the writers suggest that buying from local gardeners and farmers is the next best thing; it may be better than growing your own, because it supports the worthy goals of endangered local suppliers who are integral to the continuation of a unique southern food culture.

In each chapter of *Victuals*, Lundy features the stories of Appalachian growers and producers who advance the argument of regional distinction. For example, Lundy cites restauranteur John Stehling, of Early Girl Eatery Asheville, who commented, "Here, in the southern Appalachians, it's *always* been small farm world. And the farmers here never stopped growing these things. They *bring* you things you won't see anywhere else.... This place and its food has [sic] never died off, and it inspires me" (qtd. in Lundy, emphasis in original 21–22). The produce acquired from farmers maintains the same traditional and one-of-a-kind authenticity that home-garden-grown produce can.

While Stehling's comments echo Lundy's thesis in the introduction to *Victuals* that Appalachian foodways are not "a dying culture, a people from and fading into the past" (20), Brock emphasizes a culture under threat, propped up by farmers and suppliers. In *Heritage*, Brock writes of his intention "to help bring the small local farmer back to prominence by respecting the work of local growers and to encourage farmers to reach back beyond the hybrid varieties, wasteful practices, and chemical inputs that have transformed agriculture (and the taste of food) over the last century" (27). If consumers fail to create the demand needed to support the small farm industry, Brock's prediction is dire: "We will have lost forever a tradition that transcends the mere practice of producing food. Authentic food must engage its geographic culture—it must reflect a way of life" (27). Brock goes even further in his second cookbook, *South*, by suggesting that supporting farmers may have double the benefits beyond growing a garden: "you can not only celebrate the local ingredients of your region but also help the farmers and other producers in your area" (*South* 15). Buying excess produce from a farmer that might go to waste otherwise and preserving it yourself "is the best way to support your local agriculture," "make a big difference in the livelihood of our local producers," and come closer to "liv[ing] a little more like our grandparents" (*South* 245). Even if readers choose to avoid the potentially painful work of gardening and farming, they can still access the authentic pleasures of canning while feeling good about being good consumer-citizens in their region.

CANNING AND GARDENING AS SPECIAL WOMEN'S WORK

In most references to gardening and canning, this is gender-specific work falling to women. Though Brock describes taking on gardening and farming himself, he credits his grandmother Audrey for teaching and modeling the craft for him. Brock admires his grandmother's garden in both cookbooks, starting with the dedication in *Heritage* to "Audrey Morgan, for eternally inspiring me to work harder than the person beside me" (7). In both cookbooks, Brock attributes his interest in food and his success as a chef to his grandmother's garden (*Heritage* 13, *South* 9). He has words of admiration for her as "a master of many crafts" with "wisdom in her eyes," and "years of work worn into her hands" (*Heritage* 13). Her mastery of the garden and the kitchen "was truly a marvel;" Brock "wanted to be just like her" (13), admitting that "She's been the greatest influence in my life" (*Heritage* 14). Though Brock notes that the garden was "a passion project" of both his grandparents (*Heritage* 13), the preservation of garden produce appears to be the domain of Audrey alone. In *Heritage*, Brock associates her with the basement full of food in various stages of preservation and fermentation (13), especially creamed corn (49), mixed pickles (207), pickled cabbage (224), and rhubarb ketchup (237). In each instance, Brock notes either that the recipe is modeled on his grandmother's procedure (49, 207) or that he has memories of his grandmother growing the main ingredient (237) or making the recipe (207, 224). The association with his grandmother is so strong that jars of her mixed pickles have become heirlooms and reminders of her love and wisdom, even after death: "I still have a couple of jars in my garage that she made, but I don't reckon I'll ever eat them. I keep them as a reminder of the things she taught me when she was alive. The jars still have her gorgeous handwriting on the lids" (*Heritage* 207). Though canning and gardening have become professional activities that Brock can participate in, too, they appear first in his memory as work for his grandmother with markers of her personal authenticity.

Lundy remembers gardening and canning as work for women, too. In her own experience, whether or not a woman had a garden or canned was well known in the community. Lundy explains that "In early summer, my great-aunts, aunts, and cousins who had gardens—that was nearly all of them—canned . . ." (210); however, Lundy notes that "[her] mother did not can" (210), nor did her "Aunt Lib, who lived in Corbin" and "worked a full-time job at Belks department store downtown" (210). Lundy sums up how these activities divided women into two categories: "Women with gardens and time at home canned; women without them did not" (211). Even women who did not can for themselves assisted in canning or received gifts of canned food from female relatives. Lundy's mother assisted her aunts with all the domestic labors in the season of preserving, including helping with canning and drying, cooking for guests, cleaning, and doing laundry (75). Aunt Lib who did not can her own produce also valued the work of her relatives by keeping her cabinets stocked with "jars put up by her mother, Granny Tart, and her sister Caroline" (210).

As Lundy's comparison of women who canned and those who did not suggests, a woman's participation in gardening and preserving may suggest her worthiness to the community. Lundy cites Appalachian food historian Joe Dabney who suggests that in the early twentieth century, "a young mountain bride's merit would often be judged by her peers—and her in-laws— based on how many cans of food she put by in the first year of her marriage" (206). A store of preserved food not only signaled industriousness and hinted at fertility, but it also provided a currency for vital goods and services like midwives, doctors, school fees, and mortgage payments (207). Whether eaten as rations, sold for cash, or bartered for essential needs, Lundy credits women and their canning with "allow[ing] the family to stay on the farm during lean economic times that might otherwise have lured them to factory work elsewhere" (207). Contemporary development of canned goods for sale, or "canning for cash," as Lundy explains, is not a threat to authenticity but "is itself a continuation of tradition" (206).

Lundy also explains that the "communal work" of canning was important social time for women in the community (206). Lundy describes the important rituals of bonding in her family around canning, as well as at the "community canning facilities" set up by extension agencies in the early twentieth century. These served as "a gathering place for women and children" who could take "breaks to sit on the porch and string beans and drink iced tea, share laughter, and gossip" while they also "process[ed] more volume and a wider range of produce" than they could alone (206). In all the above examples, it is women who are most directly engaged in the processes of gardening and canning.

While Lundy continuously describes "mountain women" (205, 206) as the originators of preserving practices in the past, most of the present-day producers and suppliers she interviews and profiles in the book are men. In the "Preserving" chapter, Lundy profiles Walter Harrill and "his wife, Wendy" of Imladris Farm, "the Asheville area's premium supplier of locally crafted jams and preserves" (202–5). Harrill is the primary figure in the story, following in the footsteps of his grandfather, C. B. Harrill (202), who planted the unique mountain blueberries that Harrill now tends (207) and who opened a U-Pick farm and sold handcrafts to keep the land (208). Lundy also profiles

Doug Harrell, a farmer whose family has owned land near Bakersville, North Carolina, since 1796. When Harrell retired "from a longtime printing business in the Piedmont," he and his wife Barbara moved to the farm looking for a way to make the land profitable and support their retirement (230). Harrell repurposed his family's dairy equipment and established a business selling Sorghum syrup (230–31). Even the recipes in the preserving section credit as many male innovators—Chris Bryant (220), William Dissen (223), and Edward Lee (224)—as female—Shelley Cooper (225), Lundy's mother (236), and Emily Hilliard (237–38). The whole of the "Husbandry" chapter that includes recipes for preserving meats is devoted to stories of male innovators like Chuck Talbot and Jay Denham of Woodland's Pork Farm in West Virginia (249), Jonathan Whitt of The Chop Shop in Kentucky (251), Erik Neil of Easy Bistro and Bar (252–53) and Milton White of Main Street Meats in Tennessee (253–54), and Jim Johnson of Cloudcrest Farm in Georgia (256–59). The impression is that while canning and preserving are historically women's domestic domain, the contemporary marketplace for commercially produced canned goods is open to all genders.

An important exception to this string of male producers in Lundy's cookbook is an extended interview at the end of the cookbook with Lora Smith, a Corbin, Kentucky native (292) who established "a USDA-certified community kitchen, like the ones established in the early twentieth century to provide home canners with equipment" in Egypt, Kentucky (293). Smith specifically aims to use the facility to support women in entrepreneurial food enterprises, including making and selling preserved produce: "Think gourmet but affordably priced chowchow and heirloom tomato jams" (294). At the time of the interview, Smith told Lundy that she would "like to launch an incubator program and curriculum for women interested in becoming food entrepreneurs on their own, out of the community kitchen. Maybe it's a nonprofit incubator, or maybe we just turn it into a women's worker-owned cooperative. Not sure yet" (294). Smith's project capitalizes on the history of canning as women's economically valuable, pseudopublic work, while also recognizing that it is a deeply held part of local identity. Smith notes first the emotional value of canning work to individuals and to the region: "Everyone back home is proud of their garden or their granny's garden and that holds real value for people. The value of being able to produce your own food is something I believe Appalachians really want to hang on to." But Smith also notes that there is a wide market for "authentic" products "that could provide the opportunity for local economic development and innovation as we navigate through some uncertain times ahead" (296). This passage seems to suggest that there is still a deep association between canning and women's economic work. Even if women's canning work crossed entirely into the realm of the public marketplace of capitalism, Lundy seems to suggest that it would still maintain its connections to the past and regional distinction through a rhetoric of authenticity.

"HOT AND PAINFULLY REPETITIVE": PAINFUL OR DIFFICULT WORK

Narratives of gardening and canning do acknowledge the difficulty and danger involved in this traditionally—if not exclusively—women's work. Clearly, planting and harvesting vegetables are physical labors, but gardening is also mental and emotional labor to choose appropriate plants in the right volume, predict weather patterns, watch over growing plants and problem solve, as well as planning ahead for future shortages. Below all this planning is an undercurrent of fear and anxiety about the consequences of a failed experiment or a lost crop. Moreover, gardening and canning involve special knowledge of the science of growing and the technical knowledge to use canning equipment that functions at high temperatures and pressures. Failure to understand the processes could result in disasters ranging from food-borne illness to explosions. The cleaning, cutting, snapping, peeling, and preparing produce before canning can begin is repetitive, tedious, and boring. Narratives about canning and gardening may acknowledge the real pain of women as they also celebrate women's ingenuity and delicious foods.

One common refrain among the cookbooks is the recognition that preservation involves high temperatures in an already hot late summer season. Lundy writes that canning was "hot, hard work that began in July" (206), and she repeats again that "canning is hot and hard work" (210). When describing making sorghum syrup, Lundy notes that "raking foam from the boiling syrup is a hot and painfully repetitive job" (231). Brock is literally describing what happens when "processing the jars through crucibles of heat and pressure," but the emotional tone of the description highlights a painful process of transformation. Lundy associates summer and the season of canning with the salt of sweat: "We sweated, too, children playing hard or doing chores, women working in the steaming kitchen. Maybe that's why I remember salt so clearly as the taste of summer" (75). Canning is also boring work. Though Brock insists he "embraced and actually looked forward" to farm chores, he acknowledges "most kids would have hated these chores" (*Heritage* 13). He admits that even he "hated the tedious work then of picking long rows and preparing the beans for cooking or canning" (*Heritage* 26).

Canning narratives also emphasize the physical hard work of farming and gardening. Brock notes that even though "A vibrant garden is a social space," it is also "one that requires a lot of work, both in the dirt and after the harvest" (*Heritage* 26). In *South*, Brock describes the busy and sometimes painful work associated with the garden and canning:

> The kitchen was always buzzing at my grandmother's home in Pound, Virginia.... If you were watching television, you were snapping beans. If you were porch sitting, you were shucking corn or grating cabbage. Growing up, I thought that's what every family did. I wasn't allowed to sit back and watch my family painfully cracking walnuts (and occasionally a thumb); I had to grab a hammer and crack walnuts, too. (*South* 245)

When Brock took on the project of farming himself as an adult and chef, he appreciated anew "just how difficult it can be to grow truly delicious foods and get them out of the field and onto the plate" (*South* 9), resulting in gratitude for the hard labor of the farmers who supply his restaurants (*South* 16).

Like Brock, Lundy makes clear that much of the hard labor of canning is really only the end of a longer labor-intensive process of farming and gardening:

> Home canning to a stock a family larder and to create some extra income begins with planning for a big garden, tilling the soil, planting seed, cultivating, backbreaking weeding. It involves harvesting day after day after day as the weather allows but doesn't necessarily bless. And when crops fail, winters can become lean to desperate. (210)

The work is so difficult and so unpredictable that Lundy concludes, "It's no wonder that by the second half of the twentieth century, through much of the country, home canning was on the wane. It's actually a wonder that, in the southern mountains, it still held on" (210). Practicing canning in the present means connecting to this narrative of difficulty and traditional "authenticity."

Not only is the work of canning difficult, but the alternatives of industrially preserved foods are effortless. Lundy thinks about how her mother, who did not can, still had plenty of work to do: "I thought about my mother, who I remember working tirelessly most days of her life, cooking, cleaning, washing clothes and hanging them on the line, washing pots and pans in the porcelain sink" (213). Lundy speculates that while her mother "relished the home-canned goods that we were gifted, [and] adjusted the store-bought ones to suit her rigorous standards of taste," those inferior "grocery canned goods" might have represented "a different life ... Perhaps an easier one; perhaps one she desired" (213). Home canned goods require considerable work, especially from women, that might not have a uniformly beautiful association. Lundy is sympathetic to women who might forgo the labor intensiveness of home canning for the convenience of store-bought cans: "From our present day perspective, the arrival of commercially produced canned foods in the mountains may seem like a negative influence on the foodways, one that leads in a direct line to Big Macs and buckets of faux fried chicken. But we forget that some of those cans from the grocery brought variety, as well as vitamins and minerals, to households that largely grew their own foods" (228). Far from demonizing canned foods, Lundy "confess[es]" that she does not can tomatoes and she "like[s] to use Muir Glen Organic Fire Roasted Tomatoes in this and other recipes . . . though any good-quality canned tomato will do" (218). *Victuals* offers instructions on how to can at home and use home canned goods, but Lundy also makes space for readers to avoid this painful labor. Ultimately writers will persuade their audiences to do the work of home canning despite the pain of effort, but first they acknowledge the painful work it requires.

Brock and Lundy both emphasize the potential danger involved in canning. In both cookbooks, Brock encourages readers to consult manufacturer's instructions before trying to use canning equipment (*Heritage* 208, *South* 245). "If you want to put up fruits and vegetables to preserve the bounty of a season, as my grandmother filled her larder," Brock explains, "there are specific safety rules you must follow" (*Heritage* 208). These rules include sterilization of jars in boiling water, but never boiling the lids which will damage the seal (*Heritage* 208). All implements "need to be impeccably clean" (*South* 245). Then jars must be covered and handled with tongs to prevent contamination, filled while both the fillings and the jars are still hot. Even if these steps are followed, a jar might not seal properly, making it unsafe for storage (209). Brock reminds readers of all the ways that bacteria "can ruin all your hard work" (246). Lundy also notes that some of the vegetables that might be preserved are, in fact, poisonous. She describes preparing "Sallet" poke as "a bother to prepare," requiring careful picking, boiling, rinsing, and draining before even beginning to cook the "potentially lethal" pokeweed (55). Gardening and canning can be dangerous work if readers aren't careful.

As much as canning and gardening are connected to essential southern experiences, they can also be an entrance point to some of the South's most intractable problems. In Lundy's case, a social gathering around canning is also an opportunity to discuss "the history, the troubles in the region" (291). A conversation about a beautiful crop of okra at the farmer's market turns into concern about climate change and how warming temperatures also bring plants that couldn't grow in the region in the recent past (290).

The same landscape that provides a bounty of vegetables to preserve is also the site for historic violent labor disputes, chemical spills and pollution, and mountaintop removal (291). All of these difficult topics intersect with the practices of gardening and canning.

"THE RISK BECOMES REWARD": PLEASURES OF PLENTY

It's clear that purchasing canned or frozen vegetables from a supermarket is easier than the hot, tedious, dangerous work of gardening and canning. As Brock asks (rhetorically), "Why should we still go through all the trouble of picking, cleaning, chopping, curing, drying, boiling, sealing, smoking, or salting?" (*Heritage* 245). In short, because the pleasures in the process and in the end results are worth the pain. Frequently, Brock and Lundy will defend the practice in the same sentence that they criticize it. Poke sallet "is a bother to prepare, but we bothered because of the taste" (Lundy 55). "The hot, hard work" of harvesting and canning "was tempered by breaks to sit on the porch and string beans and drink iced tea, share laughter, and gossip" (Lundy 206). Pickling pig's feet at home is "a high risk adventure," according to Brock. "But make them yourself with high-quality ingredients, and the risk becomes reward" (*South* 294).

As with almost all cooking instructions, the first promised pleasure is flavor. Lundy reports that her "great-aunt Johnnie" preserved "tart June apples" which would sweeten through the process of drying (75). When Lundy's mother attempted to swap homegrown green peas with frozen or canned peas, the change in flavor is noticeable: "none of us would eat more than a bite or two." Lundy reports that rather than go "back to the original" made with labor-intensive fresh peas, her mother simply stopped making that dish (48). Brock is initially put off by the smell of fermenting corn, but he loved the result: "Sour corn could always be found in one of those mysterious crocks that sat in the dark and musky basement at my grandma's house. I would look at it and think, 'What on earth could be in there that I'd want to eat?' But when the contents of that crock hit the frying pan, I was the most eager one there" (*South* 272).

The communal practice of canning and sharing garden produce is highlighted among the many pleasures in these narratives. Lundy describes the canning season of her childhood as a kind of family reunion with aunts and cousins "show[ing] up every night to visit and remember" (75). Brock, too, remembers preservation "as a communal exercise" that was "a bonding experience" for his family (*Heritage* 26). These communal events were times for sharing the details of lives lived apart and to "listen to stories from the old-timers." Brock is particularly nostalgic when he imagines himself experiencing pleasure in the past and in the future: "I look forward to when I'll be the old-timer, sitting there in my overalls and peeling apples with a pocketknife" (*South* 245).

As Brock's dream scenario suggests, another part of the pleasure of canning is feeling a connection across time and space through using inherited knowledge and repeating the rituals of the seasons. Brock claims that "putting up food can be one of the most rewarding things you do in your kitchen" because of the "special and archetypal" nature of "the annual rituals of cleaning vegetables, making a solution to preserve them and processing the jars through crucibles of heat and pressure. Even the routine of cleaning the jars brings me a greater sense of meaning and purpose" (*Heritage* 206). The ritual connections to family are made stronger by repetition. According to Brock, "I can't describe how exciting it is to be able to share seeds of my grandma's greasy beans, the ones I grew up eating, with my farmer friends and then get some of their harvest in return" (*South* 16); gardening and preserving in the present helps him maintain the connection with his past.

Gardening and canning also have the added benefit of being good for the environment and a means of practicing good citizenship. Brock notes that "it's a mindful way of cooking and immeasurably rewarding" (*South* 16). Again, Brock specifically contrasts garden-grown food with supermarket offerings from big factory farms that make it "easy to be cut off from the reality" of how food is produced; knowledge about where food comes from is key to "voting with your fork." Moreover, Brock explains that the emotional connection with food that promotes living with "respect" and "responsibility" can only come from "hand-grown" foods:

> A sad-looking industrially grown carrot at the supermarket can't evoke the same emotions as a vibrant carrot just plucked from the soil and handed to you by a hardworking farmer at the market. You will look at the hand-grown carrot with a different kind of respect and therefore a different sense of responsibility. (*South* 16)

The carrots *feel* better, and they make consumers *act* better. As Lora Smith tells Lundy, "I taught my kids how to grow food . . . I'm not sure you get much more sustainable than that" (292). Besides, as Acheson remarks in *A New Turn in the South*, canning is cool: "Learning about these things will get you bonus points at the local farmer's market and points in your locavore club!" (247). The cookbooks promise the pleasure of doing good while feeling good.

The narrative of painful hard work also sets a stage for feelings of pride in effort and in resilience similar to the narratives of poverty described in the previous chapter. "Preserving food took on a whole new meaning" for Brock when he recognized with maturity "that much of this work was done to feed my family during rougher times" (*South* 245). The basement full of fermenting crocks that once was a source of fear becomes a source of pride. Brock shares that feeling of pride in a job well done with readers in the headnote for bologna: "I'm not going to sugar coat this: it takes a lot of effort to make bologna. It takes a lot of practice, too, and you're going to mess up the first few, but saying that you make your own bologna can be an incredible source of pride. Once you get it right, you'll never want to buy bologna again" (*South* 290). The list of seventeen ingredients is intimidating, and the recipe calls for special equipment like a meat grinder and a "stand mixer with sausage stuffer attachment" (290), but the promise of pride suggests that the complicated work is worth it. Brock also suggests that the work of gardening and farming—"the good and the bad, the success and the failures"—gave him a sense of "appreciation" for "good food, and perhaps, the good life as well" (*Heritage* 33). Lundy similarly claims that food writing gives her an opportunity to highlight the values that epitomize gardening and canning: "the wisdom of mountain foodways, the cleverness of cooks who could make glory out of meager stores, the profound generosity of the people who raised me" (20). In each of the stories of the hard work of this labor, the authors find ways to celebrate the resourcefulness and abundance that follows.

TOWARDS A CONCLUSION: AMBIVALENCE AT LAST

Perhaps the last word in every chapter of this book will be "it's complicated." Complication, at least, makes for a more interesting and in many ways more accurate picture of any cultural practice. Though the stories told about gardening and preserving in the cookbooks in this study are similar to one another, they each contain contradictions: exhaustion with satisfaction, tedium with community, danger with skill, inconvenience with significance. I wouldn't say Brock and Lundy are ambivalent about gardening and canning; they are boosters, for sure. But their stories are not easily categorized as simple pleasures, and Lundy especially leaves some of those contradictions standing.

For an example of ambivalence, Lundy shares a story from Leslie Boden, wife of chef Ian Boden of The Shack in Staunton, Virginia, who describes the hard labor of her grandmother Tissie. Tissie lived in the Appalachian Mountains with no running water except a spring, and when the grandchildren visited, they all helped with the work of hauling water and doing chores: "Basically we were little worker bees," Leslie says (39). Though Leslie inherited Tissie's better qualities like "strength, directness, . . . openness" (36), Leslie also notes that Tissie was not particularly warm and kind: "She was very hard, stubborn as a rattlesnake; and if we were bad, we got switched . . . But she showed us love in other ways . . ." (39). The difficulty of rural farm work, especially on women and children, is part of the story, too, and Tissie is allowed to be both admirably strong and disconcertingly harsh without having to resolve the contradictions.

Similarly, Lundy writes about chef Shelley Cooper whose "mountain grandmother" Marguerite was known for preferring to cook on an old-fashioned coal-burning stove, even though she had a newer range (278). At mealtime, there would be "five or six varieties of homemade jam and applesauce, fried potatoes, sausage, bacon," the evidence of Marguerite's labors (281). Like Leslie, Cooper worked on her grandmother's farm picking apples or digging up potatoes and beets. Cooper remembers that Marguerite and her husband "worked so hard and they didn't complain" (281). Lundy reveals near the end of the story that Marguerite only lived at the farm in the summers because the rest of the year she worked as a chemistry professor, having been "the first woman to receive a doctorate in chemistry from the University of Mississippi" at the age of fifty-seven (281). Marguerite, like the rest of us, contains multitudes. Cooper concludes, "I am so proud of where I come from, of who raised me, and ultimately, all of this is an homage to my mountain grandmother, her strength and her love" (281).

Leslie's and Cooper's grandmothers, like Brock's grandmother and Lundy's great-aunts, all participate in the practices of gardening and preserving that have become labors that signal southern authenticity. But they do not represent a single story about what that work is like or what it means to the rest of their unique identities. Canning is boring and hot and an essential contribution to family economics. It is a summer-time hobby for spending time with the girls, and it is an entrepreneurial venture for a fourth-wave feminist. It is drudgery and creativity. It is aspiration, inspiration, and a chore to be avoided if possible. While the cookbook genre's expectation of pleasure gives writers a green light to gloss over the painful parts of this story, writers like Lundy resist that convention to add complexity and nuance to the story.

In the very first academic article that I wrote for publication, I invoked canning as a metaphor for the pleasures promised in food writing. "Magazines and cookbooks are not traditional venues for troubling naturalized narratives of identity," I argued; instead, they are perfect "for preserving a season of sweetness, unproblematic in its pleasures, inside a sanitized, cut-glass

Mason jar and a hotsealed lid" ("Squirrel" 567). It's the kind of flowery prose a graduate student in English with too many credits in creative writing might lean on in a conclusion; forgive me. But the metaphor reminds me, first, that I've been wrestling with this one question about how to do *both* celebration and criticism in food writing since at least 2014, and second, that canning and preserving are iconic to the southern story. Now what I see in the metaphor is my own ambivalence about canning, about "women's work," and about my place in the southern story. When I wrote that sentence about the "season of sweetness," I was thinking about the irony of screaming matches across the rows of okra and the time I seriously considered intentionally wounding myself with the blade of a hoe to stay home. Very little about that season in my own life comes back to me as sweet.

Lundy expresses a similar kind of ambivalence when the conversation among a collection of young Appalachian farmers, producers, and activists turns toward education. Wendy Johnston and her husband Steve are farmers who sell their meat commercially and sell their produce at the farmer's market. Wendy works in a community garden that supports the Appalachian South Folklife Center where "education" includes both how to grow and use native produce and "the history, the troubles of the region" (291). Thinking about those troubles—most connected to exploitative extraction industries—brings a pause to the conversation: "We sit in silence," Lundy reports (292). In that silence, I hear the roar of ambivalence, an aporia through which the complications that are not easily resolved into sweetness can emerge. Lundy looks around at the landscape in that silence and sees, "There is green everywhere. It is easy to believe this might be Eden" (292). It is not Eden, far from it, as the forgoing paragraph explained. And in the face of "centuries of extractive economies," Lundy is perhaps right to ask Wendy if community gardens and farmers' markets are "sustainable" work (292). Though Lundy writes that she's "not at all sure" what she means by this question, I hear ambivalence again. Is it enough? Can the pleasures of food do anything against the compounding harm of real problems? Are we so in love with our season of sweetness that we are fooling ourselves into thinking we are in Eden while the world around us burns? Wendy's answer is given after another pause with a smile and a laugh: "I taught my kids to grow their own food . . . I'm not sure you get much more sustainable than that" (292). Growing food, in Wendy's answer, means sustaining traditions and connections that can provide a resistance to—or at least a means to endure—some of the region's and the world's toughest problems. Maybe this answer is too sweet; certainly, it is optimistic. But it is an answer that recognizes that sweetness is hard won.

WORKS CITED

Acheson, Hugh. *A New Turn in the South: Southern Flavors Reinvented for Your Kitchen*. Clarkson Potter, 2011.
Bower, Anne. "Romanced by Cookbooks." *Gastronomica*, vol. 4, no. 2, 2004, pp. 35–36.
Brock, Sean. *Heritage*. Artisan, 2014.
Brock, Sean. *South: Essential Recipes and New Explorations*. Artisan, 2019.
Engelhardt, Elizabeth. *A Mess of Greens: Southern Gender and Southern Food*. U of Georgia P, 2011.
Guglielmo, Letitzia. "Introduction: Re-Collection as Feminist Rhetorical Practice." *Remembering Women Differently: Refiguring Rhetorical Work*, edited by Lynee Lewis Gaillet and Helen Gaillet Bailey, U of South Carolina P, 2019, pp. 1–21.
Howard, Vivian. *Deep Run Roots: Stories and Recipes from My Corner of the South*. Little, Brown and Co., 2016.
Jolly, Susie, Andrea Cornwall, and Kate Hawkins, editors. *Women, Sexuality and the Political Power of Pleasure*. Zed Books, 2006.
Kelly, Ariana. "The Mason Jar, Reborn." *The Atlantic*, 24 Sep 2015, https://www.theatlantic.com/technology/archive/2015/09/mason-jar-history/403762/.
Lundy, Ronni. *Victuals: An Appalachian Journey with Recipes*. Clarkson Potter, 2016.
Matchar, Emily. *Homeward Bound: Why Women are Embracing the New Domesticity*. Simon and Schuster, 2013.
Mor, Ana Francis. "Laughter, the Subversive Body Organ." *Women, Sexuality and the Political Power of Pleasure*, edited by Susie Jolly, Andrea Cornwall, and Kate Hawkins, Zed Books, 2006: 286–95.
Sharpless, Rebecca and Melissa Walker. "Introduction." *Work, Family, and Faith: Rural Southern Women in the Twentieth Century*, edited by Rebecca Sharpless and Melissa Walker, U of Missouri P, 2006: 1–14.
Sharpless, Rebecca and Melissa Walker, "'Pretty Near Every Woman Done a Man's Work': Women and Field Work in the Rural South." *Work, Family, and Faith: Rural Southern Women in the Twentieth Century*, edited by Rebecca Sharpless and Melissa Walker, U of Missouri P, 2006: 42–63.
Tippen, Carrie Helms. "'Squirrel, If You're So Inclined': Recipes, Narrative, and the Rhetoric of Southern Identity." *Food, Culture and Society*, vol. 17, no. 4, Dec. 2014, pp. 555–70.
Tippen, Carrie Helms, host. "The Food We Eat, the Stories We Tell: Contemporary Appalachian Tables." *New Books in Food Podcast*, New Books Network, 25 May 2020, https://newbooksnetwork.com/e-engelhardt-and-l-smith-the-food-we-eat-the-stories-we-tell-contemporary-appalachian-table-ohio-up-2019.
Twitty, Michael. *The Cooking Gene: A Journey Through African American Culinary History in the Old South*. Amistad, 2018.
Walker, Melissa. *Country Women Cope with Hard Times: A Collection of Oral Histories*. U of South Carolina P, 2004.

KEEP SOUTHERN AND CUT THE FAT
Body Fat and Illness in Wellness Cookbooks

In the early days of writing this book, I was diagnosed as prediabetic, and by the time the manuscript was almost due and this chapter was still mostly unwritten, I had tipped over the line into an official diagnosis of Type 2 Diabetes. The discovery came, unlikely enough, from my eye doctor who, in the course of an ordinary annual exam in December 2019, saw some damage to blood vessels in my eyes that suggested diabetic retinopathy. I consulted with my primary care physician, and yes, my A1C was at the high end of normal. Prediabetic.

A few months later, I was setting up my first home office to finish teaching the Spring 2020 semester from home. I taught classes from my attic for a year. The Covid-19 pandemic wreaked havoc on whatever healthy habits I had built. No commuting four miles to work on my bicycle. No after-work yoga classes. No squash games at the university gym. Instead, there was a lot of television and what I call "happy hour creep": that thing where as the days get shorter, your end-of-the-work-day cocktail hour starts earlier and lasts longer. Like a lot of people-formerly-known-as-foodies, I get a lot of emotional comfort from eating, and lordhavemercy, did I need comforting. I live with depression and anxiety, and both of those conditions come with periods of overeating and general disinterest in taking care of my body. All this was in its most aggravated state while attempting to write this book. I wasn't expecting to be told I was diabetic while writing a book with a chapter about diabetic cookbooks, but it wasn't a complete surprise, either.

I am what fat positive circles call "small fat." (I heard the term first from Roxane Gay on *This American Life*, and read about it in *Teen Vogue*, Glass; Zoller par. 8). After a long, hard, sedentary, and emotionally fraught two years, I can no longer shop at one of my go-to stores, LOFT, because their sizes stop at sixteen. I go straight to the Plus Size section of most stores and websites, knowing there's probably nothing for me in the "straight sizes" anymore. Every "After Visit Summary" for any doctor's visit—whether it is for a cold or that one time I needed stitches from hitting my head on the breaker box in the basement—has a warning about my BMI and a huge paragraph explaining how to lose weight, like I've never heard of a vegetable or a treadmill. I sometimes feel uncomfortable in stadium seating with arms. When I took my niece to an amusement park, I felt like I barely fit in the old-fashioned rollercoaster seat, but I could still buckle my seatbelt without assistance. Usually, I can sit comfortably everywhere but a classroom desk or a roller coaster and be mostly unbothered. "Small fats" don't experience the worst of sizeism.

I think often of an article I read from Lindy West (A "Lane Bryant Fat" according to Gay on *This American Life*) from 2015. The headline in *The Guardian* reads "My wedding was perfect—and I was fat as hell the whole time." She writes about the pressure she felt to be a thin bride and how she resisted those pressures, enjoying herself in public instead of hiding her body (West par. 2). When I find myself reaching a milestone in my career or winning a karaoke contest or having a damn good time wherever I happen to be, I think, "I just got tenured, and I was fat as hell the whole time." It's a declaration of how little my round belly and thick thighs get in the way of what I want to do. It's not my first thought. I still have to interrupt the looped recording of self-flagellation that starts playing in my head. But it is the thought that opens the door for self-compassion.

You would think as a food scholar and cookbook reader that I would have a better-than-average sense of what to feed myself, but you would be very wrong about that. I sometimes think that I took on this research agenda to distance myself from that very knowledge. In my work, it's all rhetoric and marketing and story. I read *Intuitive Eating* (Tribole and Resch) in Summer 2020 like it was a lifeboat and my ship was going down. I have a general distrust of my intuition brought on by years of being a girl in an evangelical household and a woman on planet Earth, and that includes sensing my own hunger cues, understanding my tastes, and trusting my cravings. I have been told almost all my life that what I want to eat is the last thing I should be eating. What I like to eat is poison. What tastes good will certainly kill me, or I will suffer a fate even worse than death: it will make me fat.

So that's what I'm bringing with me into this chapter: a complicated personal relationship with food and fat and disease and the advice that often comes from well-meaning but insensitive corners of a ubiquitous "wellness" discourse. With my mental health care team in place, I, now thirty-eight and in some compromised health begin, hoping to cease not until death. (That was a Walt Whitman reference for the lit nerds, "Song of Myself" part 1.)

FRIED CHICKEN AND FATBACK: FATNESS, ILLNESS, AND SOUTHERN FOOD

The stereotypes of southern food as fattening and unhealthy—fried chicken and butter-and-honey-soaked biscuits—creates stereotypes of fat and unhealthy southerners. Kristen Wiig's 2010 caricature of Paula Deen on *Saturday Night Live* is a perfect example. Wiig with a padded torso and big gray wig declares, "Hey, y'all! I'm Paula Deen and my favorite two ingredients to cook with are butter and oil," pronounced *booter* and *all* (*Saturday Night Live* 0:09–0:16). In the sketch, Wiig-as-Deen is hawking a new 8-ply paper towel to suck the "fat out of your good old Southern food" (0:26–0:30) while she eats butter straight out of a dish (0:56–1:08). The cat-head biscuit she sets on the paper towel shrinks to a tiny but "healthier" thumbnail-sized cracker once all the *booter* and *all* are sucked out of it (0:44–1:13). "It tastes like fucking shit," Wiig cries with a painted-on smile (1:21–1:25).

The underside of this joke is that Deen herself was diagnosed as diabetic in 2009. She made her diagnosis public in January 2012, just a year after she released *Paula Deen's Southern Cooking Bible* (Jaslow par. 2). An article from CBS News, released on the same day Deen announced her diagnosis and her partnership with diabetes drugmaker Novo Nordisk, has the headline "Paula Deen's type 2 diabetes: Is her cooking to blame?" The connection between southern food and southern sickness, especially southern fat, is clear in the criticism that Deen received for selling sugary and fatty food while being diabetic. Even Wiig's parody notes that "health professionals are really backing up my back bumper about my food making little children fat!" (*Saturday Night Live* 1:28–1:39). The doctor that Ryan Jaslow cited for the CBS article—one "Dr. Lauren Wissner Greene, clinical associate professor of medicine, at NYU School of Medicine, in New York, who was not involved in Deen's care" (par. 14)- said "She shouldn't lose her charm, but she needs to lose her weight" (qtd. in par. 15), and "[diabetes] could strike anybody, but it's much less likely to strike someone active and skinny" (qtd. in par. 16). Deen defended her actions by explaining that she's cooking special occasion food for entertainment: "People have to be responsible" for their own health and decisions about what they eat, Deen repeats (qtd. in par. 8, par. 10). Though Jaslow never directly answers the question posed by his headline, the implication is clear: Deen got sick because she was fat, and she got fat because she cooked and ate southern food.

A wide body of medical scholarship exists about the dire sickness of southerners, usually linked to rural poverty and extraction industries with "poor nutrition that flows from food insecurity" (Engle 1050). Appalachia is especially a target for pieces like this with researchers claiming that

"Diabetes and heart disease rates in central Appalachia are also dramatically higher than in the rest of the U.S." (1050). Another study claimed that "North Carolina is consistently one of the most food-insecure states in the country, ranking tenth highest in 2018. In Durham, 13.5 percent of Durham residents were food insecure and one-third of adults had obesity in 2018, and 'Obesity, Diabetes, and Food Access' is among residents' top health priorities" (Xie et al. 3945). Bryant Simon blames "chickenization," the spread of industrial poultry farming in southern states for both low wages and low food quality. The drive for bigger, cheaper, faster-growing chickens created environmental crises, the spread of foodborne illnesses, dangerous and exploitative working conditions, and ultimately, public health crises of obesity and its attendant horrors of diabetes, heart disease, and cancer, but also "body shamming [sic] and employment and social discrimination, and drops in productivity and out-put" and rising health care costs. (Simon 69–70).

The studies in each of these articles begin with the hypothesis that "the South" (or "Appalachia") is unique in its experience of disease and illness because it is also unique in its economic and cultural landscape. The story is that South is especially poor, which is often, but not uniformly, credited to the persistence of racism or homophobia and the exploitative labor practices of bad businesses. Therefore, the South is especially malnourished, either by pervasive food insecurity, or as Simon puts it, "the so-called paradox of plenty—where the poor and the low-paid have too much of the wrong kinds of foods" (especially fried chicken parts with sugary dipping sauces, 70). Because the South is especially badly-fed, it is a region of especially sick and fat people in need of investigation and unique intervention.

The stereotype of a particularly southern fatness or sickness is corroborated in literature, too. Monica Carol Miller's *Being Ugly: Southern Women Writers and Social Rebellion* examines the grotesque female body in twentieth century southern fiction. "Ugliness" can include both thinness and fatness (20) as well as physical disability or illness, disregard of the expectations for beauty and appearance, and general impolite or unpleasant behavior. Think Flannery O'Connor's surly, badly dressed, stomping, prosthetic-leg-wearing Joy-Hulga in "Good Country People" who chooses her new name *because* it sounds ugly (22). Miller argues that in some cases, "being ugly" can be a protest against rigid gender norms by "call[ing] attention to the boundaries of normativity in society." However, "the ugly does not so much explode or reinforce boundaries as it does threaten, irritate, and call them into question." Because the norms of the "twentieth- and twenty-first-century beauty-industrial complex . . . approaches the discipline of the proper body as a duty to be enforced, the figure of the ugly woman functions as a figure of rebellion or moral failure" (22). The health and wellness discourse similarly emphasizes the duty to discipline the body and appetites, painting those who with nonnormative bodies as moral failures. At the same time, body and fat positivity discourses (like Lindy West's "fat as hell" wedding) reclaim the fat body as a political rebellion.

Between these opposite ends of a spectrum—one end marked as a painful failure of self-control and the other as a victorious pleasure over external oppression—is a wide field of play for cookbook writers with a focus on pleasure or pain in the management of weight or disease. As they negotiate the conventions of the cookbook genre to deliver pleasure, they must make decisions about how to frame the "problem" of fat and illness without alienating their audience. In the primary texts examined in this chapter, all of the writers assume that their readers have a goal of losing weight or managing the symptoms of an illness, and all must persuade readers to buy their cookbooks and use their recipes to reach those goals. They have a choice about how they present the pains of being fat and the pleasures of changing body size or the pains of being sick and the pleasures of being well. How they decide to encode the relative values of these states of "health" or body composition reveals much about their particular body politics.

In addition, the writers of the cookbooks examined here must also contend with the story of a unique southern suffering of diet-related illness and a uniquely pleasurable southern food culture. With one notable exception (Virginia Willis's self-published *Fresh Start: Cooking with Virginia, My Real Life Daily Guide to Healthy Eating and Weight Loss*), all the cookbooks self-identify as representing a distinctly southern cuisine as compatible with the goals of weight loss and symptom management (even a "culinary cure" in *My Pinewood Kitchen* by Mee McCormick) contrary to the stereotype of southern cuisine as producing negative health outcomes. This chapter focuses on how they make that argument for southern authenticity and support it with evidence and anecdote, as well as the implications of their logic on how fat bodies and people with chronic illnesses are represented and hailed as moral human beings and as authentic southerners.

One compelling argument is that a reader can restrict their eating (whether by restricting calories or eliminating components like meat, dairy, carbohydrates, or gluten) without separating themselves from their cultural practices and regional identity. In fact, according to the logic of the argument, dieting is not only compatible with performing their cultural identity, but the most "authentic" version of southern foodways is synonymous with health. It almost goes without saying in food studies circles that eating is a social and cultural activity; restricting individual eating in a social setting necessitates a separation from the group. My students love this essay by Phillip Vannini about his immigration to the US from Italy and coming to understand American snacking rituals (237). Snacking occasions like campfires (241), going out to see a movie (244), a date, a picnic, or a baseball game (245) are all opportunities to eat special foods in public that you might not eat anywhere else. Vannini argues that public snacking rituals are high-stakes "social dramas" that are "carefully scripted and enacted before a vigilant audience who demand respect toward the profound moral and aesthetic significance of the role played by food in everyday life" (238). Eating together, Vannini suggests, forms *communitas*: a short-lived, hierarchy-free zone of community (240). To eat differently at a communal table is to stand painfully out and apart from the community, or as Vannini puts it: "To refuse to eat is to sever oneself from common human biological needs and from social contractual needs of integration" (245). What's the first thing to go when you go on a diet? Spontaneous snacks of the sweet and salty variety, exactly like the ones Vannini describes.

Because eating is an important community ritual and exclusion is painful, the overarching goal of southern diet cookbooks is to promise audiences not only the pleasures of the body but also the pleasure of belonging in community, in this case, the imagined community of "real southerners." In order to accomplish this rhetorical goal of pleasure, cookbook writers lean on arguments of authenticity, convincing readers that they can have it all: the pleasure of eating in community and the pleasure of weight loss or symptom management.

I first outlined this strategy in a blog post for *Food, Fatness, Fitness*, from which I've taken the title for this chapter. In the post, I argued that *Slim Down South* offers a blueprint of the argument for authenticity that links a distinct southern food and identity with the pleasures of health, not the pain of fat and illness ("Keep Southern"). The argument for authenticity starts by reversing expectations about what southern food *really* is. Instead of the stereotypes of "*booter* and *all*" parodied by *SNL*, these books argue that the southern cuisine readers have been exposed to is not actually "authentic." It's delicious, but it's the product of marketing, not how southerners really eat. Readers can easily leave the sugary, fatty, salty version behind because there is a way of eating that is more "authentically southern." The "real" southern cuisine, writers argue, is vegetable-centric, seasonal, and compatible with weight loss and disease management. In fact, the argument goes that the author hasn't reversed or redefined what is "authentic." They've just shown readers a more accurate picture of authenticity that has been overshadowed by the more visible inauthentic food. Finally, some cookbook writers go further to argue that the southern personality and cultural practices are not only *compatible* with weight loss and disease management, but they are also actually an *asset*. Not only can readers eat like a southerner while they lose weight and relieve their symptoms, but also, they will be able to *behave* like the "authentic southerner" they already are.

The implication of the foregoing argument for authenticity is that the metanarrative of southern suffering—that the South is uniquely prone to illness and fat—is not true, not permanent, or at least, not inevitable. The cookbooks use the rhetoric of authenticity to resist narratives that mark fat and illness as essential southern experiences or qualities. To the contrary, they suggest that dieting southerners are indeed *more authentic* than their counterparts who continue to eat the stereotypical sweetened and fried foods they see in media.

Diet cookbooks don't just need to sell the South, they also need to sell restriction and limitation as a pleasurable experience. Southern authenticity is just one layer of pleasure. Diet cookbook writers emphasize both the physical pleasures of relief from symptoms of illness, increased energy, and weight loss and the emotional pleasures of living a longer, happier, more confident life as a result of restrictive eating. All the books in this sample argue that restrictive eating is as delicious and satisfying as unrestricted eating, meaning that readers can continue to experience the pleasures of the palate. Most importantly, as I've already demonstrated, diet cookbooks promise that readers can continue to feel the pleasure of community belonging and feeling "normal" while restricting their eating.

These are not particularly surprising or novel promises for anyone familiar with diet culture or diet-related food writing. However, the potential for harm becomes evident when I state the logical inverse of these promised pleasures. If the most authentic version of southern cuisine and character is compatible with weight loss and health, then readers aren't real southerners if they are fat or sick. If community acceptance, energy, happiness, and confidence are the results of weight loss and health, then readers can't be happy if they are fat or sick. If restrictive eating is as delicious and satisfying as unrestricted eating, then being fat or sick is an illogical decision a reader has made.

Disability and Fat studies theories hope to break these stereotypes by resisting labeling body fat as an illness in itself or as a problem in need of solving. As Marilyn Wann writes in the foreword to *The Fat Studies Reader*, "If you believe that being fat is a disease and that fat people cannot possibly enjoy good health and long life, then you are not doing fat studies. Instead, your approach is aligned with . . . dangerous attempts to 'cure' people of bodily difference" (ix). Wann insists that fat studies is "descriptive," approaching weight and body size as a "human characteristic" whose meanings have been constructed (ix). The subject of study is not the reality of fat bodies but "what people and societies make of this reality" (x). "Obesity," as Wann explains, is a contested term that makes body fat into an illness in need of a cure: "Cures should work; if they do not, it is the fat person's fault and a license not to employ, date, educate, rent to, sell clothes to, give a medical exam to, see on television, respect, or welcome such fat people into society" (xiii). When I use "obesity" in this chapter, it is because that's the word used by the source I am citing. While fat studies scholars want to disrupt these ideas, it is clear that the texts analyzed in this chapter are fully participating in the discourse of fat-as-illness. While the arguments about southern authenticity appear to be subverting metanarratives of a unique southern suffering, the arguments about the pleasures of weight loss and the pain of having a fat body or symptoms of disease appear to be reinforcing oppressive norms of ability.

Only one of the pleasures listed above stands out as potentially useful for subverting harmful stereotypes of body size and (dis)ability: the promise of restrictive eating that is as delicious and satisfying as unrestricted eating. One response to this argument is to blame fat and sick people for not making the effort to correct their diets sooner, but another underlying assumption of this argument is that all people, regardless of size or diagnosis, want and deserve foods that are bodily nourishing, palate-pleasing, and culturally appropriate. This chapter concludes with examples of how writers deploy the pleasure of eating as a persuasive technique, and how they might "threaten, irritate, and call . . . into question" assumptions about fat and illness in the ways they persuade readers to cook and eat.

FAT STUDIES AND FOOD STUDIES: A LITERATURE REVIEW

The central tenets of disability and fat studies are similar to other social constructionist or deconstructionist theories of identity. Disease, disability, and the presence of body fat are constructed as artificial binary opposites to "healthy" or thin bodies. On their own, metabolic processes, bodily function, and body composition are value-neutral biological facts. They take on cultural meaning or moral value through the construction of hierarchies through language, practice, policy, and repetition or transmission of dominant cultural norms. The work of scholars in these fields, then, is to historicize, problematize, and disrupt narratives that naturalize hierarchies of identity that are neither inevitable nor permanent.

Weight stigma is one consequence of naturalizing hierarchies of body size and ability. In "Obesity Stigma: A Failed and Ethically Dubious Strategy," Daniel Goldberg and Rebecca Puhl urgently argue against the pervasive strategy of using "social pressure" or "stigma" to combat the so-called "obesity epidemic." The authors define stigmatization as the process of marking "an out-group . . . as different on the basis of a common demographic characteristic," and judging "the out-group . . . deviant or inferior on the basis of that characteristic." They argue that the ineffectiveness of using public shame and discrimination as a motivator for behavior change has been proven by research which demonstrates that stigmatization has the direct opposite of the desired effect. Stigmatization makes individuals less likely to seek medical care and lowers their motivation to "improve health behaviors," increasing the likelihood of negative health outcomes (Goldberg and Puhl 5). Moreover, the authors argue that even if stigmatization worked, "its use still violates ethical norms of social justice" (5) and "should not be tolerated in a just social order" (6). Not only does shame and coercive social pressure constitute violence against individuals, the emphasis on individual behaviors and personal responsibility "fail[s] to address the societal conditions that have contributed to obesity—conditions that are themselves intimately connected to historical pathways of power, privilege, and structural violence" (6). The authors do not dispute the existence of a condition called "obesity" or that it is a problem to be solved, but they do urge medical practitioners and policymakers to look for solutions that are more just as well as more effective.

Weight stigma can be subverted through narrative. For example, in "Stories that Matter: Subverting the Before-and-After Weight-Loss Narrative," Maya Maor explains that one reason weight stigma is particularly pernicious is that the ubiquitous trope of depicting the fat body as "before" and the thin body as "after" marks body fat as temporal and temporary (89–90). If body fat is not seen as permanent, then it follows that fatness is a state to be corrected and left in the past: "presenting the 'thin' protagonist as successful, attractive, and popular and the 'fat' protagonist as ugly, miserable, and an outsider implies that the fat body should be replaced by the thin body" (90). Between "before" and "after" is an invisible but morally encoded effort. As a result of this narrative, it is seen as a moral failing not to replace the fat body. The moral value of gaining, holding, or losing body fat is constructed and repeated through narratives that privilege a "before" of suffering followed by an "after" of pleasure and relief.

However, Maor also describes a potentially useful reversal of this trope. Maor studies Israeli-Jewish women who resist weight stigma by subverting the idea that a person with body fat is "an incomplete subject eternally in the process of 'becoming' thin" (91) through narratives of their life stories with their fat bodies in the privileged position of "after." Participants in Maor's study described their "before" state as thin but suffering through "[dieting] behaviors [which] led to intense psychological and physical pain, such as shame, self-loathing and digestive problems" (96). The "after" state of the participants was increased happiness and a relief of psychological and physical pain not through weight loss but through destigmatization: "[P]articipants described their present identities as fat women, and the advantages they found in embracing this identity. Despite their increasing deviation from the thin ideal, participants experienced a greater degree of self-acceptance and a deeper connection to their bodies and identities" (97).

The reversal of the narrative challenges the idea that the thin body must be the privileged term in the binary and the suggestion that fat itself is a source of suffering. Rather, the source of suffering is weight stigma and the narratives that support it.

One study from The Ohio State University published in *Stigma and Health*, a journal from the American Psychology Association, investigated the link between the psychological pain of weight stigma and the physical pain of "excess body weight," defined as a BMI between 25 and 35 kg/m2. Researchers hypothesized that participants would report both more bodily pain and more emotional pain as their BMI increased. If they experienced less stigma, they would feel less physical pain (Olson et al. 244). The results were inconclusive at best. While the group actually reported less pain than the general population (244) and participants with the highest BMIs reported nearly identical mean scores for signs of distress from weight stigma as those with the lowest BMIs (245), the researchers still concluded that "Pain experience among overweight women [BMI 26] may be linked to social factors such as stigma, whereas pain among obese women [BMI 35] may be better explained by biological or biomechanical factors or perhaps social factors other than stigma" (245). Researchers insist—even though the participants experienced less pain than the general public—that a body with more fat must be in pain *because* of fat.

Studies like this one—and others critiqued by Francis Ray White in the article "Fucking Failures: The Future of Fat Sex"—reinforce narratives of fatness as pain even as evidence from the studies fails to support those conclusions (964). White argues that both stigmatizing public health campaigns and medical literature question the ability of fat bodies to experience sexual pleasure. White writes specifically about studies that address sexual satisfaction and reproductive fertility, but their conclusions align with the stigmatizing narratives that fatness is synonymous with suffering and incompatible with pleasure—or the perpetuation of the species.

However, just as Maor's participants found that reversing the before-and-after narrative helped them find more satisfaction, Jeannine Gailey's 2012 study suggested that involvement in the "size acceptance movement" led women to increased sexual confidence and satisfaction. Gailey describes another before-and-after narrative, this time from "shame" to "pride." Like Maor's subjects, Gailey's participants described acceptance as the means to "not only experience freedom from the pressure to diet or change their bodies, but also the freedom to be sexual" (124): a pleasure that has long been identified by scholars of women and gender as a form of protest. It is more than possible for fat bodies to experience pleasure and narrate that pleasure without losing weight, resisting the stigmatization of fat as a "failure." Given that so many of the metanarratives of fatness describe that life as a moral failure and a pain-filled experience that is "closer to death than ecstasy" of any kind (White 974), it may be a subversion—or at least an irritant to normativity—to be "fat as hell" (West) and still experience pleasure, even in eating and cooking.

Fat studies scholars are careful to remind readers that body size is an intersectional issue. Goldberg and Puhl note that fatness cannot be separated from structural inequities and "social disadvantages" (6) and neither should any attempt at "solving" or "fighting" fat. Maor's study recognizes that gender, religious belief, ethnicity, and geography all play a role in how individuals experience weight stigma and how privilege may affect their ability to resist and subvert it (91–92). Katie Margavio Strileya and Sophia Hutchens summarize that the field of food studies acknowledges, "Body size is a signifier that produces inequalities in conjunction with other signifiers such as race, ethnicity, class, gender, and sexuality.... White cisgender people will not experience size discrimination the same as people of color, LGBTQ individuals, or the differently-abled" (297). Terah J. Stewart and Roshaunda L. Breeden note that Black women's experiences of fatphobia, stigma, and discrimination are imbricated in "white supremacist racial politics" which has been used to "degrade black women and discipline white women" (qtd. in 223). The authors conclude, "Black women have specifically become the antithesis of what beauty, 'health,' or 'wellness' is or can be, especially as it relates to the body" (223). Like all experiences of oppression, fat stigma does not operate in isolation.

While much of the discourse of southern fat and illness seems to emphasize class as the key intersecting identity, with scholars citing industrial labor and unemployment as the causes of food insecurity (Simon 68) and experimenting with solutions like an additional forty dollars a month for purchasing grocery store vegetables (Xie et al. 3945), it is clear that individuals who call themselves southerners may also experience and understand body size differently based on the interlocking hierarchies of race, gender, sex, sexuality, and age, as well as based on their perception of regional identity. Any discussion of a resistance to or subversion of discrimination based on body size or ability must consider how other aspects of identity may hinder or help an individual to accomplish that resistance.

PAIN AND PLEASURE IN THE FAT BODY: CASE STUDIES

With these definitions and understandings of pleasure and pain as points of resistance, I will be analyzing three cookbooks marketed as representing southern cuisine with an emphasis on "healthy" eating, weight loss, or food restrictions for the relief of symptoms of illness.

The first category includes general "healthy cooking" cookbooks that may make recommendations for reducing sugar, fat, and salt in southern canonical foods but without specifically addressing weight loss or any particular illness as either a cause for picking up this book or an effect of using it. Books typical of this category include Matt and Ted Lee's *The Lee Bros. Simple Fresh Southern* from 2009, *Paula Deen Cuts the Fat* from 2015, and Eric and Shanna Jones's 2022 book *Healthier Southern Cooking*, along with an array of vegan and vegetarian cookbooks that promise southern authenticity without meat, like Jenné Claiborne's *Sweet Potato Soul: 100 Easy Vegan Recipes for the Southern Flavors of Smoke, Sugar, Spice, and Soul* from 2018. I focus specifically on Virginia Willis's 2015 book *Lighten Up, Y'all* as an example of how these books formulate an authentic southern cuisine that counters stereotypes of "unhealthy" foods.

Weight loss-specific cookbooks, by contrast, convince readers that their version of healthy eating results in weight loss. The explicit rhetorical purpose of these books—like the *Southern Living* branded book *Slim Down South: Eating Well and Living Healthy in the Land of Biscuits and Bacon* by Carolyn O'Neil—is to provide a pleasant solution for the painful problem of body fat. Willis's *Fresh Start* is examined here to demonstrate the contrast in rhetoric when weight is added to the conversation. This section also includes a reading of *Skinny Southern: 90 Reinvented Classics Without the Guilt!* by Lara Lyn Carter (2019).

The final category contains cookbooks that restrict particular ingredients for the relief of symptoms of illness. These books address conditions like diabetes, heart disease, and gastrointestinal disorders like Crohn's disease. Often these books are self-published on Amazon as free e-books, but typical of the commercially published genre are books like *The Southern Comfort Food Diabetes Cookbook: Over 100 Recipes for a Healthy Life* written by certified nutritionist Maya Feller. Natasha Newton's *Southern Keto* (2018) presents a low-carb diet as a solution for her diagnosis of Crohn's disease. While Emily

Bailey's *The Southern Keto Cookbook* (2020) is less specific about her own "medical conditions beyond [her] control" (ix), she does emphasize that a keto diet that restricts carbohydrates "can offer incredible health benefits including weight loss, improved blood glucose, decreased inflammation, improvement in other health markers, increased energy and mental clarity, and so much more" (3). This section focuses on *My Pinewood Kitchen: A Southern Culinary Cure* by Mee McCormick (2020) which promises on its cover "130+ crazy delicious, gluten-free recipes to reduce inflammation & make your gut happy." In each cookbook, the recommendations are not for general health in moderation but specific relief of painful symptoms of disease by the elimination of specific ingredients.

Taken together, these books demonstrate a rhetoric of southern authenticity that reverses an assumed expectation that southern food is by nature "unhealthy," offering a version of the authenticity argument that resists stereotypes and invites readers to change their cooking and eating habits without compromising their regional identity. They also offer a range of possibilities for how writers can define southern authenticity, healthy foods, healthy bodies, and the various pleasures of belonging and the pain of illness.

GENERAL HEALTH AND WELLNESS: LIGHTEN UP, Y'ALL

Virginia Willis's *Lighten Up, Y'all*, which was a James Beard Award winner and International Association of Culinary Professionals (IACP) nominee for Best American Cookbook in 2016, is the chef's fifth cookbook, following in the pattern of *Bon Appetit, Y'all* and *Basic to Brilliant, Y'all*. After *Basic to Brilliant* Willis wrote two slim volumes on single ingredients: *Grits* for the iconic Short Stack series in 2013 and *Okra* for the University of North Carolina's Savor the South series in 2014. *Lighten Up, Y'all* is presented as a guide to making southern food that is compatible with a healthy lifestyle. The inside cover explains that Willis "needed to drop a few pounds and generally lighten up her diet," and the recipes that follow are "packed with real Southern flavor, made with healthier, more wholesome ingredients and techniques." While Willis's weight loss appears to be the exigence for writing the cookbook, the overall theme of the book is to help readers "wherever you are on your health and wellness journey" (Cover copy).

Like all the cookbooks examined in this chapter, *Lighten Up, Y'all* is predicated on the argument that the "unhealthy" dishes we've come to recognize as "southern" are inauthentic while an older, more authentic way of cooking waits to be discovered. While the subtitle "Classic Southern Recipes Made Healthy and Wholesome" suggests that the "classic" recipes need the intervention of the chef-author to "make" them healthful, the front matter of the book argues that the real southern food is already naturally "healthy and wholesome."

The foreword, provided by celebrity chef Art Smith—who also writes southern cookbooks with an eye towards health like his 2013 book *Healthy Comfort*—frames his endorsement of *Lighten Up, Y'all* in the argument that the cuisine commonly known as "southern" is an unhealthy "caricature" of an older and healthier way of cooking. Smith marvels how "'Southern food,'" in scare quotes, "became all about butter and bacon fat, deep-frying anything that didn't move fast enough to get away, and sugar, sugar, and more sugar." The result of this inauthentic way of eating caused southern families to "lose their connections" and become "increasingly unhealthy and overweight" (vi). Smith's own diagnosis of diabetes was "a wake up call," and he describes losing over one hundred pounds by "eating the old fashioned way" with a focus on vegetables. Smith claims that the secret to "becoming healthier and happier was just a matter of returning to the Southern food traditions that I knew from my childhood" (vii). Smith praises Willis for her "classic and wholesome" recipes, believing as he does "that Southern food can be healthy and delicious, and actually make you feel good rather than guilty" (vii). Smith's brief foreword focuses almost exclusively on reversing the stereotypes of southern food, convincing readers that the older, more "authentic" southern food is compatible with health.

In the introduction, Willis concurs with Smith's assessment that what readers may think of as "southern" is a false stereotype. Willis notes that "the media" is responsible for the "proliferation" of a stereotype of "unhealthy Southern cooking," but that stereotype bears no resemblance to the authentic southern food that real southerners eat: "Let me tell you, I have never had a bacon-wrapped, deep-fried macaroni and cheese square or a hamburger on a donut bun in my entire life. My Southern grandmother . . . would have been absolutely appalled" (4). The over-the-top examples are contrasted with the "okra, green beans, tomatoes, and corn" that Willis notes as abundant in the South (2). To essentialize southern food as "just fried chicken" is as ignorant and insulting as "saying Chinese food is just eggrolls or Italian food is just spaghetti" (2). Willis takes down the reputation of southern food as unhealthy so that she can reverse reader expectations and present her version of healthful cooking as continuous with an older, more "authentic" cuisine.

Willis argues that "authentic" southern food is vegetable-centric and unprocessed. Willis reports that "like many Southern families," hers ate a diet "filled with fresh, in-season vegetables, plenty of from-scratch food, and very little of the processed stuff that is so common today" (1). Willis argues that "traditionally," almost inevitably, "Southern cooking was a vegetable-based cuisine" because of the South's unique climate, long growing season, and "fertile land" (2). Willis argues that "the origins of Southern cuisine" teach us that we should "[eat] in moderation and [rely] mostly on plant-based cooking" (4), in contrast with the excesses of the "fried chicken and fatback" stereotype.

Willis also attributes this plant-based diet to poverty, another essential southern experience of suffering discussed at length in this book: "For the most part, the plant-based diet was a symptom of the poverty that affected the entire South, both black and white—eating a lot of meat was simply too expensive. In fact, that bit of pork in the greens might have been the only meat in the pot" (3–4). In the past, Willis suggests, poverty inadvertently led to a healthier way of eating, but in the present, ironically, the most expensive foods are "fresh produce and organic, wholesome ingredients," pushing poorer families to buy cheap and convenient food. Willis directly correlates "the South's obesity epidemic" with the fact that the southern states with the highest rates of "obesity" also have "some of the highest poverty rates in the nation" (4). The overall message is that the answers for eating healthfully can be found by looking to the southern past for a more "authentic" way of eating.

Similarly, Willis equates healthful cooking with an essential southern personality trait. Willis learned the ways of southern cooking from her grandmother and mother who were expert cooks as an extension of their authentic southern identity: "It's not surprising that my family is full of good cooks; after all, food is central to the South's personality and character. We define ourselves and our lives by the food in our kitchens and the food on our tables" (2). Willis learned from her grandparents "that it was possible to cook healthy Southern food" (4); in other words, it is possible to follow the common advice for healthful eating (i.e., eat less, mostly plants) and still rely on her instincts as an "authentic" southerner, true to inherited family knowledge and belonging to a regional community.

While *Lighten Up, Y'all* is not marketed as a weight loss cookbook, Willis opens the book with a discussion of "the F-word ... *fat*" (1), suggesting that a healthy body is a thin body. Willis describes her weight as a lifelong "problem" starting with being a "chubby toddler" and growing into "one sturdy girl" who has "most often been at least a little overweight" (1). Willis attributes her weight to eating "too much," even though the food served by her parents and grandparents was "homemade, wholesome," but she also acknowledges that "my genetics weren't working with me" (1). Willis describes herself as being at her healthiest when she was also at her thinnest. While training in a French culinary school, Willis reports that she was "the thinnest I had ever been in my life. I was actually skinny." Though she was eating lots of delicious, "rich," and butter-laden foods, she was also "walking several miles a day both to culinary school and to work at a restaurant" and skipping processed convenience foods. Willis calls this "a healthy lifestyle": a combination of physical activity and diet that leads to a thin body (2). Later, when Willis determines she needs to "take a stand, make a change" (4), she reports losing forty pounds and experiencing better health in terms of cholesterol and glucose levels (5). Throughout the introduction, body size is the first indicator of being healthy, though health is not measured in body size alone.

Willis is careful in *Lighten Up, Y'all* not to demonize any food in particular as "unhealthy," with the exception of overprocessed convenience or junk foods. Processed foods have "a lot of sugar, salt, and fat" (4), and Willis also suggests that readers avoid highly processed no-fat and low-fat diet foods that have added sugar, salt, and carbohydrates (9). "The type of fat matters more than the amount," Willis argues before listing "Cooking Fats for the Healthy Southern Kitchen" (9–10). Trans fats and saturated fats are to be avoided; butter and various unsaturated fats are fine (10). Of course, the basic principle of *Lighten Up, Y'all* is making "classic Southern dishes . . . lighter," which is defined as "lower in fat and calories, and higher in fiber than their more traditional counterparts" (5). Though there is a bit of a logical paradox in defining the most traditional southern foods as "naturally" healthful while also claiming to improve the healthiness of "traditional" foods, the implication is only that fiber is better than fat, not that fat is something to eliminate from food altogether.

Willis continues the pattern of approaching ingredients with neutrality by offering tips for "Lightening Things Up" that are less about restricting foods than achieving balance and avoiding feeling hungry. Willis suggests that readers choose foods that are satisfying including lean proteins to feel full and well-seasoned dishes that "stimulate your tastebuds" (12). Some of Willis's tips are not directly food-related but generally accepted healthful practices like drinking water (12), measuring portions, and making social events into opportunities for exercise (13). Willis's attitude about health can be summed up in her gentle encouragement to readers: "Do what you can when you can—it doesn't have to be all or nothing" (12). Willis explains, "this is not a book about saying 'no.' This is a book about saying 'yes!' This book is about what you *can* have, not what you can't" (5). Though she states clearly that she is "not a nutritionist, dietician, or a doctor," she promises "nutritional information you need to make good decisions" (5). Moderation and neutrality are embedded in her definition of southern food and in her definition of healthy eating. These rhetorical moves emphasize that "healthy" eating is pleasant, or at least her approach avoids the pain of restriction or separation from community.

The kind of pain most clearly on display in *Lighten Up, Y'all* is weight stigma. Willis makes a distinction between the "clinical diagnosis" of being "overweight" and the socially stigmatized word *fat*: "*Fat* ... is an ugly word that's cruelly used in taunts on the playground ... *Fat* is a nagging constant in the internal dialogue about self-worth. *Fat* is the word that makes fully competent adult men and women feel like a failure" (emphasis in original, 1). Willis confesses to readers, "I know firsthand how crippling the F word can be to self-esteem" (5). While fat studies as a field seeks to neutralize the word *fat* as a valueless descriptor and abolish the idea of body weight alone as an indicator of ill health, Willis appears to experience these words in the direct inverse: *Overweight* is a term that neutrally describes a body's size relative to a medically determined "healthy" norm, while *fat* is a damaging personal insult. Willis argues that the word *fat* is associated with pain, wielded as a weapon by others and by ourselves. Fat seems incompatible with feelings of self-worth, success, and self-esteem. For Willis, pain does not necessarily come from having body fat but from living in a thin-privileging society that causes her to feel a painful state known as "fat" even when her body weight was "'normal'—[defined as] well within the doctor-recommended weight range for someone my height" (1). Willis claims that she "struggled with weight" and sought to lose weight as a way "to quell the voices in my head," (4) implying a painful fight between expectations for herself and her reality. A lower body weight offers pleasant relief from that painful conflict between social expectations and medical recommendations.

Willis also notes that body weight is dependent on gender expectations. She describes herself as breaking gender expectations by resembling her father in body type, "big-boned with broad shoulders." Though her father's body type is suitable for him as a man who was a boxer in the Navy, it is not desirable for her as a woman. Willis speculates, "if I had been a boy, I would have played offensive lineman," implying that a larger body would have been an asset for her father's son, not the liability that it seems to be for his daughter (1). Willis's "struggle" to see her body as anything but "fat" appears to be a condition of gendered expectations, and being outside of those social norms is experienced as pain.

Willis may start the book with talk about the pain of being fat, but most of the introduction is given to describing the pleasures of good food. "Food and cooking have always given me joy," Willis claims (1). "The kitchen is a place of happiness" because of the connection she feels to her family there (2). Willis writes with obvious pleasure about the delicious foods she learned to make in France: "I made quiche with triple-cream cheeses that were heady and dense with the flavors of the pasture; served platters laden with spicy, meaty saucisson that was nearly primal with animal essence; and prepared delicate, flaky, tender pastries that seemed to consist of layers of buttery air and flour" (2). In the same paragraph where Willis describes losing weight and lowering her cholesterol and blood glucose, she reports, "I feel really good. I am strong and healthy. I am happy. Is this a lifelong journey? Yes. Will I continue to have to watch what I eat and exercise? Yes. Do I still love food? Yes—a big, loud, resounding YES!" (emphasis in original, 5). The suggestion is that weight loss has given Willis feelings of physical pleasure (feeling good and strong) that she did not have at a higher weight; however, the pleasure that has been consistent and that she most wants to emphasize with capital letters and exclamation points is the love of good food. When Willis writes, "I don't eat for fuel; I eat for enjoyment and pleasure," (2) she defies the most basic tenet of wellness discourse that all food is calories that must be used up by the body or burned away with exercise. Instead, she presents the pleasure of eating as compatible with "health," a definition that includes good emotional and embodied feelings, not merely weight loss.

Readers of *Lighten Up, Y'all* are promised the pleasure of taste and flavor. Willis states explicitly that "the first and most important criterion" for choosing recipes for the cookbook "was that it had *to taste delicious*" (emphasis in original): "After all, at the end of the day I'm still a classically trained chef who loves to eat, so if a healthy variation doesn't taste as good or authentic as the original, well, it didn't make the cut" (5). Willis flaunts her own pleasure in eating while promising the reader that they can expect to experience pleasure, too, both in taste and in "authenticity."

In addition to the pleasure of good-tasting food, Willis also reassures readers that they can participate in the social eating events that form a community while making "good choices" about what they eat. Willis introduces the "Starters and Nibbles" chapter by noting that appetizers, "which despite their small size are often loaded with fat and calories," are also key elements of social events like "a game day party," "cocktail gatherings," and "supper clubs." Willis promises that the chapter will provide something that the reader can serve at events like these "that tastes wonderful, is good for you, and will make your guests smile" (15). These three distinct pleasures ensure personal satisfaction as well as a successful exchange of social capital in the community. Willis emphasizes that her version of healthy cooking is indistinguishable from good cooking: "Forget counting calories—this food is just flat out good!" (16). With Willis's guidance, a reader-cook can blend into social eating events by contributing something indistinguishable from—or even superior to—any other offering on the buffet and by publicly eating in community.

Overall, *Lighten Up, Y'all* attempts to minimize the pain of dieting by emphasizing the pleasure of being part of an "authentic" southern community through eating food that is consistent with the most traditional version of southern cuisine and sharing in public meals that won't alienate the reader as a "dieter" separate from the community. Willis does reinforce the idea that a thin body is a healthy body and that general wellness includes losing weight, but she does so without making food into a dangerous enemy or losing the pleasure of eating. The reader is promised the pleasure of community, flavor, and good health with minimal inconvenience or judgment from the author.

Willis's most recent publication, *Fresh Start*, stands out in this analysis as an exception to many of my rules for choosing cookbooks for analysis in that it is both self-published and not explicitly southern. However, as an established southern food writer, chef, and personality with six southern-specific and professionally published cookbooks, Virginia Willis's name comes with a southern branding. Willis explained to me in an interview that she chose to self-publish *Fresh Start* in the interest of speed. Social media followers were clamoring for advice after Willis's weight loss became obvious in her profiles, and the fastest way to get recipes into their hands was through self-publishing in digital form (personal interview). *Fresh Start* is tiny by comparison to her commercially published cookbooks; it contains only twenty-seven recipes. While each recipe has a full-page, full-color photo and a headnote, the book is not divided into chapters and has only the introduction and a short "Seven Smart Tips for Healthy Eating" for paratext—nothing resembling the journalistic essays in *Secrets of the Southern Table*. Unlike *Lighten Up, Y'all*, *Fresh Start* is explicitly focused on weight loss but not a distinct southern cuisine, and I use it here to compare how the narratives around pain and pleasure may be different when authentic southernness is off the table but weight loss is front and center.

Weight loss cookbooks like the ones examined in this chapter often begin with a narrative representation—if not a photographic one—of the author's "before" and "after" journey from illness to recovery or fat to thin, reinforcing the weight stigma that Maor describes. Virginia Willis opens *Fresh Start* with before and after photos of her face to illustrate her weight loss (v). Though *Lighten Up* is presented as the "after" of Willis's weight loss, there are no photos of a "before" body in its pages.

Willis is far more explicit about the pain of being at a higher weight (before) and the pleasure of losing that weight (after) in *Fresh Start* than in *Lighten Up*. The text of Willis's introduction is her story of losing forty pounds (the impetus for writing *Lighten Up*), her disgust at gaining it back ("Ugh."), and the pain and unhappiness that she was feeling at a higher weight. "I was not taking care of myself," Willis remembers, "stress eating, drinking too much, and not exercising. I was very unhappy." Her attempts at weight loss were beset by personal and professional setbacks and a back injury that limited her mobility and required medical intervention for pain control (v). But as she lost weight, Willis reports that "my back has healed itself" and "I weaned myself off all medications." In true before-and-after style, Willis writes, "I've now lost sixty pounds and I feel better than I have ever felt in my life. I recently had bloodwork done and all of my numbers were better than they were over a decade ago" (vi), right around the time Willis was writing *Lighten Up*. The very title of the book, *Fresh Start*, suggests that life may not even begin until the journey to leave fatness does. This type of before-and-after story reinforces the metanarrative that fatness and illness are states of pain to be left behind for the pleasures—physical and emotional—of being thinner and "healthy" (defined here as being pain-free and within medically defined measurements of normal body functions).

WEIGHT LOSS: SKINNY SOUTHERN

Laura Lyn Carter opens *Skinny Southern: 90 Reinvented Classics Without the Guilt* with a one-page introduction accompanied by a full-page, full-body photograph titled "Becoming a Skinny Southerner." The brief essay is a before-and-after narrative, though the photo is only of the "after." Around her forty-seventh birthday, after having a baby at forty-three, Carter "decided to make a lifestyle change" which resulted in losing forty-six pounds (viii). *Skinny Southern* is Carter's second cookbook; Carter also works as a private chef, host of food television program, and brand founder for a "gourmet line of clean-eating sauces" (viii). "Clean eating" is defined here as gluten and dairy free with reduced sugar. The cookbook ostensibly contains recipes that Carter developed in the first 120 days of her diet when she committed to creating new recipes each day. *Skinny Southern* follows a similar pattern of persuading readers that they can change the ingredients in recognizably southern dishes without compromising flavors or their connection to an "authentic" group identity.

Carter doesn't directly engage with the premise that there is some version of southern food that is unhealthy. She notes that "no boring baked chicken and plain salads were going to grace my southern table," suggesting that she and her family expected her to continue to cook recognizable southern food even as she attempted to lose weight (viii). The implication is that Carter's first instinct was to replace southern food with more obvious "diet" foods like salad and lean protein; "Southern food is comfort food!" Carter exclaims (viii). Southern food provided a challenge to "clean eating," but it was worth it to keep herself and her family from feeling the pain of losing their connection to southern food.

While Carter notes that some southern foods are breaded in flour and fried, only the gluten in the wheat flour is identified as a problem. She notes that "Fried chicken, cornbread, fried green tomatoes, pound cakes, and, of course, grits" are all traditional southern dishes (viii), and Carter provides a "clean" recipe for all of them. Her recipe for shrimp and grits is accompanied by a headnote that emphasizes the southern origins of the dish: "Never has there been a dish more Southern! Just like the South, the recipe varies from one part of the South to the others. Mine takes a Georgia twist with the incorporation of Vidalia onion, local olive oil, and local grits" (44). Though the headnote doesn't address the idea of "clean" eating (the recipe includes eight ounces of parmesan, presumably dairy-based), Carter seems to be assuming that her audience is as interested in the "southern" part of her title as they are in the "skinny." Carter argues that her style of eating for weight loss is compatible with maintaining "authentic" southern flavors and traditions.

Carter does admit that she is "reinventing" recipes and deviating from her grandmother's version of southern food, which stands in as "traditional" or "authentic." In some cases, like the headnotes for "Oyster Stew," Carter reports staying faithful to her grandmother's original recipe (51). However, at least twice in the cookbook Carter notes that the recipe on offer is not what her grandmother would have served. In the headnote for "Classic Southern Pound Cake," Carter mixes evidence for authenticity with her story of "reinventing" the recipe:

> Every Southern lady passes down her grandmother's pound cake recipe to the next generation. My grandmother was famous for hers and made literally hundreds of them. I even have her pan with all of the dings and dents in it—talk about a precious treasure. My pound cake is, of course, altered and lightened, but I think that she would be proud of me and what I am doing. (117)

Carter authenticates the recipe by citing her grandmother as the contributor of the recipe. The dented and inherited cake pan is added evidence of the continuity of the cake with its original source. Even though Carter has admitted to changing the recipe (gluten-free flour, dairy-free and almond-based cream cheese), she assures readers that her grandmother's conditional approval of the alterations preserves the authenticity of the recipe. Carter relies on the same rhetorical move in the headnote for "Pecan-Crusted Catfish." Her grandmother is cited again as loving the original dish but approving of Carter's decision to substitute pecan meal for flour and bake the fish instead of frying it (102). While Carter is not claiming to be accessing an older or more traditional plant-based southern food as Willis does, she is still invested in making an argument that preserves a link to a historical, "authentic" southern cuisine in the form of her grandmother.

Carter defines "healthy" food as "clean." Carter's suggestions for weight loss are to "avoid processed foods, gluten, and refined sugar; limit dairy; and add more plant-based foods to replace dairy" along with exercise. As we have seen in the examples above, the recipes tend to replace wheat four with gluten-free alternatives and dairy with nut milks and cheeses. The sugar in sweet tea is replaced with honey or stevia (36, 170). Maple syrup stands in for refined sugar in the "Banana Nut Smoothie" and "Pumpkin Spice Latte" (167, 169). In the recipes, another food to be avoided appears to be potatoes. Potatoes are replaced with cauliflower in "Cauliflower Soup" (40) and "Mashed Cauliflower" (81), though no explicit explanation for why potatoes are not "clean" is given for the substitution. Carter is not often explicit about what makes a particular recipe compatible with weight loss, except in the headnote for "Pico de Gallo," she notes that it is "the all-around nutrition-popping topping! Full of veggies and heart-healthy avocado, you can't go wrong" (82).

While Carter's list of "unhealthy" foods is short, she has more to say about the kinds of "healthy" foods she is not interested in eating. She uses "bored" and "boring" three times in the single-page introduction: "no one in the family was going to be happy if I cooked boring food. . . . No boring baked chicken and plain salads. . . . The thought of being bored with cooking, when it is what I love so dearly, was terrifying" (viii). Bad food, in this case, is not only tasteless and unappetizing diet food, but also food that is not creative or fun to cook. One marker of "good" food, then, is that it challenges her creativity as a cook.

Not only does Carter suggest to the reader that they can maintain ties to southernness on a diet, she also argues that they can diet invisibly within their own family. Carter often identifies recipes as being delicious or pleasing to her family who would not be happy with diet food. In the introduction, Carter notes that cooking for her husband and children's tastes made it difficult to change her diet because their happiness was important to her. Her solution was to "create delicious meals, just as I always had, but healthier and cleaner," almost so that they didn't notice anything had changed. Several recipe headnotes include the endorsement of her children as evidence of the goodness of the recipe. Beau is the family "smoothie expert" whose favorite is the "Sunrise Smoothie" (173), and mashed potato lover Christopher gives mashed cauliflower "the stamp of approval" as a substitute (81). Dylan is named in the recipe title, "Dylan's Favorite Chocolate Chip Cookies," because "My little Dylan loves to make these to share with his big brothers" (144). An entire chapter is devoted to recipes designed for "Kids in the Kitchen" (139–56). The argument here is that Carter's adaptation of recipes to make them compatible with weight loss does not make them incompatible with feeding others who are not attempting to lose weight. Good food for weight loss, then, should not be discernably different from "regular" food.

Carter's representation of a healthy body in *Skinny Southern* is obviously a thin body. The book's title and the title of the introduction, "Becoming a Skinny Southerner," privilege "skinny" as desirable. Carter claims that she "had to get back in shape and lose weight after having a baby at almost forty-three years old" (viii), but the sentence does not make clear why she "had to" lose weight or who was making this demand for her to "get back in shape." The implication is that she gained weight during pregnancy and "had to" return to a prepregnancy state that did not include having visible fat on her body. Carter works as a private chef and has appeared on television (viii), so perhaps readers can assume that the pressure to be "camera ready" might make the success of her career depend on appearing thin. This is not stated in the introduction, however. What is stated explicitly is that her body at a size twelve was a "before" problem and that losing 46 pounds to become a size two was an "after" success (viii). While no images of her "before" body are included in the cookbook, Carter's body is photographed throughout with two full-body photographs before the recipes begin (iv, viii), and a photograph of Carter in her kitchen accompanying each chapter. The "after" body that readers see in the cookbook stands in as ideal.

Carter does not describe her "before" body as experiencing any particular pain. The cookbook has a distinct lack of suffering, though Carter expected that losing weight would be unpleasant. She imagines that cooking healthy food would be boring and bland, but she discovers that "you can eat healthy without sacrificing pleasure" or creativity (viii). A common headnote structure that Carter uses is identifying an ingredient or dish that she expected to have to "give up" to lose weight, the absence of which would have been painful, and providing a solution that is pain-free. For example, fried green tomatoes might seem off limits because of gluten and deep frying in oil, but Carter reassures readers that "You can still have those summer green beauties without frying or gluten. I promise, you will never know the difference!" (74). Carter declares, "Asking me to give up ketchup would be like asking me to give up water! But most are full of refined sugars, so I made my own!" (29). She predicts suffering, but it never comes because her version preserves the essence of ketchup that is necessary to sustain life. Carter's predictions about exercise are similarly dire but turn out to be unfounded: "I actually love working out. I discovered muscles and strength I never knew I had" (viii). Carter describes her whole experience in this same pattern of predicting pain but finding pleasure instead: "What began as something that I thought I would suffer through to reach my goals of becoming healthy and fit has become a new passion" (viii). It seems clear that Carter is expecting objections from her audience who assume that eating to lose weight must be unpleasant, and so she emphasizes pleasure to persuade them to use the book. Even though she makes her "before" body invisible and absolutely reinforces the "after" body as the desired state, Carter does not mark her fatter body as painful or a source of suffering. The process of weight loss is expected to be painful, but it is not; no point in the transition from having fat on the body to being "a Skinny Southerner" is presented as suffering. Perhaps there is some little resistance in avoiding the depiction of fat as inherently suffering.

I described Carter's book as having "a distinct lack of suffering." It therefore follows that it has an excess of pleasure. Again, contrary to my expectations, the pleasure of a thin or "healthy" body is minimized. Even in the introduction where Carter describes losing weight, she does not describe her thin body as experiencing specific pleasures beyond enjoying working out and finding "muscles and strength." The pleasures emphasized most are of flavor and of avoiding the pain that she expected. "I haven't given up anything," Carter claims. "I have simply added a new culinary passion—glorious food that is delicious, beautiful, healthy, and clean!" (viii).

Skinny Southern suggests in its subtitle, *90 Reinvented Classics Without the Guilt* that one unpleasant feeling a reader might have is guilt for eating classics that haven't been reinvented with Carter's "clean" approach. The text of the cookbook doesn't directly address this feeling of guilt. There is a hint that Carter might feel guilty about altering her grandmother's recipes, but she dismisses that feeling easily by imagining her grandmother's approval of the changes. Even though the headnotes and introductory material don't elaborate on guilt as a consequence of "unclean" eating, the title implies that the painful feeling of guilt can be eliminated by following the recipes. Carter provides a pleasant solution to a painful problem, even if she does not elaborate on the source or experience of that problem.

Like *Lighten Up, Y'all*, *Skinny Southern* persuades readers that they can maintain connections with an authentic regional identity even as they change their eating behaviors. Carter is more explicit than Willis in suggesting that a reader could diet in public and in front of family without being detected. This preserves the possibility of *communitas*, of ritually bonding with the social environment around the dieter (Vannini 240). While Willis identifies her heavier body as painfully fat in both *Lighten Up* and *Fresh Start*, Carter only suggests that fat is painful through the absence of evidence of her heavier body and the unexamined statement that she "had to" lose weight. Perhaps this is because the size twelve body she sees as fat is firmly within "straight sizes" and smaller than the average American woman (size sixteen, according to Tali par. 1). Instead of addressing pain, Carter follows the conventions of the cookbook genre by remaining stubbornly positive, turning every expected annoyance into a pleasure. In the next section, we will look at illness-related cookbooks that are far more explicit about the pain and suffering associated with sickness.

RESTRICTING INGREDIENTS FOR ILLNESS: MY PINEWOOD KITCHEN

In cookbooks focused on restricting ingredients, illness is the exigence and restrictions are the cure. Fat is not typically the problem, though it may be concomitant with illnesses like diabetes, heart disease, gastrointestinal disorders, thyroid disorders, and other health issues. Diet may or may not be the cause of the illness, but these cookbooks emphasize that changes in diet can lead to relief of symptoms or eradication of disease.

In *My Pinewood Kitchen*, Mee McCormick, chef and owner of Pinewood Kitchen in the small town of Pinewood, Tennessee (about an hour's drive from Nashville), defines "health" in terms of the microbiome—the colonies of bacteria that live in and on the human body—and the functioning of the digestive and immune systems. This focus extends from her experiences with a number of digestive issues and autoimmune disorders that she has "healed" or managed with a diverse prebiotic and probiotic focused diet (32). McCormick is explicit from the title onward that a "Southern Culinary Cure" is available for illness. "Part One" of *My Pinewood Kitchen* describes McCormick's journey through illness, likely inherited from her mother who also suffered from debilitating digestive issues, and into restaurant ownership (6–27). "Part Two" details what McCormick has learned about the relationship between diet, the microbiome, and gut health. She outlines ingredients that are helpful and which to avoid, often citing medical research as evidence for her conclusions (29–58). The final section of the cookbook contains about two hundred pages of recipes. Most of the recipes do not come with their own headnotes, but McCormick begins each section with a short introduction and interjects frequently with sidebars (111) and captions on full-color photos of food (102) that highlight the benefits of certain ingredients or convince readers of the superlative quality of dishes. McCormick promises an end to the pain of digestive illness while highlighting the pleasures of taste and community.

McCormick is not as invested in crafting a distinct southern cuisine as Willis and Carter are. Apart from the title, she only names the South as a region four times (3, 85, 138, 153) and labels an ingredient or dish "southern" nine times (3, 14, 85, 96, 113, 169, 195, 231, 254). However, the introduction constructs a kind of southern authenticity for McCormick by placing the town of Pinewood, Tennessee, and the McCormick family in a recognizable southern location and culture. McCormick's history of the small town of two hundred begins in the 1830s with the purchase of land by one Samuel Graham who "did not support slavery" but paid all his workers "equally" in "Pinewood dollars" which could be spent at the "commissary store—the original Pinewood store" (6). When you read it out loud, you can hear that Pinewood dollars are company scrip, and we all know that paying your laborers to buy products from you is exploitation, even if you don't call it slavery. But McCormick uses it as evidence of Graham's progressive politics and the formation of something like a utopian community. In "the late 1800s," possibly during the era of Reconstruction, McCormick reports that "the land was divided and people moved away" (6), though the reason for this change is not explicit. The history that McCormick tells as the beginning of the story for her restaurant places its origins in the South, but not *that bad South*. Graham is a planter, but not an owner of enslaved humans. Pinewood Plantation is not haunted by *that* painful story. I'm not fooled by the whole "Pinewood dollars" business (photographed on the same page), but McCormick's story is a challenge to the stereotype of slavery as essential to being an authentic southern place.

McCormick's own southern bona fides are established in the opening sentences of Part One, where she dreams of being like Loretta Lynn and leaving her northern Appalachian home. Though she travels widely from Maryland, New York City, and Los Angeles to Israel and Mexico, she starts and ends in a recognizable southern place in the first three paragraphs (6). The photography of those first pages also signals southernness. The cover features McCormick dressed in plaid flannel on an aged red tractor with a cowboy hat in one hand, a smiling farmer. The first image on the dedication page is McCormick's family on the front steps of the restaurant. She is wearing a white chef's coat over denim overalls with the bib folded down and one strap still buckled to it over tan work boots with visible dirt (iii). The combination of chef whites with a humble laborer's denim signals both authority and down-home authenticity. Behind them is a chalkboard with a drawing of a Mason jar filled with flowers and partially obscured writing that I assume reads "Farm-to-Table" (we only see "RM- O- BLE" [iii]). The hand-drawn jar, the distressed wood decking, and the casual family pose all are suggestions of a simple agrarian South.

McCormick's reversal of expectations about what is "authentic" to the South appears most clearly in discussions about what her customers at the restaurant like. The unnamed "good-ole-boy-chef" who was initially lined up to run the restaurant represents McCormick's antithesis and a stereotypical version of southern cooking based in canned vegetables and deep-fried sides that please the masses (13). "You have to know your audience," he warns her. "[F]olks in these parts don't want any of your California food. I know what they want" (14). The chef's assumption is based in the stereotype of southern food as fried, fast, and unsophisticated. He calls her probiotic and food-allergy-aware cuisine "California food," a knock on her own authenticity as a "real southerner" for having lived and worked in LA and Malibu (14). However, McCormick makes the "good-ole-boy-chef" into a straw man whose arguments are flawed and who is ultimately proven wrong by the success of the restaurant. His food may be a stereotype of the South, but hers is "authentic" by being "real." When McCormick struggles with whether to hire this chef or not, she thinks to herself, "How can you allow this chef to serve processed, fake food when you have an abundance of real, living foods on the farm?" (14). His food cannot be authentic to the South because it isn't even food. Hers comes from southern ground, making it real and really southern.

She also explains that the "good-ole-boy-chef" has underestimated the tastes of locals. Though she sells lots of hamburgers and fries when the restaurant is getting started, she introduces locals to falafel as a meat substitute. There is a humorous misunderstanding when the customers call it a "full-on awful burger," having never heard the word *falafel* before (17), but McCormick is not patronizing of her customers' developing palates: "I knew that regular folks wanted to spend money on real food and wanted to feel good when they left a restaurant . . . they wanted to make better choices and still enjoy their favorite recipes" (14). She listens to their requests and "[begins] to master their favorite flavors while adding superfood ingredients" with great results (18). Her customers from Pinewood and Nashville "were loving that Pinewood was serving Southern food that wasn't sending folks home loaded and bloated" (19). McCormick makes the chef's stereotypical southern food look inauthentic by presenting a "more authentic" cuisine based in "real" ingredients that can be satisfying to "real" southerners while also being the antithesis of what they've been served, even by their own regional compatriots.

McCormick continues the argument that her restaurant's food is more authentically southern than the stereotype by connecting to an agrarian South of the past. McCormick argues that "It's no longer just coastal hippies wanting organic food; deeply seated southerners are also conscious of the environment." She explains that southerners' interest in the health of the environment extends from an essential relationship to farming. Her customers "had mainly grown up on farms and craved that old-school connection at the table" (19). By this logic southerners have more right to want organic food than Californians because their connection to farm-to-table cuisine comes directly from personal experience in the past. This kind of authenticity argument is both personal and traditional.

McCormick also connects her restaurant's mission to the essential Southern characteristic of hospitality (See Anthony Szczesiul's comprehensive *The Southern Hospitality Myth* for more). Not only is it "authentic" for southerners to eat farm-to-table organic foods, it is also "authentic" to serve food to others with a level of individual care that is more typical of home entertaining than restaurant service. The restaurant's kitchen observes a strict food allergy protocol that prevents cross-contamination (19–20), and McCormick claims that "everyone who works in the restaurant—from dishwasher to server—knows what's in the food and can serve customers with care and knowledge" (20). The attention to care is an extension of McCormick's personal views on service and empathy, but she also connects it to an essentially southern characteristic when she claims, "our tiny little kitchen is leading the way with a new level of hospitality, and there isn't a better place to kick this off than in the warmhearted South" (3). The South is the ideal place for her healthful, compassionate kind of service because the South is especially generous, open to giving and receiving hospitality. The food she serves—and the attitude with which she serves it—is presented as authentically southern.

McCormick defines "healthy food" quite narrowly in relationship to digestion, specifically in how foods affect the "microbiome" of bacteria that live in the human body. "Prebiotics" are foods that encourage the growth of "probiotics," or bacteria that are helpful to the body's functions. McCormick calls these "good" bacteria our "gut homies." Poor health comes from improperly nourishing our good bacteria: "If we don't feed them properly, they will die, and unhealthy bacteria will multiply, leading to high levels of inflammation and illness" (30). McCormick is careful to note that each person's microbiome is unique and that bodies react differently to certain bacteria, and so the prescription for what is good for one person might be different for another (31). While fermented foods are offered as healing for the gut for folks with Chron's (36–40), they are "off the table" for individuals with histamine intolerance (53–54). McCormick suggests experimenting to understand how each person's body responds to foods based on their individual microbiomes and illnesses, allergies, sensitivities, or intolerances before declaring any food healthy or unhealthy.

However, McCormick is clear that unhealthy foods include those that slow digestion, irritate or inflame the intestines, or kill good bacteria in the gut: namely, highly processed foods. McCormick describes growing up poor with a mother who suffered from digestive disorders, too, and eating processed foods like Cheerios and "chipped ham sandwiches on white bread with ketchup" bought with food stamps (9). As an adult, she thought healthy cooking meant "purchasing mainly processed foods and serving them along with salads and fruits," but later learned that this was not compatible with her digestive illnesses (10). McCormick attributes the severity of her illness to eating processed foods since childhood, even suggesting that she didn't inherit her mother's disease so much as she inherited her mother's unbalanced microbiome and unhealthy habits (31). She blames industrial food systems and soil depletion for reducing the nutrient values in foods, introducing chemical pesticides and genetically modified organisms (31), and pushing ultraprocessed "fake food" (14), all of which "caus[es] an imbalance in our guts and a lack of diversity in the microbiome" (30).

Healthy foods, by contrast, are those that contain probiotics including fermented foods (36–40); walnuts (40), beans (40–41), olive oil (42), mushrooms (43–46), and berries (48–49); and prebiotic foods like arugula, broccoli, cabbage, chickpeas, dark chocolate, and kiwi that are "powerhouses" for encouraging probiotic bacteria growth (47). Fresh and organic produce is recommended to limit exposure to chemical preservatives and pesticides. Sugar in all forms is regarded as inflammatory, but honey, coconut sugar, monk sugar, and stevia are recommended in small amounts (50). McCormick uses three pages and a considerable number of superlatives to recommend seaweeds and sea vegetables like kombu, hijiki, and wakame to add minerals and prebiotic nutrients to flavor dishes like beans, rice, and soups (66–69). "Fake food" of the industrial food complex is contrasted with the "real food" of small, organic farms like theirs at Pinewood (27). McCormick describes the farm itself as a biome: "Because Pinewood Farms is a biodynamic farm, our gardens are created with the biodiversity of a natural ecosystem.... All this supports the giant organism of our farm. This organism feeds us and our community's microbiome as we serve these foods in Pinewood Kitchen" (35). Healthful food in *My Pinewood Kitchen* is defined exclusively in this context of harmonious living with naturally occurring biodiversity, especially as it applies to digestion.

McCormick's view of good and healthy foods can best be summed up by the conversation she recounts with the "good-ole-boy chef" described above. McCormick asks him about his vision for the restaurant, and his answers put profiting from cheap and easy industrial food above flavor and health.

He plans to use canned vegetables and fry with "corn, soy, and vegetable oil [which] had the best price point and usually had an anti-foaming agent and preservatives (aka chemicals), which would extend the life of the oil so we'd only have to change the oil every couple of weeks" (13). The oils especially concern McCormick who explains that corn and vegetable oils are "cut with cottonseed oil, which isn't a food." Cotton is "one of the crops with the most pesticides on the planet," and ingested cotton causes "intestinal inflammation even for healthy people." Frying in this cheap oil creates an unappetizing and sinister sounding "chemical stew." His indifferent attitude toward food allergies gives her pause, too (13). In the end, McCormick dismisses the potential chef and decides to run the restaurant herself, sourcing beef and pork from their own farm (15), chicken and eggs from Amish neighbors (16), non-GMO rice bran oil for frying and olive oil for sautéing (13), produce from a local organic farmer (16), and very carefully chosen premade products like "buns and bread, dried goods, cheeses, and more" acquired with considerably extra effort from Sysco, "the world's largest broadline food distributor" (16). She admits later in the introduction that these costly choices put the business in precarious economic straits (25), but as the success of the restaurant demonstrates (27), "healthy food" is not necessarily incompatible with profitability.

McCormick makes a unique argument by suggesting that another marker of good and healthy food is the emotional environment in which it is produced. "I'd never worked in a kind kitchen," McCormick claims. From the aggressive, fast-paced, hierarchical structure of a restaurant kitchen (22) to the anger that seemed to attend domestic work modeled by her mother and grandmother (22–23), McCormick suggests that the "culture" of the kitchen matters as much in producing good food as the ingredients. She marvels that people enjoy restaurant food when the toxic workplace environment of professional kitchens produces "anxious food" made by stressed-out employees (24). Instead, McCormick emphasizes that her energy and care for customers and employees is part of the healthfulness of her food: "This is the most important ingredient—kindness. It takes self-kindness to make the time to learn to cook for our own wellness and kindness to cook for the wellness of a loved one" (24). McCormick often frames her work as a "service" that extends from gratitude for her recovery (10), praying for opportunities to keep serving (10, 11, 26). McCormick implies that her vision of healthy food includes preparing it with attitudes of kindness, compassion, and empathy along with equitable working relationships and care for others (20, 21).

McCormick's representation of a healthy body is similarly focused on gut health and digestive function. Healthy bodies are not necessarily thin bodies. In McCormick's introduction, her most unhealthy state was also her thinnest:

"I was rail thin. I couldn't eat much of anything. Even drinking water brought me to my knees with pain" (9). The doctor who writes the foreword notes that when she met McCormick only a few weeks after giving birth, "Mee was so frail and thin that baby Lola was practically bigger than she was" (xi). Extreme thinness is a sign of ill health. However, McCormick also considers "obesity" to be a result of unbalanced microbiomes and something to fight with a probiotic-friendly diet (33). According to McCormick, the short chain fatty acids produced by probiotics absorb the fat we eat for use in the body. "If fat isn't absorbed," because of imbalance of microbes, unused fat "hangs out on the side—usually of our jeans!" (32). The picture of fat hanging out of too-tight jeans is marked as unhealthy because it is the product of an unhealthy microbiome, but the image thrown in as a cheeky aside suggests that the physical appearance of fat is also a symptom of ill-health. Moreover, McCormick notes that "by supporting the gut microbiome, we can get back to our spry, energetic, quick-witted selves and lose weight and the bloat" (32). The suggestion is that body fat makes a person slow physically and mentally. A healthy body, then, is one with enough fat to be used by the body, but no visible signs of "excess" fat.

Apart from the mentions above (and the twenty photographs of the author's body in the introductory chapters), McCormick spends little time on the body's appearance, and much more on the feelings of good health and the mobility of a healthy body. McCormick uses some version of the word *heal* thirty times in the book, mostly describing the body's ability to heal itself with a balanced microbiome. Though McCormick admits that "My body still struggles at times with Hashimoto's fatigue, my rheumatoid arthritis kicks up when I'm stressed or overworked, and if I eat out and I'm 'glutened,' I miss at least three days of work recovering" (25); she more often describes herself as healed and healthy. Healthfulness is described as high in energy and physical movement: "I think people come to see me play the tambourine and dance around the kitchen because they know how hard it was for me to climb up off the floor and now feel so good again" (21). This sentence appears just above a photograph of McCormick playing a tambourine while her husband Lee plays a guitar in front of a microphone as proof of her vitality. McCormick unequivocal in her belief that healthfulness comes from diet:

> I still wake up every day full of energy (sometimes I'm even up with the roosters). I'm physically able to work on the farm, be goofy with my girls, and dance with my cowboy husband to our live jam sessions on Saturday nights. I don't think I'd be this healthy if it were not for the real food I've been putting in my body. (57)

To be healthy, then, means to be without symptoms of illness, energetic, active, and happy.

Unlike the other cookbooks examined in this chapter, McCormick is fairly explicit in framing the pain and suffering of digestive illness. The foreword claims that McCormick's "journey from death's door to Pinewood kitchen is a page turner" (xi). Her illness is severe and lifelong, starting with being born with an "intussusception, meaning my intestines collapsed inside themselves" due to "an ulceration I was born with." As an infant, McCormick had surgery to remove part of her intestines, and it seemed unlikely that she would survive (8). McCormick's mother was ill with undiagnosed Crohn's, too, unable "get up off the floor to cook or go to work" and often hospitalized (8). As a child, McCormick was thin and had food allergies that "no one paid much attention to." She grew up into adulthood with "chronic pain, bloating, and occasional partial bowel obstructions" (8), "suffering" from many of the same issues that her mother had (9). Her health became a crisis after the birth of her second child when her digestive issues were so acute that she could not eat or drink, and she began to recognize that her first-born child may have inherited similar digestive problems (9). After seeing many doctors, one found "an ulceration the *total* circumference of my small intestines" and recommended life-saving surgery and medication (9). Even the treatment of the illness is described as painful, life-threatening suffering: "I knew I wouldn't survive the side effects of the medicine, and I could barely swallow the pills" (10).

Even after finding some resolution of symptoms in treatment, McCormick describes in some detail an episode of getting "glutened" by a restaurant that didn't take her gluten intolerance seriously, causing a "bad bout of digestive issues" as she boarded a plane from New York to Nashville. McCormick is explicit about having diarrhea and nausea: "I barely made it off the plane without an intestinal explosion! . . . I was green and sweating, hoping I could hold it together until we reached the farm." The pain continues when her daughter, glad to see her mother after her absence, climbs into McCormick's lap for a hug. Instead of being delighted by the affection, McCormick's reaction is physical pain: "*Ouch, not my lap!*" (emphasis in original, 11). Later in the chapter, McCormick describes the seriousness of this discomfort on her ability to function: "If I eat out and I'm 'glutened,' I miss at least three days of work recovering" (25). It must be a cookbook-taboo to describe diarrhea and farts, but McCormick does it, warning readers to scoop the foam off of cooking beans or else "your tummy will fo'sho be in a state of methane suffering!" (61).

Apart from the physical suffering of digestive disorders, McCormick also describes emotional suffering that comes along with illness and poverty. Her mother's illness certainly caused her mother pain, but it also affected

McCormick and her sister. McCormick writes that her older sister "didn't have much of a childhood" because she was responsible for taking care of the family when her mother was ill, "therefore her inheritance of my playfulness passed her by" (23). Even as an adult, her sister isn't capable of the same kind of pleasure because of this early suffering. McCormick's decision to serve even customers who cannot pay extends from her childhood of poverty and her mother's illness: "We watched our momma suffer, not being able to eat or provide food for her kids, and we were helpless, hungry children.... If there had been a Pinewood Kitchen when I was a little girl, I wouldn't have gone as hungry, and my momma could have eaten without pain" (23). Her mother's physical suffering became her own emotional anguish. Not all of these emotional wounds are healed by diet, but McCormick reports that "I have seen a huge positive change in my emotional self since healing my gut" (34), and she and her sister have worked through their childhood trauma by working in the kitchen together (23). When McCormick writes, "I can't begin to tell you the healing Pinewood Kitchen has given my sister and me," she isn't talking about physical healing but emotional healing (23).

Of course, McCormick describes the pleasure of the relief of symptoms from illness. Many of her own issues have been resolved through diet changes (10), and she describes all the positive health effects of probiotic-friendly food from reduced inflammation, lower cholesterol, and protection against blocked arteries (32) to a healthy colon, faster wound healing, and weight loss (33). McCormick also suggests better "emotional health" because probiotics "reduce stress and anxiety through a unique gut-brain interaction" leading to "lowered rates of depression, which by the way, is the second leading cause of disability in the US" (33). Her description of a healthy body includes a feeling of emotional wellbeing, a sense of purpose, and happiness. McCormick's enthusiasm for emotional health through diet is explicit: "Y'all should know I'm jumping outta my seat cheering as I write this. Because if we can get in our kitchens and use food as a way to help us find emotional balance, we gain back our confidence and our ability to create joyful, incredible lives" (34). The promise of this cookbook is a pleasure that extends well beyond the relief of physical symptoms to an emotional well-being that means a better life as a whole.

TOWARDS A CONCLUSION: SOLVING THE PROBLEM OF FAT

Like Lara Lynn Carter looking at her running shoes (iii), I also expected to suffer through the investigation of these cookbooks. "Principle 1" of *Intuitive Eating* is to withdraw from diet culture which thrives on making us believe we can't trust ourselves to know what to eat to be healthy (64–83). I had intentionally separated myself from thinking about "dieting" or any kind of restrictive eating. I expected the cookbooks to hold the kind of shame that this discourse always made me feel, but I didn't find it. I shouldn't have been that surprised. The premise of this book is that cookbooks as a genre have an imperative to deliver pleasure; weight loss cookbooks would not be an exception to that rule.

The rhetorical challenge at the heart of the southern diet cookbook is not convincing the reader that they should want to lose weight or change their diet to improve symptoms of disease. The authors begin with the assumption that their audience has already been convinced of this need by acquiring the book. Rather, the complicated logical knot is convincing them that changing their diet won't change their relationships within their social circles, from their immediate family to their regional identity. Each of the cookbooks examined here acknowledges the potential pain of separation from the community by choosing to eat differently from those around them. The ritual of eating together and in public has the effect of binding diners in a common identity; refusal to participate isolates the individual as deviant.

Each in their own way promises a solution to avoid the pain of separation. Willis locates her "lightened" cuisine in a tradition of southern cooking that is older and more authentic than the indulgent and stereotyped "fried chicken and fatback" that dominates media representations of southern food. Carter assures readers that her amendments to recipes are undetectable by her family circle and approved by the most authentic source of traditional knowledge, her grandmother. McCormick follows Willis's pattern of rejecting an inauthentic and unhealthful version of southern food and connecting her way of eating to a cuisine that emerges naturally from the *terroir*. With this argument of "authenticity" firmly in place, the authors can then go on to advance an argument about what they determine to be healthful ingredients and preparations.

While Willis and McCormick describe their "before" states as experiencing physical and emotional pain, all three writers emphasize the pleasure of their "after" states as well as the pleasure of the process of getting there. The tenets of fat and disability studies ask us to be critical of representations of fat as an illness in need of a cure. None of the books in this sample meet that standard. Certainly, none of them express pleasure in living in a fat body; all present weight as a key measure of health. These support the status quo that underpins fatphobia and constructs fat as a medicalized problem in need of a solution.

If there is any political resistance in the pleasure taken in these books, it is the pleasure that each writer takes in eating flavorful and culturally appropriate foods, even as they restrict or alter their eating habits. All three recognize the value of pleasure as a motivation for change and a key part of a healthy life. As the last chapter demonstrated, women taking pleasure in their own sensual experiences (in this case, the sense of taste) runs counter to messages about appropriate gendered behavior.

I suppose, in a way, I am asking for blood from a turnip. It is too much to expect for a cookbook whose rhetorical purpose is weight loss to present weight as a value-neutral description or even a pleasant experience. It wouldn't be a diet cookbook anymore but something else entirely. Just as pleasure is a convention of the cookbook genre at large, stigmatizing fat is an inviolable convention of the diet cookbook subgenre. Still, the cookbooks in this chapter at least acknowledge that pleasure—especially the pleasure of blending in—is available to people with fat and sick bodies.

WORKS CITED

Bailey, Emily. *The Southern Keto Cookbook: 100 High-Fat, Low-Carb Recipes for Classic Comfort Food*. Callisto Media Incorporated, 2020.

Carter, Lara Lynn. *Skinny Southern: 90 Reinvented Classics Without the Guilt!* Familius, 2019.

Claiborne, Jenne. *Sweet Potato Soul: 100 Easy Vegan Recipes for the Southern Flavors of Smoke, Sugar, Spice, and Soul*. Rodale, 2018.

Deen, Paula. *Paula Deen Cuts the Fat*. Paula Deen Ventures, 2015.

Engle, Jill C. "Improving Outcomes in Child Poverty and Wellness in Appalachia in the 'New Normal' Era: Infusing Empathy into Law," *West Virginia Law Review*, Spring 2018, pp. 1047–61.

Feller, Maya. *The Southern Comfort Food Diabetes Cookbook: Over 100 Recipes for a Healthy Life*. Rockridge Press, 2019.

Gailey, Jeannine A. "Fat Shame to Fat Pride: Fat Women's Sexual and Dating Experiences." *Fat Studies*, vol. 1, no. 1, 2012, DOI:10.1080/21604851.2012.631113.

"Tell Me I'm Fat." *This American Life*, hosted by Ira Glass, WBEZ Chicago, 17 June 2016, https://www.thisamericanlife.org/589/transcript. Transcript.

Goldberg, Daniel and Rebecca Puhl. "Obesity Stigma: A Failed and Ethically Dubious Strategy." *Hastings Center Report*, vol. 43, no. 3, 2013, pp. 9–10. Doi: 10.1002/hast.167.

Jaslow, Ryan. "Paula Deen's Type 2 Diabetes: Is Her Cooking to Blame?" *CBS News*, 17 Jan 2012, https://www.cbsnews.com/news/paula-deens-type-2-diabetes-is-her-cooking-to-blame/.

Jones, Eric and Shanna Jones. *Healthier Southern Cooking*. Page Street Publishing, 2022.

Lee, Matt and Ted Lee. *The Lee Bros. Simple Fresh Southern*. Ten Speed Press, 2009.

Maor, Maya. "Stories That Matter: Subverting the Before-and-After Weight-Loss Narrative." *Social Semiotics*, vol. 24, no. 1, 2014, pp. 88–105. http://dx.doi.org/10.1080/10350330.2013.827359.

Margavio Strileya, Katie and Sophia Hutchens. "Liberation from Thinness Culture: Motivations for Joining Fat Acceptance Movements." *Fat Studies*, vol. 9, no. 3, 2020, pp. 296–308. https://doi.org/10.1080/21604851.2020.1723280.

McCormick, Mee. *My Pinewood Kitchen: A Southern Culinary Cure*. Health Communications Inc., 2020.

Miller, Monica Carol. *Being Ugly: Southern Women Writers and Social Rebellion*. Louisiana State UP, 2017.

Newton, Natasha. *Southern Keto: Beyond the Basics*. Victory Belt Publishing, 2018.

Olson, KayLoni L., Jacob D. Landers, Tyler T. Thaxton, and Charles F. Emery. "The Pain of Weight-Related Stigma Among Women With Overweight or Obesity." *Stigma and Health*, vol. 4, no. 3, 2019, pp. 243–46. http://dx.doi.org/10.1037/sah0000137.

O'Neil, Carolyn. *Slim Down South: Eating Well and Living Healthy in the Land of Biscuits and Bacon*. Oxmoor House, 2013.

Saturday Night Live. "Paula Deen's Paper Towels—Saturday Night Live." YouTube, uploaded by Saturday Night Live, 10 Sep 2013, https://www.youtube.com/watch?v=46sVCxEjExI.

Simon, Bryant. "Chickenization and Public Ill-Health in the American South." *Southern Studies*, vol. 25, no. 1, Fall/Winter 2018, pp. 55–77.

Stewart, Terah J. and Roshaunda L. Breeden. "'Feeling Good as Hell': Black Women and the Nuances of Fat Resistance." *Fat Studies*, vol. 10, no. 3, 2021, pp. 221–36, DOI: 10.1080/21604851.2021.1907964.

Szczesiul, Anthony. *The Southern Hospitality Myth: Ethics, Politics, Race, and American Memory*. U of Georgia P, 2017.

Tali, Didem. "The 'Average' Woman Is Now Size 16 Or 18. Why Do Retailers Keep Failing Her?" *Forbes.com*, 30 Sept 2016, https://www.forbes.com/sites/didemtali/2016/09/30/the-average-woman-size/?sh=7e29e1c52791.

Tippen, Carrie Helms. "Keep Southern and Cut the Fat: Negotiating Identity and Authenticity in Diet Cookbooks." *Food, Fatness, Fitness*, 1 Dec. 2020, https://foodfatnessfitness.com/2020/12/01/keep-southern-and-cut-the-fat-negotiating-identity-and-authenticity-in-diet-cookbooks/.

Tribole, Evelyn and Elyse Resch. *Intuitive Eating: A Revolutionary Anti-Diet Approach*. Updated edition, St. Martin's Essentials, 2020.

Vannini, Phillip. "Snacking as Ritual: Eating Behavior in Public Places." *Food for Thought: Essays on Eating and Culture*, edited by Lawrence C. Rubin, McFarland, 2008, pp. 237–47.

Wann, Marilyn. "Foreword: Fat Studies: An Invitation to Revolution." *Fat Studies Reader*, edited by Esther Rothblum and Sondra Solovay, New York UP, 2009.

West, Lindy. "My wedding was perfect—and I was fat as hell the whole time." *The Guardian*. 21 Jul 2015, https://www.theguardian.com/lifeandstyle/2015/jul/21/my-wedding-perfect-fat-woman.

White, Francis Ray. "Fucking Failures: The Future of Fat Sex." *Sexualities*, vol. 19, no. 8, 2016, pp. 962–79.

Whitman, Walt. "Song of Myself 1." *Leaves of Grass: The Deathbed Edition*. Modern Library Edition, 1993.

Willis, Virginia. *Fresh Start: Cooking with Virginia, My Real Life Daily Guide to Healthy Eating and Weight Loss*. 2022.

Willis, Virginia. *Lighten Up, Y'all*. Ten Speed Press, 2015.

Xie, Julian, Ashley Price, Neal Curran, and Truls Østbye. "The Impact of a Produce Prescription Programme On Healthy Food Purchasing and Diabetes-Related Health

Outcomes." *Public Health Nutrition*, vol. 24, no. 12, 2021, pp. 3945–55. Doi: 10.1017/S1368980021001828.

Zoller, Charlotte. "What Terms Like 'Superfat' and 'Small Fat' Mean, and How They Are Used." *Teen Vogue*, 6 Apr 2021, https://www.teenvogue.com/story/superfat-small-fat-how-they-are-used#:~:text=Small%20Fat%20%E2%80%94%20sizes%2014%2D18,trouble%20with%20size%2Dbased%20accessibility.

"USEFUL IN A FEARFUL TIME"
Responding to Grief and Death in Funeral Cookbooks

When I was twenty-three, my best friend from work was having trouble conceiving a child. She and her husband were both in their late thirties, and she had been diagnosed with uterine and ovarian cysts. I jogged with her in the park in the morning before work and sat with her through many lunch breaks while she talked about just how out of control it all felt. How something that was supposed to be so natural and so easy was so impossible for her.

I wrote a poem for my creative writing class (later published in the magazine *Entropy*) about how guilty I felt to sit so close to her grief and not be able to soothe it or help relieve the burden. "The Southern woman in me brings food to a misfortune," I wrote, "an apology for not bearing the blow of fate myself" ("Dinner," lines 1–2). I listed all the things I would make for her if I thought it would do any good: herbed and brined chickens, rich stews, crusty artisan breads. I would feed her so well that her nourished body would have no choice but to be fertile ground for the baby she wanted so badly. That is, I would if I could cook.

Even as a brand-new adult with absolutely no useful domestic skills, I knew that the proper response to other people's pain was to feed them, and I noted it as a special aspect of my southernness and womanhood. I had good reason to believe this. When I was six years old, my father had a kidney transplant. In my earliest years, while he was in and out of the hospital and dialysis clinics, my family was regularly fed by our church, friends, and family. Our church friend Cula Jo Trout was famous for a banana pudding that my father adored, but bananas are forbidden for a person with failing kidneys that can't remove excess potassium from the blood, so he hadn't eaten it in his sickest years. When he came home from that last hospital stay after transplant and he was cleared for banana-eating, there was a big bowl of pudding waiting for him in the refrigerator. He ate it all in one sitting. Devouring this bowl of banana pudding was a victory lap. He lapped up other forbidden foods, too, like peanut butter and watermelon. (I wrote and published a poem about this, too, "Food Chain"). From then on, there was a bowl of banana pudding with Nilla Wafers at every church dinner, and my father would pretend to claim the bowl for himself, even though he always served himself last as a devout expression of humility.

Now that I live outside the South, it's still important to me to be the one who brings food, to practice my southern identity for my western Pennsylvania friends. I mastered a buttermilk biscuit that freezes beautifully during my Covid-19 lockdown, and I can whip them up in a jiffy to deliver with a carton of eggs from my backyard chickens almost at a moment's notice (see Splawn for the recipe). I got to do this three times while writing this chapter: for a colleague who had heart surgery, for the family of a colleague who died of cancer, and for the family of my neighbor who died unexpectedly. Since my Texas accent is fairly neutralized, sometimes delivering food is the most legibly and intentionally "southern thing" I do.

This chapter explores the food practices that surround death and grief as another intersection of suffering and pleasure in southern foodways. A moment of profound sadness in the life of an individual is transformed into an occasion to feel the love and support of a community expressed in gifts of food. I argue that the peculiar pleasure promised by the exchange of funeral foods is to ritually construct belonging and reinforce the social bonds of the community. This is true of most death rituals and communal meals, but southern funeral foodways—and the texts that represent them—interest me most because they are self-conscious attempts at crafting a distinct regional identity through public acts of feeding and eating.

You might be surprised to learn that there is a niche subset of southern cookbooks that provide instructions for feeding, behavior, and rituals of southern funerals with quirky titles like *Being Dead Is No Excuse: The Official Southern Ladies Guide to Hosting the Perfect Funeral* (Metcalf and Hayes, 2013). These cookbooks promise delicious food and fellowship as a balm for suffering death in a community while highlighting foods, emotions, values, habits, and rituals that they argue are specific to the US South and local funeral customs. While these cookbooks empathetically describe the painful feelings that must accompany a death, they also offer advice and recipes to ease the social awkwardness of grief, providing comfort and a path to the end of suffering through culinary pleasure. They describe the communal meal and sharing food as a key part of performing a distinct southern identity and creating a localized community.

Anthropological and sociological theory supports this interpretation of ritual communal meals as socially important moments of bonding. Gwen

Kennedy Neville describes "kin-religious gatherings" like reunions and homecomings as "a process of gathering and dispersing of geographically scattered people who share religious beliefs and who are related in networks of kinship (130). Neville highlights the sacred nature of food in the rituals of the "folk liturgies" surrounding kin-religious gatherings as a means of reinforcing social networks and community bonds through "repeated partaking of the sacred foods of the reunion." Repetition is key: "Specific dishes are often made by the same cooks year after year and laid out in the same order for consumption." Though the foods themselves have no power, Neville argues that "they are made holy by . . . the *communitas* of eating together with one's own" (136). Funerals become an opportunity to ritually perform a distinct and continuous identity that transcends both time and geography. The repetition of the same meals, "year after year," creates a feeling of collapsed time and continuity with a stable identity connected to a distinct southern homeplace. Funeral food cookbooks offer a script to novices for entering this community ritual and feeling the pleasure of belonging.

SELF-CONSCIOUSLY SOUTHERN: A BRIEF HISTORY OF SOUTHERN FUNERALS

Being generally suspicious of claims of essentialism and having attended no funerals in any other region, I was prepared to be skeptical that southern funeral customs were unique in the US. But according to Charles Reagan Wilson, a scholar of southern religion, funerals in colonial Virginia differed from those of the Puritan New Englanders. Part reunion, part celebration, Virginia funerals were elaborate public affairs that included "the firing of guns, the consumption of liquor, and the funeral feast tradition brought from England." However, by the nineteenth century, Wilson reports that southern funeral rites were indistinguishable from the rest of the United States. Differences in practice were more likely to be related to race and class than region (102).

Of course, because of chattel slavery and racial segregation, Black and white southern funeral traditions developed in separate but often parallel lines. The "Funeral Rites" entry in the *Encyclopedia of African American Society* describes antebellum funeral rites among African Americans as "among the few occasions in which family and other people could get together and socialize" (Jaynes 356). The suffering of being enslaved or free but marginalized and the novelty of gathering as a community gave funerals in Black communities a dual purpose as events of mourning and celebration, "as the deceased was regarded as finally 'free' and was said to be 'goin' home'" (356). Beverly Bunch-Lyons explains that Black-owned southern funeral homes, created out of necessity because of segregation and racism, serve as important social centers in black communities and opportunities for entrepreneurship (58). The material differences between Black and white southern funerals are less distinct in the twenty-first century, according to Jaynes's encyclopedia entry, but they remain significant events for community gathering and publicly performing local and familial traditions (357).

No matter how similar the rituals of mourning may appear between Black and white southerners, Wilson argues that the historical origins of white southerners' self-conscious attempts to create regionally distinct funeral rites is inseparable from white supremacy and celebrations of the Confederacy. Wilson argues that it was only after the Civil War with the public funerals of Robert E. Lee and Jefferson Davis that southern funerals began to take on an intentionally distinct formula that was self-consciously regional, and by extension, exclusively white ("Funerals" 102). As Wilson explains, the funerals of these figureheads of the Confederacy "were true ceremonies of the southern identity. Symbols of Dixie were prominently displayed, while eulogies explained the contribution of the deceased to the South as a region" (103). Wilson writes much more about this in "The Death of Southern Heroes: Historic Funerals of the South" for the journal *Southern Cultures* (3–22). Postbellum funerals offered a perfect moment to make an argument for a distinctly southern culture and identity separate from the rest of the United States. At the same time that the South's cultural arbiters were invested in distinguishing the South politically, culturally, economically, racially, and even genetically from the rest of the United States (see Watson's *Normans and Saxons: Southern Race Mythology and the Intellectual History of the Civil War*), there were also hundreds of thousands of too-young dead to mourn and public ceremonies for marking their deaths as a consequence of an armed conflict over these same sectional distinctions. In other words, white southerners had many occasions within a short period of time to practice and repeat rituals of death that naturalized regional and racial differences (Wilson, "Funerals" 103). Black and white southerners may have settled into similar patterns for funerals in the twenty-first century, but it is clear that the very idea of a regionally specific funeral practice is an echo of these exclusionary and violent origins. Whatever comfort these funeral rituals bring to a community now, we cannot read them as unmixed pleasure shared equally by all people who call themselves southern.

Karla Holloway, professor of English, African American studies, and law at Duke University and author of *Passed On: African American Mourning Stories*, reminds us that death, dying, and mourning are deeply embedded in African

American art and culture because of the violent realities of racism: "Instead of death and dying being unusual, untoward events, or despite being inevitable end-of-lifespan events, the cycles of our daily lives were so persistently interrupted by specters of death that we worked this experience into the culture's iconography and included it as an aspect of black cultural sensibility" (6). Even if the menus and protocols of funerals look similar, Holloway cautions us to be aware of differences in emotional responses to and cultural meanings of death as they intersect with race. I take this as a warning to be skeptical of white writers' attempts to bring the practices of Black southerners neatly into a unified whole with the practices of white southerners.

PLACE: GEOGRAPHIC SPECIFICITY AND COMING "HOME"

Within the South, there are of course microregional differences in cuisine and custom, including the ultradistinct tradition of the New Orleans "Jazz funeral" and the "Second Line" parades that attend a burial (Regis 38–56). These variations only support the argument that funeral gatherings, with their ritual sameness and formal calling of kin-networks home, would be an opportunity for any community (whether it be regional, local, religious, racial, kin, or any other group identity) to self-consciously craft a ritual of distinction that is bound to that particular place. Neville's description of sacred *communitas* at kin-religious gatherings depends as much on the location of the table under the same oak trees as on the presence of the same ritual dishes (136). The first step in creating a distinct regional community is to put it in a specific geographic place. The funeral is a convenient opportunity because it is a place-based ritual, gathering mourners into one location and placing the deceased person's body permanently into a final "resting place" through burial, spreading ashes, or other ritual. The idea of a uniquely southern funeral evolved to create cultural differences associated with geography.

Though all funeral rites to some extent become an opportunity for family reunions or homecomings for family members who have moved away, geographic mobility in the twentieth and twenty-first centuries may have added regional significance to funerals as opportunities to draw relatives who might have migrated to urban areas or outside of the South back to ancestral homes. The gathering of relatives and friends from "off" back to the "homeplace," would create an opportunity for solidifying bonds between members of a community in relation to a specific geographic place identified by unique practices distinct from those in the places they would return to. These already self-consciously distinct rituals become moments to perform unity for a community in diaspora, maintaining a "home" and legible identity in the geographic South, and taking "home" practices with them.

Though this drawing together a community bound to place sounds like pleasure, too often the bonds of community are as restrictive as they are comforting, and the place itself becomes fraught with layered meanings. Anissa Wardi complicates the vision of the "home-coming" or "home-going" as an easy and pleasurable experience for Black southerners. In her examination of death and home in twentieth-century African American literature, Wardi argues that authors represent the South as a haunted "landscape of the dead" (2). The patterns of exile, migration, and return in African American literature are representative of a deep ambivalence and paradox that defies the simplicity of coming home and feeling connected to place: "Graveyards—both sacred ancestral grounds and reminders of southern violence—are overarching metaphors of belonging and exile, inheritance and disinheritance" (2). The segregated graveyards are a final insult to a life lived in segregated housing, dining, shopping, working, medical care, and embalming. This is to say nothing of the many, many unmarked graves of African Americans in the South, as well as those marked but anonymous or bearing the surname of their enslaver. The ambivalence toward death and a southern "homeland" is right there in the tradition of the "home-going" celebration: only the deceased ever really get to go home.

Reta Ugena Whitlock, editor of *Queer South Rising: Voices of a Contested Place* and author of "Season of Lilacs: Nostalgia of Place and Homeplace(s) of Difference," explains that home-going to the South is complicated for LGBTQIA+ folks, too. Whitlock suggests that some level of "yearning for a homeplace," may be a generalizable southern trait (7), but as an adult "going home queer," Whitlock suggests that coming out means never quite going home to the same place as before (12). When being bound to a community means having to hide or alter important parts of one's identity to fit expectations, it can hardly be painted with broad strokes as pleasure. Therefore, attempts to bring all the experiences and emotions of death, grief, and funeral rites into one geographic place called "the South" defies, elides, and erases the various lived experiences of the many millions of people who would gather for a funeral there, going far beyond even the brief discussion of sexualities, genders, and races described above.

Despite the many individuals who would feel pain by being associated with the South, the cookbooks examined in this chapter suggest that an audience exists of people who elect to use the occasion of a funeral to perform an identity legible as "southern." Food and hospitality remain common markers of southern identity in general discourse, and food is a central feature of the southern funeral from the colonial feasts to today's communal meals after funeral services and visitation luncheons in the homes of the bereaved. Wilson notes that "the funeral remains a prime ceremonial occasion for eating southern food, hearing southern music, and nurturing the region's renowned sense of family and community" (104). The funeral event called by the name "southern," as Wilson describes it, is self-consciously aligning with recognizable markers of southern distinction. Funeral cookbooks operate on this same logic of geographic specificity as an argument for authenticity and a key first step in the process of social bonding. The first implied step in each recipe is to decide you want to be southern.

TIME: CONTINUING BONDS

The funeral meal collapses space by bringing a dispersed community into one geographically specific southern place. It also has the effect of collapsing time, giving an illusion of a continuous and stable group identity over many generations. Anthropologist Joshua Graham notes a particularly understudied aspect of the southern funeral feast: the "highly gendered phenomenon" of serving dishes recognized in the community by a possessive title, "e.g., Maw Maw's Chess Pie" (89). Graham argues that by connecting dishes with their specific practitioners and innovators, the community practices what in death studies is known as "continuing bonds theory." The theory of continuing bonds describes practices "in which the bereaved actively seek to maintain or reclaim connections with the deceased" (89). By continuing to use the recipes of the dead and repeating their names and stories, mourners keep the dead vital to the living community. Since funerals are an occasion where many such recipes can be used and served at once in a communal meal, Graham argues, "traditions marking one person's recent death have the net effect of resurrecting the social influence of the long-dead. There is a collapsing of meaning here: the recent dead provide a gateway to the long-dead and sometimes stand in for them" (89). In other words, the communal meal reenacts a community of living and dead into a unified group collected over time and space into *now* and *here*. The effect of preparing and serving dishes connected with long dead matriarchs is to give women a social afterlife where they continue to "exert influence" on social and cultural practices, shaping the group identity, and acting as "guardians of the community" (93). Graham continues, "When a memorial dish is not prepared on a regular basis, the individual loses any agency or power to influence the social world. If the dish is rediscovered, however, the individual has a chance of regaining agency," essentially amounting to a "social resurrection." (95) Though Graham never quite draws this conclusion, what I find fascinating about this prolonged social influence is that it may give women in death *more* social life and agency than they experienced while living.

If southern funerals are in any way unique to the South in practice, it is because of an intentional and self-conscious attempt to craft a distinct, temporally continuous, and place-based identity for the community of mourners, attached through kinship and friendship to a particular southern homeplace across time. The food practices associated with southern funerals are a tangible, if temporary, means of performing, embodying, and perpetuating a community identity. The accounts of southern funeral traditions examined here also highlight the contradictory mingling of pain, suffering, and grief with the pleasures of eating, drinking, bonding with kin and non-kin networks, remembering and storytelling, feeling belonging, and expressing a communal identity. If funerals are an opportunity to ritually perform a unique and timeless southern identity, then funeral cookbooks provide the recipes for belonging.

The remainder of this case study examines three books with recipes focused exclusively on funeral rituals in the US South: Jessica Bemis Ward's *Food to Die For: A Book of Funeral Food, Tips, and Tales* (2004), Gayden Metcalf and Charlotte Hays's *Being Dead Is No Excuse: The Official Southern Ladies Guide to Hosting the Perfect Funeral* (2005, reissued 2013), and Perre Coleman Magness's *The Southern Sympathy Cookbook: Funeral Food with a Twist* (2018). It is important to note that all the authors are white and cisgendered females. The conclusions that we draw from these books may suggest a model for feminine agency in defining social identity, but they are limited in their ability to speak for the entire southern experience.

PAIN AND PLEASURE IN COMMUNAL BELONGING: CASE STUDIES

Like a recipe, the logic of an argument for belonging to a particular group is a procedure with steps in order. The first piece of a cookbook writer's argument that following their advice will lead to community bonding is to provide recipes and advice for behavior that will mark the cook as a southern insider. All three cookbooks use the rhetoric of authenticity to argue that their recipes are unique to a southern place. When readers participate in funeral rituals with the advice of this cookbook, they will be noted as belonging to the geographical space. As Graham and Neville argue, the performance also must be "timeless," making a clear connection to southerners of the past.

The cookbooks stand in for inherited local knowledge by explicitly connecting recipes to the past and authoritative sources in narrative. Now that the cook is embedded in the community in time and space, they can begin to distinguish themselves within the community in displays of social capital, investing in their community in exchange for social status. Superlatives in the cookbooks promise that the cook will be remembered in the community as impressive, thoughtful, and helpful, and they may even become a necessary part of the community by developing a signature dish without which the ritual would be incomplete. The pleasure here is what Graham calls "continuing bonds," and if performed properly over time, the cook may achieve a kind of social afterlife, continuing their presence in the community through repetition of their recipes and stories of their place in the community.

It bears repeating that the gift of a good funeral performance is eternal life. The wages of sin may include a kind of social death. The stakes are life and death. Perhaps not literally, but in the lived experience of women in communities like the ones represented in these cookbooks, the benefits of bringing the right dish at the right time in the right way could be as concrete as guaranteeing a dish will appear when your time of need comes or securing a favor from a grateful recipient. The benefits may be as abstract as social power or even love. Bringing a good dish puts your name on a list of the kind, the generous, the aware, the involved. Bringing a bad dish puts your name on a list of the ignorant, the obtuse, the inconsiderate, the excluded. Failing to bring a dish at all is to be erased and irrelevant. The cookbooks for funeral foods promise far more than something that will taste good. They offer instructions for living forever.

It is not surprising that there are very few American cookbooks explicitly marketed as containing recipes for funeral foods. Like other cookbooks with a focus on painful subjects, the three funeral cookbooks examined here challenge some of the conventions of the cookbook genre, making them "exceptional" or unusually genre-blending. In many ways, *Food to Die For* (Ward) is a traditional community cookbook. It was produced locally as a fundraiser for the Old City Cemetery in Lynchburg, Virginia, a landmark in the city that is maintained in a public-private partnership between the city and a sixteen-member board called the Southern Memorial Association. The group has ties to "a group of women . . . organized to mark the graves and to oversee upkeep of the Confederate Section" of the cemetery established in 1866 (147). According to Ward, Lynchburg served as a Civil War hospital center. The 2,200 soldiers from fourteen states who died in Lynchburg were buried in this Confederate Section and marked with uniform headstones (147). In 1980, the Southern Memorial Association consisted of four women including Ward (147–48). The group expanded and formalized in the early 1990s to care for the cemetery at large, raising funds and overseeing a clean-up and redesign of the area into a multi-use public park and historical site (148–49). *Food to Die For* serves as a fundraiser for the Association and its activities like most community cookbooks. Ward's history of the Old City Cemetery towards the end of the book is reminiscent of the kinds of organizational histories one might find in a community cookbook. There are no images of food in this book, only photographs of the cemetery's past and present. All of this, plus the book's spiral binding and the shiny gold sticker announcing it as the National Winner of the Tabasco Community Cookbook Awards on my copy of the eighth printing from 2006, clearly mark *Food to Die For* as a community cookbook.

However, Ward is ostensibly the only author of this cookbook. She writes with a first-person pronoun and features many of her personal experiences and recipes. The prose surrounding the recipes bears the distinct mark of a single author's unique voice rather than the composite, anonymous voice representing a group that is more typical of the collectively authored community cookbook. The list of acknowledged contributors may be more reflective of Ward's social network than any particular geographic community. In other words, what this community of contributors most uniformly has in common (at least as evidenced by the text) is a relationship with the author. The traditional organization of the recipe section, the focus on practical advice, and the book's spiral binding all point toward a book that aims to be useful in the kitchen.

Of the three cookbooks, *Being Dead is No Excuse* presents the greatest challenges to the cookbook genre, functioning more as satire or parody, more like a creative nonfiction essay collection with recipes than a traditional cookbook. It seems intentionally unhelpful to a cookbook user in a hurry. The book is not organized in the expected courses or categories of dishes like *Food to Die For*. Instead, each chapter begins with a lengthy humorous essay, full of hyperbole, charming southern witticisms, and gossipy tales of Greenville, Mississippi. The recipes that follow are related to the topic of the essay. For example, one chapter essay focuses on the differences between the Episcopalian funeral customs at St. James's Church—more elite and alcohol-friendly—and the Methodist traditions—rich with condensed soup and nothing stronger than tea (27–38). Recipes are provided for dishes named in the essay: "The Ladies of St. James's Cheese Straws" (39–40) and "The Methodist Ladies' Chicken Lasagna Florentine" (54–55). *Being Dead is No Excuse* is first published in 2005, and it bears much in common with a series of imaginative cookbooks that came after it authored by Patsy Caldwell and Amy Lyles Wilson. The narrative elements of Caldwell and Wilson's cookbooks are set in the fictional town of Lucketville: *Bless Your Heart: Saving the World One Covered Dish at a Time* (2010), *You Be Sweet: Sharing Your Heart One Down Home Dessert at a Time* (2012), and *Y'all Come Over: A Celebration of Southern Hospitality, Food, and Memories* (2013). Caldwell and Wilson organize their chapters with recipes to follow fictional stories of a small town and its quirky characters. An afterword to the 2013 edition of *Being Dead* notes that the stories and characters are real to Greenville (237), but the tone and humor are nearly indistinguishable from the fictional counterparts.

In sum, *Being Dead is No Excuse* is what I call a literary cookbook, one with more interest in being read than being used. In fact, the size, shape, and binding of the cookbook has more in common with the paperback novel than a guide for cooking. The book contains no photos of food, people, or places, and only a few cartoony line drawings at the beginning of the essays. Unlike *Food to Die For*, with its helpful essays on decorum and practical advice, *Being Dead is No Excuse* is more focused on representing the spirit or character of a particular place than helping a reader in a practical sense. The audience is far more likely to be casual readers interested in the macabre humor of the title than eager cooks looking for information and advice. Ironically, the cookbook that is the least traditional in genre is also the most focused on pleasure, emphasizing the potential for fun and humor in the rituals surrounding death.

The Southern Sympathy Cookbook: Funeral Foods with a Twist is the newest of the cookbooks and the most faithful to genre conventions. It is organized by courses, and the chapter introductions and headnotes are generally instructive rather than humorous or chatty. Magness is a professional writer and cook living in Memphis, Tennessee. She is the author of the popular blog *The Runaway Spoon* and two other southern-themed cookbooks: *Pimento Cheese: The Cookbook* (2014) and *Southern Snacks* (2018). While Ward and Metcalf and Hays are locally bound to specific communities, Magness is more generalized. She makes references to her home in Memphis, her childhood spent in Columbia, Tennessee, as well as some dishes and sources that are specific to those places. Overall, Magness signals that she intends to represent the South as a whole. Magness frequently references her process of researching for the book by "asking every single person you encounter what they think of when they think 'funeral food'" (80). The crowdsourced nature of the book gives Magness the credibility to speak not just for her own peculiar family traditions or local customs, but to confidently speak for the entire cultural group known as "The South."

While funeral cookbooks are clearly about death and grief, they are never written with the bereaved as the intended audience. This is for good reason.

According to all three books, southern funeral traditions dictate that the people in the immediate circle of the person who died are not responsible for the food. They may need instructions for other protocols surrounding funerals and mourning like writing obituaries and thank you notes (Ward) or choosing a burial plot and venue for the funeral (Metcalf and Hays), but they don't need to know what to cook or how to serve it. That is the job of the social network of friends and relations. Metcalf and Hays explain: "A legion of friends working behind the scenes, coordinating the food, makes sure that the essential Delta death foods are represented in sufficient quantities. The best friend of the lady of the house, along with members of the appropriate church committee, swing into action without prompting" (2–3). Though the authors note that "Funeral procedure is something that we all just know" (2), the other two cookbooks seem intentionally directed at making what might be inherent or inherited knowledge explicit in text for the community surrounding the bereaved.

Ward notes explicitly that one of the purposes of *Food to Die For* is "to provide suggestions for lending thoughtful, practical, nonedible support to those who are dealing with loss. Offered here is the wisdom of people who have experienced the death of loved ones. They know which gestures are helpful and which are complicating" (1). The "tips and tales" that "herein lie" are for those with a degree of separation from the death. The "young friend" who asked Ward for advice "about what to say when a friend has died, but when he is not acquainted with anyone else in the friend's family" (10) is a prime example of the kind of distance from death that describes the audience of the cookbooks. Except for "Writing Thank You's for Funeral Foods," (15) the book is directed toward those lending support, not those dealing with loss. Even the hints for writing obituaries (usually the job of an intimate friend or family member) are mostly for the reader who will die someday to start writing their own obituary or to collect information that will help someone write their obituary (11–14). Of course, Ward acknowledges in her suggestions for writing condolence cards and obituaries that friends of the deceased will feel pain, too, at the loss of a friend and community member, but the aim of the book—and the appropriate response of this outer ring of the community—is primarily to bring comfort to someone else, though that act of support may be personally healing, too (7).

It is clear from the opening pages of *The Southern Sympathy Cookbook* that the pain in this cookbook is not the reader's pain. There is a pain in the reader's community, but at a distance from them. If there is any pain here, it is only sympathetic or empathetic pain, not direct. The introduction focuses on the occasion of comforting "a grieving family" (8–9). The southerner's "first thought" in times of trouble is "How can I feed them?" (8). The pronouns suggest again that the suffering is at some distance from the reader, happening to *them*. The only mention of the reader's potential sadness is in the suggestion that feeding those closer to the trauma can relieve difficult feelings: "We often express our emotions and process our grief through the act of nourishing our neighbors" (8). Whatever pain the reader may be in, the cookbook suggests that they may be able to experience comfort while comforting others. Though death and grief are moments of suffering for the bereaved, the function of the funeral extends beyond that immediate locus of pain into a community with easier access to feelings of pleasure and enjoyment.

Metcalf and Hays's *Being Dead is No Excuse* is especially free of suffering. Its sarcasm and irreverent humor disarm the sting of death, turning the funeral into "a social occasion" for delicious food, drinking, gossip, and humor (3). From the minister who accidentally falls into the open grave (9) to the "overserved" Sis McGee who passes out at the reception (101), funerals are full of moments to laugh at the absurdity of death and southern affectations. The audience is "Southern Ladies," those women whose class status and community connections mean they are called on to participate in many local funerals, not just those of close relations. The authors even report the words of a friend who may be called on to cook without a personal connection to the deceased at all: "When somebody dies, I may not know them well enough to go to the house or attend the funeral . . . but I can always take the family a cake or a casserole" (143–44). Personal pain is not required for participation in funeral rituals of food.

Though the pain that is the focus of funeral cookbooks is not directly experienced by the reader, funeral cookbooks do spend some time describing the pain of grief. In Magness's *Southern Sympathy Cookbook*, the experience of the bereaved is vague but includes: "a time of particular stress and sadness" (34), feeling a need for "a little sunshine in a dark time" (72), having "no will to cook" (96), looking for a solution for private family meals "in the gloomy days following [a funeral]" (118), and generally feeling too busy or overwhelmed with grief to perform the routine tasks of hosting guests in the home. Most of the time, Magness describes grief as simply needing comfort (98). *Comforting* or *comfort food* is a common refrain. It is often found paired with superlatives describing the dish as "incredibly comforting" (56), "the essence of comfort food and the perfect gift for a bereaved family" (84), "classic comfort food" (104), or "the most satisfying and comforting food gifts I know" (152). "There is something comforting" about "a creamy baked spinach dish" (74), and Magness notes that "something with the words gooey and butter in the name can only be immensely comforting" (34). Gifts of food can provide pleasant solutions to discomfort.

Magness is clearest about the specific suffering of children during a time of loss in the headnote for a baked spaghetti dish:

> It's important not to forget kids in times of trouble. Funerals and visitations can be confusing and sad and momentous all at once. Lots of old people patting you on the head. And a parade of congealed salads and unfamiliar casseroles on the table aren't exactly comforting to little ones. So here I present a casserole that will please everyone with its sheer comfort. This is the one to sit down to as a family after all the hullabaloo has quieted down. (130)

Magness invites an adult reader to empathize particularly with the grief of children, perhaps because adults need to be reminded of this distant experience in more detail than the more immediate feelings of other adults in bereavement. Like so many cookbooks examined in this volume, the cookbook only raises the specter of pain and suffering to provide the antidote to it, this time in the form of a familiar and kid-friendly spaghetti to eat quietly within the immediate family circle.

On two occasions in the book, Magness notes her own experience with being bereaved. She notes an unexpectedly delicious purple congealed salad that appeared around the death of her grandmother. Feeling obliged to politely sample the suspicious-looking dish, Magness and her mother and aunt "each scooped the smallest possible spoonfuls" to taste: "We all went back for seconds and scraped the dish clean" (71). After the death of her father, "Friends brought us a pork shoulder meal after my father's funeral and it was the perfect remedy. We absolutely devoured it" (124). In both instances, the hearty eating and return of appetite through delicious food is evidence of comfort.

The cookbooks acknowledge that the reader-cook may not be in the direct epicenter of suffering after a death in the community, but Ward allows that there are still painful feelings. The suffering that Ward describes most often in the introductory pages is feeling awkwardness and uncertainty. Her young friend, who is ostensibly the intended audience of the book, "feels uncertain about words that will be meaningful and sensitive when he is face to face with the family at a post-funeral reception or at a calling hour at the family's home" (10). "*Everybody* has anxiety," Ward acknowledges, but she "will not tell you that it gets any easier. Becoming an old hand at funeral going makes the ritual only a *little* less threatening" (emphasis in original, 10). Ward describes the feeling of awkwardness at showing up without an invitation (it's not a wedding; no one gets invited to a funeral) and the fear of adding to the person's pain by saying the wrong thing (you won't have time to say much anyway; don't be original). Ward acknowledges these feelings as valid and natural and then smooths them over by reminding the reader that their presence is wanted (10) and that they can trust that their sincerity and intuition will carry them through (11). Ward gently reminds the reader to keep their pain in perspective by praising their bravery with just a hint of irony: "You have done a kind thing by overcoming feelings of awkwardness, rigging up in Sunday clothes and by making contact. You may have experienced some discomfort, but I assure you that your presence is remembered with gratitude" (11). You may have felt awkward and uncomfortable and had to put on pinchy shoes, but these are minor inconveniences for the benefit of the social circle.

Because pain is held at a distance from the reader and it has a concrete solution in the form of food, the tone of the funeral cookbooks is light and airy. Metcalf and Hays especially take humor and minimizing painful feelings as a *raison d'etre*. Magness's book is peppered with jokes from Mark Twain, humorous stories of funeral faux pas, and unusual passages from obituaries interspersed throughout the recipes. It can be easy to forget that these are foods to make and take to a funeral, a visitation, or a homegoing. The dishes in the cookbook are crowd-pleasers, inexpensive and portable in portions for large groups. In fact, Magness notes that many of the recipes in the book have been tested in other kinds of social gatherings like a "book clubs, supper clubs, family dinners," (100, see also 44, 121, 128, 150), or that they have traditions in communal meals beyond the funeral like a "baby shower, wedding party, holiday celebration, or tailgate" (42), "church supper, dinner on the ground," (62), "Christmas Eve and New Year's Eve" parties (84), "wedding showers and ladies' birthdays" (184), or "ladies' luncheons and church potlucks" (98). They may even be appropriate for other kinds of food gifts like hams (66) and divinity (a meringue-like candy with nuts) (164) for Christmas.

Ward provides a recipe for "Sweet Briar Cookies," so named because they are served at Sweet Briar College functions (106), and Metcalf and Hays note the tradition of "Methodist Party Potatoes" that are essential to but not exclusive to that Delta Methodist funeral (58). The reminders of these other community meals take readers away from the funeral and visitation from time to time, and it invites them to use the cookbook more often for less fraught occasions. It is a rhetorical move that centers pleasure more frequently than pain.

When a cookbook writer shares recipes connected to the funeral feast and the stories that accrue to the dishes served, they are essentially enacting the pleasurable storytelling and communal aspects of the funeral that Graham and Neville describe without the painful occasion of a death. Readers may encounter the funeral cookbook at any time. There need not be pain in the community for the reader of a collection of funeral recipes to experience the resurrection of ancestors in story or the embodied practice of cooking and eating food that ritually binds them into a community. No pain must be endured to experience the joys of the locally-bound and communally-practiced traditions of southern funerals, even if only experienced in the reader's imagination. The genre of the cookbook and its requirement for pleasure gives ample opportunity for writers to emphasize the many pleasures of cooking, eating, and imagining what is presented as a distinctly southern experience.

THE PLEASURES OF BELONGING: INTEGRATION AND DISTINCTION

First, and perhaps most obviously, the food produced with these recipes should bring pleasure to those in pain. The goal is to produce "comforting, sustaining, and well, practical food" (Magness 8). It should be "wholesome, satisfying, and most of all, enjoyable. Something that will be truly appreciated and do what it is meant to do—provide comfort, show kindness, and hopefully bring some joy" (9). At the very least, the gift of food should "remove at least one mundane worry" (9). Metcalf and Hays note that "You get the best food at funerals," (2) and "Nobody in the world eats better that the bereaved Southerner" (143). Ward, too, writes, "Practically, and psychologically, the edible offering provides sustenance and comfort," and the ideal funeral food gift is "delicious, familiar, and portable" (1). All three cookbooks also suggest that the giver of the gift of food receives pleasure in this exchange as well in the form of emotional satisfaction, the feeling of being helpful and significant to your community, "to feel useful in a fearful time" (Magness 9).

I argue that the greatest pleasures promised by funeral cookbooks are first, to be integrated into the community through food-based rituals of mourning, and second, to earn distinction within the community as especially knowledgeable, generous, thoughtful, or skilled. If funerals are an opportunity to ritually perform a unique and timeless southern identity, then these cookbooks provide the recipes for belonging.

The recipe for belonging looks something like this:

1. Connect to your local community through a food contribution that is appropriate to place.
2. Incorporate yourself into the collapse of time by bringing a "timeless" or traditional dish that has roots in a place-based community past.
3. Distinguish yourself within the community with an impressive display without looking like you want to distinguish yourself.

4. Secure an afterlife as an essential part of the community, a link in a chain of inheritance.

COMMUNITY IN PLACE

If Graham is correct, the recipes for funeral foods emerge from the local community and its matriarchs of the past; social resurrection of the dead cannot occur when recipes come from outside the community or from contemporary sources. Funeral foods are also local expressions of local identity, most often archived in personal manuscript collections and community cookbooks (especially those created by religious bodies where funeral services may be held). If southern funerals are such hyper-local affairs, what would be the purpose of a commercially published and nationally available collection of recipes explicitly for southern funerals? The widely circulated cookbook seems counterproductive to the place-based and timeless folk-liturgy that Neville describes. However, the cookbooks are careful to locate their recipes in an authentic southern place, recognizing that their readers need a cookbook because they can't connect to place using the culinary knowledge in their own network.

The existence of the commercially published funeral cookbooks examined here suggests that southern food traditions around funerals need some explaining or marketing to a wider audience which may include some self-identified southerners without a southern matriarch to resurrect or a deep well of local knowledge to draw upon. A reader-cook with a weak personal network must look outside for information about how to behave in their own community. Similarly, even deeply connected southerners, like my writing partner and Appalachian foodways scholar Erica Abrams Locklear, may know what place-based dishes are appropriate, but they do not know the steps for preparing them. Erica left me this note when she read this paragraph in draft form:

> I suspect there are plenty of people (myself included!) who consider themselves southerners, who have the repository of local knowledge and deep connection to place, and know what to bring (Mabel Duckett's ham biscuits) but lack the culinary knowhow to actually prepare the dish .... I can rattle off the important foods for days, but put me in the kitchen and tell me to make them, and I'm immediately googling to find recipes. A cookbook would help!

In both instances, a reader has the desire to fit into a local community but is missing key information to successfully perform their role as an "authentic" southerner and support to the bereaved.

The story of "Elizabeth" that appears in the margins of the recipe for "Brown Sugar Angel Food Cake" in Magness's *The Southern Sympathy Cookbook* explains most clearly what role the commercial cookbook can play in connecting a reader to their local community. In the anecdote from "many decades ago," Elizabeth moves to a new town with her husband. When her husband's boss dies, she prepares a cake from her family's repertoire that she thinks is appropriate for the funeral. It's a hit until she reveals that the cake contains rum, and the entire congregation of "teetotalers" spits their cake out in horror. Magness concludes: "Elizabeth bought *The Joy of Cooking* and learned to make a chocolate cake" (149). The fact that Elizabeth is so startled to find her new southern town to be morally opposed to alcohol consumption suggests she is from some other nonsouthern place in need of a helpful guide to understanding the intricacies of southern funerals and communities. She only has *The Joy of Cooking* and an embarrassing episode to guide her, but Magness's readers now have access to insider information Elizabeth could not have had many decades ago. Readers like Elizabeth who don't have a local network can count on *The Southern Sympathy Cookbook* to fill in that gap.

Like Magness, Ward recognizes that the audience of *Food to Die For* lacks experience and local knowledge. Instead of writing for folks like Elizabeth from out of town, Ward aims her advice at young people and novice cooks who are more like Erica, lacking procedural knowledge (10, 28). More than once, Ward specifically notes that she is writing to "new cooks" who will need some things explicitly written down that more experienced cooks have "taken for granted" as obvious (67) such as how to wrap sandwiches in paper towels to keep them fresh when made ahead (28). Presumably, the readers of this book are those who aren't experienced with death and don't yet know what part they will play in the rituals of their place to be a comfort to their community. They need the advice of adults who are not in their kinship networks.

Metcalf and Hays seem to be addressing an audience that is already self-identified as southern but may need more information about hyperlocal customs. The subtitle is *The Official Southern Ladies Guide to Hosting the Perfect Funeral*, but the narratives focus more locally on the specific location of Greenville, Mississippi, by addressing a second-person *you*, an implied audience who needs to know how to behave in Greenville. The opening chapter, "Dying Tastefully in the Mississippi Delta" describes what happens in the community when a death occurs, assuming that the reader does not already know this (1–2). The chapter contains a lot of insider information specific to behavior in Greenville including where the deceased is likely to be buried and how to get a "good" spot in the exclusive old cemetery: "The old cemetery is one of the best addresses in Greenville, Mississippi. Being buried anywhere else is a fate worse than death in Greenville" (3). The authors suggest which local churches to belong to in life to get the best funeral upon death:

> Anyone in our neck of the woods who is not counting on immortality might want to give serious thought to taking the appropriate steps to becoming a communicant of St. James' Episcopal Church before it's too late. No, belonging to St. James' won't necessarily get you into heaven. But it will ensure that have a tasteful sendoff. (27)

The rituals around death are part of belonging to the community. "We're people with a strong sense of community," Metcalf and Hays write. "Being dead is no impediment to belonging to it. We won't forget you just because you've up and died" (4). This message is borne out in the narratives when Metcalf and Hays make references to the long dead in Greenville and name recipes after their innovators (Aunt Hebe's coconut cake [12] and Virginia's butter beans [49]). The cookbooks are built on the assumption that the reader needs place-based information that they cannot get from their own local network. So the first step in the process of creating belonging is to locate the recipe in place with geographic specificity and southern authenticity. All three cookbooks mark southern funeral rituals and the foods that support them as unique to place.

The cookbooks suggest that the southern funeral is self-consciously and intentionally unique among American funeral practices with its own specific language and traditions. Ward introduces a section called "Funeral Phrases" to explain "colloquial" language surrounding death that is particular to central Virginia including a definition of "cortege" (funeral procession [3]), what it means to be "on the door" (friends who serve as gatekeepers at the home of the bereaved [4]), and a meditation on keeping a home and life "in dying order" (so organized that you could die at any moment and not leave a mess for your mourners [4–6]). Magness, too, uses side notes throughout the book to define and explain unusual customs like "The Visitation" (the local name for a gathering before a funeral [13]), "The Funeral Fan" (a paper fan on a wooden stick to keep cool [43]), and the "Home-Going" (services that focus on a celebration of life and sending the deceased "home to heaven to be with Jesus" [79]).

The cookbooks characterize rituals beyond food that are authentic by being geographically specific. All three cookbooks argue that the tradition of writing obituaries is unique to the South. Ward devotes four pages to giving advice on writing obituaries with an outline to follow. While her general advice is "a 'just the facts, ma'am' approach," she provides a sample of a 2004 obituary from the Lynchburg *News and Advance* newspaper that flouts all her advice. Linda Thomas, the daughter of the deceased Edna Lollis Thomas, packs her obituary with self-deprecating humor and charming jokes at her mother's expense. "She had two daughters, one of whom died at age 16," Thomas writes, "She would have been a greater comfort and joy to her throughout her life than the other, but the surviving one did the best she could and will miss her" (14).

While Ward notes this as an "unconventional obituary," it is exactly the kind of obituary Magness includes throughout *The Southern Sympathy Cookbooks* as exemplary of the form. Magness fills interstitial spaces between recipes with quotations from obituaries in southern newspapers that represent a unique memorial tradition. The first of these quotations is the worst of them, a cautionary tale: "She had no hobbies, made no contribution to society and rarely shared a kind word or deed in her life. I speak for the majority of her family when I say her presence will not be missed by many, very few tears will be shed and there will be no lamenting her passing" (14). This brutal posthumous takedown from Galveston, Texas, printed just below the recipe for buttermilk banana bread, is a shocking example of an "only in South" obituary. The next quotation Magness takes from an obituary is its opposite: "Heaven now smiles with the addition of this precious soul from our midst whose radiant spirit shall now join with the elders, the angels, the saints, and the heavenly chorus in singing praises unto God throughout the eternal ages" (18). The implication is that obituaries may range in tone from extremes, but the obituary is practiced in the South in ways that make it distinct.

Metcalf and Hays devote most of the chapter "Who Died? Stuffed Eggs, Etiquette, and Delta Pate" to the obituary, especially the little exaggerations and euphemisms that can hide the truth. "A glowing obituary is practically a birthright in the Delta," the writers explain (67). "While Bubba Boone [the local undertaker] prettifies the mortal remains for the visitation, somebody else touches up the incorporeal remains for the newspaper" (68). No matter how degenerate the deceased—like a "well-known local roué and cad" who was murdered for philandering (69) or the "Janis Joplin of the plantation set" who lived as an expatriate hippie in New Orleans (70)—all reputations can be rehabilitated with a creative obituary.

From funeral fans to flower arrangements and hymns sung, to the order of events in the days before and after a funeral, the cookbooks argue that the funeral rituals are unique and local to the South, supporting Wilson's conclusion that what makes the southern funeral unique is its self-conscious insistence on being distinct. This uniqueness certainly carries over to the dishes appropriate to southern funerals. All three books attempt to catalog the essential dishes for southern funerals. One of the ways that Magness highlights the appropriateness of dishes is to note that they sometimes go by the shorthand name of "funeral X": including "funeral beans" (76), "funeral baked beans" (78), "funeral chicken" (102), "funeral sandwiches" (121), and "funeral brisket" (128). In addition to being essentially appropriate for funerals, the recipes in *The Southern Sympathy Cookbook* make reference to being essentially—even "quintessentially"—southern. Of the seventy-eight recipes in Magness's book, forty-two have headnotes that mention being a uniquely southern tradition or including a distinctly southern ingredient. Sweet tea (12, 38), home baked biscuits (31), roasted pecans (41), pickled shrimp (48), black eyed peas and cornbread (60), tomato aspic (68), black walnuts (73), collard greens (74), and ever so many more dishes are all described as "truly a Southern standard" (80), "classic" (16, 56, 74), or otherwise "ubiquitous" in the South (12). Magness even claims that "full Southern lady credentials" include "be[ing] able to make an aspic" for a funeral (68). All of these provide evidence of the authenticity of the recipes for performing southern identity.

Metcalf and Hays distinguish essential southern funeral foods as rich and especially unhealthy: "Southern funeral food won't bring back the dead—in fact, it's so rich it may be food to die *from*" (144). They describe two "tiers" of funeral food: "*haute* funeral food, which includes aspics, homemade mayonnaise, and dainty homemade rolls," and the "Campbell's soup based" dishes that rely on convenience ingredients like "Velveeta cheese, almond slivers, French-fried (canned) onions, and Ritz crackers" (144). The reliance on convenience ingredients is partly to keep the community ready to provide food quickly in times of crisis (145), and partly because "Food is grief therapy in the Delta" and these foods are "guaranteed to bring comfort" (144). The authors are clearest in a headnote for "Parmesan Squash Casserole" when they note, "We understand that outsiders consider [casseroles] tacky, but they are the essence of funeral food in the South" (160).

Ward notes that regional foods are good for bringing to funerals, especially if the giver needs to rely on preprepared or catered food. Ward admonishes the reader to "Think what foods, available to you any day, you would really miss if you moved to another place. Or if the food provider shut down" (21). Ward even provides space on that page for the reader to write in "your own favorite take-out possibilities. Think most particularly of good versions of regional favorites" (22). In the chapter on vegetable side dishes, Ward attempts to codify recipes so familiar to regional cooks that they often do not get written down: "These are the foods that often define what we think of as Virginia food and for which most good cooks would be hard put to give definite proportions" (67).

Though Ward does note that appropriate funeral foods are connected to the South or to central Virginia, she seems less invested in the regionally place-based aspect of the food offerings than on the appropriateness of the food to the situation where it is being eaten, i.e., at a church table, on a lap in a living room, standing around a funeral home, etc. Ward explains that there are a number of events surrounding a funeral in the South where a gift of food is appropriate, and each one has specific needs and considerations. Whether it is "the potluck meals to provide for gathered family" or "organized meals and receptions that often follow a funeral service," there are specific food related protocols to follow (117). But more typical of Ward's definition of essential funeral food is that combination of "familiar" (read: local) and "practical" (read: appropriate to the setting) found in this headnote for ham biscuits:

> Ham Biscuits are the quintessential offering at bereavement. They abide by all the rules of Funeral Food. They are pickup food that require no additional fussing over. They can be eaten for breakfast, lunch, or supper. They are familiar and comforting. Virginia ham does not require refrigeration, though it would be a good idea to refrigerate if they last overnight. (131)

Ward's insistence on Smithfield-branded Virginia ham is a nod to an essential local practice, but the rest of the note makes clear that in Ward's opinion, what makes funeral food successful is how it "behaves" in the place where it is served. Her greatest praises are reserved for foods like Chicken Tetrazzini which "can claim all the attributes of well-behaved Funeral Foods. Is it a food that almost all people like. It can be made ahead, it freezes well, and it expands to feed crowds, if needed. Goodness knows it is familiar! It is smooth and rich and comforting" (35).

The foods are described as essentially southern, but the authors go even further by suggesting that the impulse to bring food is innate to southerners. Magness mentions that southerners have a "particular way . . . of combining sorrow and joy" (79). Feeding neighbors in pain is an essential southern practice. "Funerals in the South are synonymous with food," Magness claims. The "first thought" is food. Magness hails the reader as an authentic southerner when she notes: "There are times when your instinct, your heart's reaction, is to prepare food" (8). This reaction to grief is at the reader's core. The instinct to seek out a cookbook to learn to prepare food after a death is itself a sign of authentic southernness. Being truly southern means fitting into the local southern community or practicing southernness wherever the reader may be.

The challenge presented by these commercially available cookbooks is that they are a replacement for a more "authentic" source of knowing. Graham and Neville both emphasize that the rituals of funerals that result in community bonding start and end with in-network and local recipes. The cookbooks take on this challenge in part by locating themselves geographically in the South, but more importantly, they validate the sources of their recipes as local and authoritative. Most single-authored and commercially published cookbooks would get their ethos from originality and professional chefs, but the nature of the funeral ritual places far more authority on the "tried-and-true" and humble authorities of home cooks.

Magness convinces her audience that she is providing local information by citing regular cooks and friends, not professional chefs. The crowdsourced nature of the book gives Magness the credibility to speak not just for her own peculiar family traditions or local customs, but to confidently speak for the entire cultural group known as "The South." She also notes that her recipes are not always completely original inventions; she frequently researches community cookbooks for basic recipes that she can innovate with. The existence of the recipe as "a stalwart community cookbook recipe" (56) or something "you'll find ... in almost every Southern community cookbook" (80) connects Magness's collection back to that local community source of authority. The sources for Magness's recipes are authenticated as grassroots innovations, emerging from inside the community (especially of ordinary women contributors) rather than coming from the outside.

For example, Magness decides to include macaroni salad as an essential funeral food after finding it in one of the most southern places on earth:

> I never thought of macaroni salad as a funeral food until I was attending a wedding at a very, very small church in a very, very small Mississippi town. As I was waiting in the vestibule to be ushered down the aisle, I glanced at a church bulletin board and saw a sign up sheet for the funeral reception of a congregation member, three people had signed up to bring macaroni salad. (64)

This episode is offered as evidence of authenticity, endorsed by the people with the most authority on what is appropriate for a southern funeral: church ladies from rural Mississippi.

Ward, too, locates her expertise in a network of local experts. *Food to Die For* also includes contributions from named local figures in the spirit of the community cookbook. Ward states explicitly in the introduction, cleverly titled "Herein Lie Tips and Tales," that the book is meant to capture something of the local community and its local foodways: "It will be a by-product of this book to tell you something about the characters and interesting people of Lynchburg.... We hope this book captures the traditional recipes of Lynchburgers before they are lost" (1). Though I argue that Ward's book has more in common with the single-authored commercial cookbooks that are the center of my research, Ward markets the cookbook as a community cookbook—a far more authoritative source for "authentic," place-based recipes than a commercial book.

Ward makes ninety-one mentions of other people who innovated or contributed recipes, from her college roommate Julia (55) to "the first First Lady Bush" (108). Twenty-two other textual sources are cited including community cookbooks (*Hot Springs, Virginia Presbyterian Cookbook* 92), commercially published cookbooks (Julia Child's *The Way to Cook* 81), and recipes printed on packages (The Hellman's Mayonnaise label 75). The nature of her sources is humble and local. She tells her readers, "get your recipes from good non-cooks." Do not trust celebrity cooks "who do not have to wash their own pots and pans," but look to a real local who serves good food but claims they hate cooking (23). These are the people who will have recipes that are easy and accessible for any kind of cook. The real authorities for what to bring to a funeral are local and ordinary. Mixed in with recipes for bringing food to a funeral, Ward also offers instructions for how to integrate the reader into their own local community by finding the right authorities and asking the right questions.

Ward gives the reader permission to consider their own special locality as they read. Ward's book even has a special page at the back for writing your own favorite recipe into the book with an invitation to submit it to Ward for inclusion in future volumes of the cookbook (180). There is also a space for the reader to collect local information about restaurants and stores that sell "good versions of regional favorites" that can be purchased instead of making a dish (22). Along with Ward's repeated instructions to look locally for good recipes, these suggestions point readers to a performance that will connect them to the essential qualities of their local place and the region at large.

COMMUNITY IN TIME

While commercially published recipes may not be able to collapse time through continuing bonds to specific people in the same way that cooking from the family recipe card box can, these cookbooks do offer "timeless" suggestions that will help relative outsiders join the fabric of a local community by giving them instructions on how to act like an insider. Ward notes that traditional dishes at funerals "are connections to the past at a time when those connections are important" (1). The suggestion is that a death is a time to solidify temporal continuity in a community, despite the obvious rupture of loss. The funeral highlights continuity and chains of inheritance. One person has passed, but they came from somewhere in the past and they are survived by future generations if they have been influential in life. Though readers who would look to a commercial cookbook for instructions may not have inherited place-based knowledge, the cookbooks mark recipes as timeless, classic, traditional, or connected specifically to deceased contributors so that the reader may create the illusion of inherited knowledge and join the temporal confluence created by the funeral ritual.

The rhetoric of "timelessness" often appears side-by-side with statements of place-based authenticity. For Magness, "tradition" and "classic" mark the age of a recipe, but they also mark continuous practice in the South. Cranberry salad is presented as "a truly classic congealed salad" served with "Southern black walnuts," (73) and "Classic Chicken Salad with Grapes and Poppy Seeds" is "the classic southern tea room chicken salad" (96). Magness simply notes that "you can't go wrong with the classic" (157) or the "old-school comfort" that comes with nostalgic dishes like "Pineapple Upside Down Bundt Cake (146). In each case, Magness highlights the timelessness of her offerings.

However, unlike the other writers in this sample, Magness is also invested in updating or modernizing "classics" by removing the convenience ingredients that give southern funeral foods a bad reputation (or authenticity, depending on who you ask). Her recipe for cucumber ring with a smoked salmon centerpiece—a gelatin mold surrounding slices of fish—speaks to "a certain Sixties chic" trend, but Magness's version is "modern and sophisticated without a hint of lime Jello or packet seasoning." The ring mold is made with white wine, plain gelatin, cucumber, onion, buttermilk, mayonnaise, lemon, and dill (52). Similarly, Magness removes all the canned ingredients from "Southern Three Bean Salad with Bacon Vinaigrette." Magness argues that she protects "the spirit of the dish" but makes it "fresher and crisper," a change that her father would approve (62). Invoking her father's approval ensures that the recipe is close to its roots in the past even as it is improved for the present.

Magness attempts to convince the reader that her amendments to the recipes are not actually "updating" at all but removing a marker of time. Ambrosia—a ubiquitous citrus salad-slash-dessert—is both "traditional" and "a piece of Southern culinary history." Magness claims, "I stick to the truly classic version, not the creamy Cool Whip and marshmallow calamity that followed." Instead, she is following "the most traditional ambrosia recipes" that focus on fresh fruit and a simple syrup (82). Magness redefines *when* the tradition starts. She presents what might look like updating a recipe as a return to a deeper past. Again, convenience ingredients are a mark against authenticity. What is more dated than "red dye number three jello"? (73). What could be more timeless than cooking with seasonal produce? "Fresh, in-season, local strawberries are one of life's great pleasures, so why muck them up with chemicals and additives and fake gunk?" (15), Magness asks. The "return" to simplicity before industrial food is itself an argument for "timeless" authenticity.

Ward's cookbook includes chapters on nineteenth-century foods and funeral traditions to advertise the work of the cemetery museum, but they have the added benefit of marking the whole book as historical, arguing that the present performance is continuous with the distant past. The activities of the cemetery's public museums bring the past into the present, and the text around Ward's recipes promises historical connections. Ward introduces a nineteenth-century "Funeral Pie," described as ideal in one cookbook because it "'was easy, made from non-seasonal ingredients, and could be taken long distances without spoiling.' Those are good twenty-first-century virtues for funeral food as well, but were essential in the nineteenth century" (161). The past is good enough for the present. The recipe is perfectly sensible and accessible to a twenty-first-century cook despite its distant origins. Ward's most common synonym for timeless is "familiar," an appellation given to chicken tetrazzini (35) and ham biscuits (131) and pimento cheese (134). Ward highlights the familial chain of inheritance that is the preferred method for creating that sense of timelessness in evoking "Our grandmothers' recipes" (1). Though these recipes "have evolved" and "have been made easier by microwaves and processors," Ward assures readers that "the essentials remain for familiar food that has brought us together for generations" (1). Ward seeks to codify the recipes that are so familiar that they "are known by heart" and "taken for granted" (67): recipes that are unwritten and liable to disappear with the passing of a generation (1) who will not experience a social afterlife if their recipes are "lost." Timelessness is guaranteed by repetition.

Metcalf and Hays create a sense of a timeless and unchanging southern culture. Though they joke about how women in their forties (in 2005) are disappointing their mothers by having jobs and not staying up all night, this seems to be one of only a few acknowledgments that the present is any different from the era of southern belles attending cotillion (133). Essays refer to the antebellum South with nostalgia for a past not too far gone. Plantations still exist with private family cemeteries (5), and the narrator wishes enviously that her family "still had a private cemetery. Note the *still*" (emphasis in original 6). *Still* suggests a direct familial connection to an antebellum planter class. The Civil War is invoked sarcastically as "The Wah-wuh" (33, 176), and throughout the essays, "Yankee" is used as an insult (72). A section on which hymns to choose for a funeral puts a firm limit of nothing newer than 1940 (174). Mostly, timelessness is achieved by simply stating that rituals are the way they have always been. *Always* is a keyword repeated often in the essays and headnotes: "We always plan to have a good time at the reception" (3); "Southern women always want to look their best" (7); "Somebody always brings a supermarket platter of deli ham" (23); "You can always tell when a Methodist dies—there are lots of casseroles" (34). The nostalgic tone and broad generalizations suggest that things in Greenville don't change; the advice in the book will be as timeless as the unchanging place.

DISTINCTION IN COMMUNITY

The funeral meal binds the diners together in a community, but within that community, individual members may distinguish themselves. Magness and Metcalf and Hays are most open in their recognition that a good performance in a funeral can be a social benefit to the cook. Just as easily, a poor performance can have devastating effects on the cook's reputation. Contemporary food scholars Lisa Heldke, Josee Johnston and Shyon Baumann, and Peter Nacarrato and Kathleen Lebesco have authored three separate interrogations into the culture of the food connoisseur, drawing on Pierre Bourdieu's *Distinction* to describe how today's consumers food culture gather cultural and social capital through food discourse to form their identities. Distinction is the cultural project of developing and displaying "taste," in both uses of the word. When individuals read cookbooks, perform recipes, eat the results, share food with others and talk about their process, they are actively engaged in processes of taste education and class distinction. Bringing food to a funeral is an occasion for publicly displaying taste and class, exchanging food (culinary capital) for praise and status (social capital).

Magness notes frequently in the headnotes within the recipe sections that certain foods and actions will earn the cook significance in the community. Often, this significance looks like winning: earning the most social capital by being the most helpful, the most thoughtful, the most comforting, most memorable, most skilled, or most unique. Magness notes which recipes "look impressive" or have a "spectacular presentation" (50, 52, 71). The dual (and equal) purposes of the "Visitation" are for guests to reminisce while eating and "for the ladies in the equation to show off their skills in the kitchen" (13). The funeral is the time when "everyone always puts their best foot forward, bringing the dish they are particularly proud of—one that is sure to impress" (50). It is an essential part of the funeral ritual to show off a little, Magness argues, including in the visual presentation of the dish in a crystal bowl (48), an heirloom Jello mold ("an absolute mainstay, in fact the pride and joy, of any hostess's table" 71), or the good silver (117). The dish, the artistic presentation, and the material object of the container are all displays of social and culinary capital that grant the giver local distinction.

Magness uses the potential to impress as an argument to persuade the reader to stop reading and start cooking. "People will swoon over your homemade rolls," Magness promises, "as much for the flavor as for the fact you made them yourself" (33). This extra effort to be homemade and fresh (avoiding the convenience ingredients that Metcalf and Hays argue are essential) is key in earning distinction as a cook who can connect to the traditions of the past while demonstrating better taste and culinary skills than one's forebears. Those recipes filled with "canned green beans, canned soup, and fried bits of something" are deemed by Magness to be a "sulfurous, chemical abomination" (76). Magness deems recipes "impressive" when they require additional difficulty in the procedure or higher-quality, more expensive ingredients. Magness's call to use "the best" ingredients like "European style butter and farm fresh local eggs" (152) or "fresh, in-season, local strawberries" (15) and "a minimum of the truly odd ingredients you sometimes see in old recipes" (68) is meant to help the reader earn distinction in the community by simultaneously being faithful to the spirit of the traditional while providing something that tastes better and shows better taste.

While Ward is less focused on standing out as "impressive"—a move she would certainly consider selfish and self-aggrandizing—she particularly encourages her readers to find a way to distinguish themselves in the community as a predictable source of a particular food. She gives the example of her friend Duane Nelligan who "frequently delivers tenderloin as her Funeral Food. She is a mighty welcome sight when there are several days between death and a funeral with gathered family needing breakfast, lunch, and supper" (42). By being someone who can be counted on for a special contribution, Nelligan is a "welcome sight" and a valued member of the community. Ward tells her readers to collect recipes into their own bound manuscript cookbooks in order to establish their own "signature" dishes:

> Into this cookbook will go the recipes you return to over and over, year in and year out. Your cookbook will contain foods you feel really comfortable serving.... This will be your signature food book. Whatever the original source, you have cooked the dishes so long and

so often that they are yours! . . . When you are at a loss for what to serve, you can open your book and be reassured by the recipes and menus that have successfully appeared at your table many times. (26)

This advice is not only about making life easier for the cook and reader, but also about making a "signature," a unique identity in the community.

Perhaps when Nelligan herself has passed on, her association with the tenderloin will be strong enough that the presence of a tenderloin at a funeral meal will be evidence of her ongoing social influence, a continuing bond after death. Ward's advice is less oriented towards a temporary experience of appreciation or improving social status than it is oriented towards establishing the kind of reputation that would make a cook's name synonymous with a highly valued dish. The true sign that a cook has become embedded in a local community is that their signature dish is so firmly associated with the ritual of the community that it is taken for granted while alive and reintegrated into the fabric of the community practice when they are dead.

When the afterlife is on the line, the stakes of the funeral food performance are high. As I argue above, success can mean a permanent place in the community that outlives the cook, having agency on the community long after death. By the same token, poor performance in this situation can have the opposite effect, excluding the cook from the process of identity-making, essentially a social death-in-life. Graham defines social death as "being forgotten by individuals" and "ceasing to exert influence and exercise agency within a particular group" (91). *Social death* as a concept is intricately connected with race; the term was coined by Orlando Patterson in 1982 to describe the state of enslavement as a still-living person with the social agency and power of a corpse (13). To be socially dead means to be biologically alive but considered unworthy of taking time and resources from the living. Social death precedes, even predicts, a physical death—usually violent or painful. When using "social death" as a term to describe upper to middle class white women and their social and culinary reputations *after* physical death, it's worth considering in context. No, it is not likely that the consequences of a bad funeral dish would be equal to the dehumanization of being enslaved, but in communities like the ones imagined in these funeral cookbooks, social networks are small and social capital moves through them rapidly with high social stakes.

When I mentioned in the opening pages that my family had been fed by our church, friends, and family, these were all the same people. My elementary school's principal—my mother's employer—was also a member of our church, and they shared a Sunday School class that my father led. The principal's father was a local judge. When my mother brought a covered dish to his mother's funeral, it was not only a gesture of friendship but also a tribute owed to a family with power over her job. Remember the cautionary tale of Elizabeth who served the dry church a rum cake? That was her husband's boss's funeral. They had just moved to town for him to take this job, and the funeral was likely her first opportunity to meet women in the community (149). Consider the risk of being the new hire at a business whose founder has just died. What consequences could he have faced at work for showing himself a true outsider? Consider the loneliness of being new in town. What relationships were over before they began as a result of Elizabeth making this bad impression? Social life may depend heavily upon a good performance in a tense time.

Metcalf and Hays note with some disdain how a poor performance can identify the cook as an outsider with serious material consequences. Asking for a Cobb salad instead of enjoying the cream-of-mushroom laced casserole gets a niece from California written out of her aunt's will (145), and a bad thank you note earns the criticism, "I bet her mother wasn't a Southern girl" (75). Though the authors give a wide latitude in terms of food quality that is acceptable to bring to a funeral, there are things that are simply "not the done things," like paper napkins, drinking too much, and eating too early (104). Perhaps the greatest consequence of a bad performance is getting written up in *Being Dead is No Excuse*.

The right actions performed with the wrong motives are as damning as any social misstep. Ward notes that a self-centered supporter is worse than no support at all. In the glossary of funeral phrases, she notes two figures who may be overstepping the boundaries of propriety by using a death in the community as an opportunity for attention. A "Funeral Fairy" is "a person who is inspired into action by news of a death no matter how remote the acquaintance. She has that casserole ready. This is a thoughtful person, though perhaps a little too eager to share the spotlight focused on the recently departed" (4). Ward seems to be aware of a delicate boundary between being thoughtful and wishing to be thought of. The actions of the "Funeral Fairy" and a concerned friend are identical—bringing a casserole— but the giver must give without appearing to even *want* a benefit from the action, or else the benefit will not come.

According to Ward, the "Funeral Tsar" is "the person who takes command, whether bidden to do so or not, and issues commands to food donors so that the resulting potluck covers all the food groups" (4). A very necessary person, the hint in "whether bidden to do so or not" is perhaps to wait to be invited into this role. In Metcalf and Hays's book, this person is called "The Handmaiden of the Bereaved" "because she always shows up and takes over (or tries to) when there is a death" (101). The sarcasm of "Tsar" and "Handmaiden" suggests a power grab that would be indelicate and inappropriate to take by force. The most distinguished roles in a funeral ritual cannot be taken or even visibly sought without the risk of appearing self-interested, ruining the effect of community cohesion and the chances of social advancement.

For Ward, the worst kind of performance in a funeral ritual is one that does not take into account the practicalities of space, time, temperature, and numbers. "Arbitrarily presenting a casserole or other large item before knowing the situation can cause problems for those in charge of the kitchen," Ward warns. "Refrigeration limitations and oversupply, in general, can make the casserole more a threat than a promise" (33). Ward has a special disdain for "fussy" foods that require special utensils for serving or eating (20–21) because they show a lack of care and awareness for how that food comes into contact with real people. The person wishing to be caring turns out to add to the stress: "Go on and make your salad from baby greens that you have to be tending at the eleventh hour fray of the preparations in the kitchen of the bereaved," Ward threatens (79). See if that earns you any thank you notes. The wrong gift, given in the wrong way is worse than a failed social coup; it's annoying to people already in pain.

Ward notes with some disdain those "people who give, even Funeral Food, with an eye to the thank you to be received" (15). Ward implies that the better behavior is to be humbly less concerned with being thanked and more compassionate toward the bereaved (15). She remarks with humor that a good thank you note has "the warmth to make me feel that my gift was indispensable, brought the collected gathering to halt while they oohed and aahed, and will be remembered forever and ever, amen" (15). It is a joke, but Ward highlights how pleasure is a key part of the exchange of food, bringing comfort to the receiver and reflecting a pleasant glow of social capital back to the giver. However, as Ward makes clear, that pleasure is always very near to a painful misfiring. No wonder Ward's "young person" is anxious to perform well and is uncertain about the rules.

Metcalf and Hays devote an entire chapter to embarrassing funeral fails. "I Was So Embarrassed I Liketa Died" catalogs all of the ways that a funeral goer can make a fool of themselves while having "*too* much fun at a funeral" (99). Overdrinking is a key theme of the chapter. But the overall message is that even when "well-meaning" guests make a faux pas, it is up to the host—the bereaved—to smooth over that mistake with "grace" (103). For example, a "local grocer" sends a plebian meal of hot tamales, barbecue, and spicy pork to the funeral of an elite family. It's all wrong, but "holding her head up high, Betsy Minor Millsaps Miller put the ribs in a place of honor, alongside the aspic, the dainty homemade rolls, and Aunt Hebe's coconut cake" (103). While the grocer is honored at the meal for his gift made in poor taste, the misstep is not forgotten, nor is his status raised. The tony Millsaps are distinguished for their grace while the lowly grocer is made into an example of what not to do. The material consequence to the grocer is not outlined here, but the reputation of the small business owner among the elites is forever tarnished.

Magness, too, offers cautionary tales of the consequences of a bad performance. Elizabeth, who committed the grave error of bringing rum cake to an alcohol-abhorrent congregation is only one such embarrassing encounter. "Mary" and her husband go to the wrong address for a house party and accidentally stumble into a funeral visitation. When they recognize their error, they excuse themselves with condolences for the host. "Thank goodness we hadn't eaten any of the food yet!" Mary exclaims as they make their exit (65). Certainly, gate-crashing a stranger's funeral is unacceptable, but Mary's exclamation makes clear that it could have been worse. Eating food not intended for you, a meal that you did not contribute to, in a community that you do not belong to is a violation of the funeral ritual and its purpose as a builder of community identity. "Susan" tells a story about a funeral for a relative that was marred by a faux pas by a church lady who volunteered to bring napkins. They turned out to be a sack of paper napkins from a fast-food chain. The punchline is that the napkins are from Jack-in-the-Box and "the deceased, unfortunately, was also named Jack" (131). Even if the deceased hadn't been named Jack, bringing paper napkins—especially ones that may be pilfered from an ignominious burger joint—is distinguishing the giver in the wrong ways, showing poor taste and perhaps even poverty. The cookbooks demonstrate the high stakes of the funeral ritual and how the wrong moves can turn an opportunity to find belonging in a community into a public excommunication.

TOWARDS A CONCLUSION: SCRIPTS FOR COMMUNITY

As a coincidence, while I was working on this chapter, I recognized Perre Coleman Magness's *The Southern Sympathy Cookbook* for sale in the gift shop of the Country Music Hall of Fame in Nashville, Tennessee. It wasn't there in case the bereaved stumbled into the gift shop looking for a recipe; it was there as a souvenir of the South. The rest of the building spoke to the uniqueness of country music and the southern culture it emerged from and created, just as the cookbook is designed to speak for the peculiar southern customs of funeral foods. I wondered who was picking up this book and taking it home with their keychains and stickers and postcards. Would it be people who were going to use it to embed themselves in their southern communities by contributing to funeral food rituals as the conceit of the cookbook suggests? Or would it be curious travelers who were going to take this souvenir of the strange South to some other place where they could imagine the unusual people who lived and died there? I am humbled once again by the reminder that a cookbook is an object that circulates in the hand of a reader-user who will read, not read, use, not use, however they see fit. My analysis always runs into the caveat: a cookbook user is not always a cookbook reader.

It is important, then not to give the food itself too much credit for making a community. The caloric compounds of potato salad and pork tenderloin alone do not make the funeral meal a site for establishing community bonds that exceed the boundaries of time and space. Neither does a nice book of recipes get used exactly for its stated intentions or by its hailed audience. Rather, it is the ritual—the repeated menus, the relied upon contributors, the "folk liturgies"—that give the script for performing community. The cookbooks turn the unwritten script into a document, a set of procedures and instructions for making the performance count. There is an opportunity in ritual for pleasure that can be a balm to pain. There is an opportunity for pleasure that can forestall forgetting. There is a threat of failure, of pain, but the cookbook promises a way to avoid it.

In this instance, the self-consciously southern rituals surrounding death are an opportunity to reinforce a regional identity around easy-to-recognize "essential" southern cultural markers. In the discourse of southern distinction from *I'll Take My Stand* to the *Bitter Southerner* email newsletter, the uniqueness of the South is always embattled, on the verge of being absorbed into a homogenous national identity. The ritual of the funeral meal—and the unusual cookbooks that attempt to capture the ritual in text—may be one more attempt to at a resurrection of a continuous and "authentic" southern identity.

However, only one kind of southerner is speaking for the ritual in this sample of texts. Middle to upper-class, white, cisgendered women dominate the texts about funerals and offer us only one view of one section of the South. What are we missing?

Karla Holloway and Anissa Wardi remind us that Black southerners experience death, time, and a southern homeplace through the inescapable lens of an identity and a past not shared by the writers of these cookbooks. In many ways, the model of community formation and distinction presented here is too easy. It does not allow for ambivalence toward place or conflict with the past endemic to life on the margins of a community.

Reta Ugena Whitlock writes eloquently about her ambivalence to "homeplace" as a place that is lost in the past and not quite recoverable. It is a funeral that brings Whitlock back home and to the questions at the heart of "Season of Lilacs: Nostalgia of Place and Homeplace(s) of Difference." Over Sunday meals as a child, Whitlock heard her mother and grandmother tell stories of an ancestral homeplace where none of them lived anymore, a place that shaped her sense of identity and belonging and generated intense nostalgia that was hard to satisfy. "Southerners, like me," Whitlock writes, "spend an endless quest yearning for homeplace, trying to go home" (Whitlock 7). The longing for a lost homeplace is complicated by the loss of love and connection that may follow coming out as queer. Whitlock quotes poet, activist, and essayist Minnie Bruce Pratt who makes clear the risk of coming out and then going home: "We don't want to lose the love of the first people who knew us; we don't want to be standing outside the circle of home, with nowhere to go" (qtd. in 12). Whitlock concludes that tying identity to a lost place "paralyzes us to growth, to our own becoming" (9) and that white southerners, particularly, needed to interrogate their devotion to place as a troublesome part of a Lost Cause mythology that serves white supremacy:

> When memory is Dixiefied, grounded in Old South "lies of normalcy" (Segrest, 1985, p. 57), we become complacent—and complicit—in the lies, protective of the veil that makes home and Dixie the Most Holy Place (Exodus 26:33) in homeplace ideology... For the white Southerner, memory (home)work means uncovering indicators of conflation of home land and home place with the Dixie ideal. (15)

As Wilson's history of the southern funeral ritual makes clear, the distinctly southern funeral is a direct product of Lost Cause mythologies. When funeral cookbooks link the rituals with "authentic"—timeless and geographically specific dishes—in order to determine who is valued within a community and who is outside of it, Whitlock asks us to interrogate what place and what past we are connecting with and who we might be leaving standing outside the circle of home.

WORKS CITED

Bourdieu, Pierre. *Distinction: A Social Critique of the Judgement of Taste*. Harvard UP, 1979.
Bunch-Lyons, Beverly. "'Ours Is a Business of Loyalty': African American Funeral Home Owners in Southern Cities." *The Southern Quarterly*, vol. 53, no. 1, fall 2015, pp. 57–71. *Gale Academic OneFile*.

Caldwell, Patsy and Amy Lyles Wilson. *Bless Your Heart: Saving the World One Covered Dish at a Time.* Thomas Nelson, Inc., 2010.
Caldwell, Patsy and Amy Lyles Wilson. *Y'all Come Over: A Celebration of Southern Hospitality, Food, and Memories.* Thomas Nelson, Inc., 2013.
Caldwell, Patsy and Amy Lyles Wilson. *You Be Sweet: Sharing Your Heart One Down Home Dessert at a Time.* Thomas Nelson, Inc., 2012.
Graham, Joshua. "Funeral Food as Resurrection in the American South." *Dying to Eat: Cross Cultural Perspectives on Food, Death, and the Afterlife*, edited by Candi K. Cann, U of Kentucky P, 2018, 89–106.
Heldke, Lisa. *Exotic Appetites: Ruminations of a Food Adventurer.* Routledge, 2003.
Holloway, Karla. *Passed On: African American Mourning Stories.* Duke UP, 2002.
Jaynes, Gerald D. "Funeral Rites." *The Encyclopedia of African American Society*, edited by Gerald D. Jaynes, Sage Publications, 2005, 356.
Johnston, Josee, and Shyon Baumann. *Foodies: Democracy and Distinction in the Gourmet Foodscape.* Routledge, 2010.
Locklear, Erica Abrams. Personal Communication. 11 May 2021.
Magness, Pere Colman. *Pimento Cheese: The Cookbook.* St. Martin's Griffin, 2014.
Magness, Pere Colman. *The Runaway Spoon.* https://therunawayspoon.com/.
Magness, Pere Colman. *Southern Snacks.* U of North Carolina P, 2018.
Magness, Pere Colman. *The Southern Sympathy Cookbook: Funeral Food with a Twist.* The Countryman Press, 2018.
Metcalf, Gayden and Charlotte Hays. *Being Dead Is No Excuse: The Official Southern Ladies Guide to Hosting the Perfect Funeral.* Hachette, 2013.
Naccarato, Peter and Kathleen Lebesco. *Culinary Capital.* Berg, 2012.
Neville, Gwen Kennedy. "Kin-Religious Gatherings: Display for an 'Inner Public.'" *Southern Heritage on Display: Public Ritual and Ethnic Diversity Within Southern Regionalism*, edited by Celeste Ray, U of Alabama P, 2003, 130–43.
Patterson, Orlando. *Slavery and Social Death: A Comparative Study, With a New Preface.* Harvard UP, 2018.
Regis, Helen A. "'Keeping Jazz Funerals Alive': Blackness and the Politics of Memory in New Orleans." *Southern Heritage on Display: Public Ritual and Ethnic Diversity Within Southern Regionalism*, edited by Celeste Ray, U of Alabama P, 2003, pp. 38–56.
Splawn, Meghan, "How to Make Southern Biscuits," *The Kitchen*, https://www.thekitchn.com/how-to-make-southern-biscuits-237815.
Tippen, Carrie Helms. "Dinner," *Entropy Magazine*, https://entropymag.org/dinner.
Tippen, Carrie Helms. "Food Chain," *Entropy Magazine*, https://entropymag.org/food-chain.
Tippen, Carrie Helms. *Inventing Authenticity: How Cookbook Writers Redefine Southern Identity.* U of Arkansas P, 2018.
Ward, Jessica Bemis, *Food to Die For: A Book of Funeral Food, Tips, and Tales.* Southern Memorial Association, 2004.
Wardi, Anissa Janine. *Death and the Arc of Mourning in African American Literature.* UP of Florida, 2003.
Watson, Ritchie Devon, Jr. *Normans and Saxons: Southern Race Mythology and the Intellectual History of the Civil War.* Louisiana State UP, 2008.

Whitlock, Reta Eugena. *Queer South Rising: Voices of a Contested Place*. Information Age Publishing, 2013

Wilson, Charles Reagan. "The Death of Southern Heroes: Historic Funerals of the South," *Southern Cultures*, vol. 1, no. 1, 2012, pp. 3–22. *JSTOR*.

Wilson, Charles Reagan. "Funerals." *The New Encyclopedia of Southern Culture*, edited by Glenn Hinson and William Ferris, vol. 14, *Folk Life*, U of North Carolina P, 2009, 102.

TOWARDS A CONCLUSION
Intersections and Implications

A PLEASURE-CENTERED GENRE

At the most essential level, cookbooks are defined by their promises of pleasure and readers' expectations and trust in the author's ability to deliver on that promise. The pleasures that a cookbook can provide range from the obvious and concrete pleasures of delicious food and easy procedures to the subtle and abstract pleasures of self-efficacy and even love. Whether these pleasures are experienced in the imagination or in the kitchen and at the table, cookbooks are texts that are written, designed, and marketed for the enjoyment of readers and users.

A cookbook that does not promise pleasure or intentionally delivers something unpleasant is no longer a cookbook, but something else. Tyler Kord's *A Super Upsetting Cookbook About Sandwiches* plays on the expectations of the genre by representing the author as a self-deprecating and sometimes unreliable narrator. Though Kord makes jokes about working in a kitchen through sickness because he wanted "to make people *emotionally* sick because of how exciting the food was," he ultimately promises that "anything can make a good sandwich as long as it is good food" and that readers "can make food that is insane(-ly good) if you let go of how things are supposed to be" (1). His irreverent play with the genre does not violate the essential promise of pleasure; to the contrary, his creative play with humor heightens the experience of pleasure in reading and imagining the voice and character of the chef. Kord prepares readers to experience the book as "Super Upsetting" in the title, but he ends up conventionally promising good food and good stories.

CHALLENGING CONVENTIONS

The story of the South is often one of pain. While John Egerton bemoaned the loss of southern distinction in *Southern Food: At Home, On the Road, and In History*, he also noted that South's "checkered past now belongs to myth and memory" while "its food survives . . . intact in its essence and authenticity" (3). Perhaps Egerton spoke too soon in 1993 about the South's painful past being left behind. Many of the sins euphemized behind that innocuous adjective "checkered" remain perennial and intractable: racism and violence against people of color, poverty and exploitation, gendered and sexual inequality in labor, weight stigma and discrimination of ability. Even the South's beloved rituals of hospitality and community care surrounding death and painful feelings of grief extend from white supremacist scripts and Lost Cause mythologies. To write about any of these experiences is to break cookbook genre conventions by invoking pain.

PAIN AS EVIDENCE OF AUTHENTICITY

If the story of the southern past is one of pain, then aligning a dish or a person or an ingredient with those painful experiences is to link to something recognizable as unique to the South as a cultural group or geographic place. If the South is known for its "peculiar" investment in the institution of slavery, then recipes and traditions emerging from that institution—whether invented by enslaved people or imposed upon them by their enslavers—are peculiar to the South. If people in the South are statistically fatter and unhealthier than Americans in other regions, then the causes and solutions to these "problems" are also unique to that place. The examples throughout this book demonstrate that writers can and do talk about pain, contrary to the genre expectations, to serve the rhetorical purpose of making arguments of "authenticity."

PLEASURE, PAIN, AND PLAY

Because the genre demands pleasure, stories of the painful parts of the southern experience must eventually end in pleasure. In some instances, bringing up pain highlights resilience and overcoming adversity through creativity, community, and character. Pain is almost always left in the past as Egerton hoped, just like the "before" body of a weight loss cookbook writer or the long-dead ancestors of a Black southern chef. The present and the future are full of the promise of delicious food, an easy process, delighted diners, and a story to tell.

Genre conventions are not like the laws of physics. They can be defied without having to reconcile quantum mechanics with theories of relativity. I've always loved the definition of play as movement within rigid structures. The game of tennis has lines to determine in and out-of-bounds, an order for who serves when and from where, and rules for what happens when a ball touches the net, but the players can create infinite variety in the game by how they hold their racquets and where they aim their volleys, how they run and how hard they hit, what they wear and how they celebrate or curse. So, too, cookbook writers (and their editors and publishers and publicists and teams of designers) decide how to operate within the expectations of the genre. There is always room for creative play, and frequently it is deviation from convention that causes a writer or text to stand out from the crowd.

Unlike the laws of physics (but much more like the rules of tennis), genre expectations are socially constructed, defined by community stakeholders, and subject to change. The "expectations" in the phrase *genre expectations* are agreed upon between writers and readers through experimentation, reader response, and repetition over time. Each time a cookbook writer is successful in writing, publishing, marketing, and selling a cookbook that deviates from convention, genre expectations can change. Once a deviation has proven successful (read profitable), it is often imitated until it, too, becomes an expected convention, *de rigueur* for the author in the know.

I argue that when southern cookbook writers invite pain into their narratives in defiance of genre expectations that prioritize pleasure in order to critique institutions and problematize normative metanarratives, they move the boundaries of the game and make space for other writers to follow suit. I argued in *Inventing Authenticity* that maybe a cookbook wasn't the right place, rhetorically speaking, to make complex and nuanced arguments about serious social and political issues. For a reader (or scholar) to ask them to do so is user error, not the cookbook writer's mistake or an intentional oversight. But after writing this book and reviewing the field of cookbooks on offer today, it seems clear to me that cookbooks as a genre are perfectly capable of sustained arguments, ambivalence, complexity, and critique. Writers are consistently pushing the boundaries of how many pages of writing readers are willing to read before a recipe appears in the text, how personal and political they can get with their readers, how much research and interview they can conduct to support their conclusions. They ask more of their readers, and their readers continue to respond by buying their products.

Even within the work of a single cookbook writer I can see changes in the genre. Virginia Willis writes about the same white farmer, Will Harris III, in both *Basic to Brilliant, Y'all* in 2011 and in *Secrets of the Southern Table: A Food Lover's Tour of the Global South* in 2018. In 2011, Willis praises Harris for recognizing the environmental and ethical problems in industrial farming of animals for meat and responding with more humane and small-scale operations (133). However, in 2018, Willis returns to Harris's story as a contrast to the story of Matthew Raiford, a Black farmer who did not have to make the dramatic changes Harris had to make because he and his family had been consistently operating in more humane and sustainable methods for generations (11–14). As I argued in the chapter on slavery and racism in this book, Willis uses the opportunity to make her own apology for ignorance and complicity in acts of racism. Willis first introduces Harris as part of a critique of animal suffering and an argument for ethical meat eating; when he next appears, it is part of a critique of racism in the South. In just seven years, Willis has pushed the boundaries of the genre to hold space for topics she avoided in earlier cookbooks. Similarly, Nicole Taylor's first book *Up South* (2015) avoids direct references to slavery and enslaved innovators. Her second book *Watermelon and Red Birds* (2022) is devoted to celebrations of Juneteenth and the end of legal slavery in the US. By coincidence, another seven-year gap shows movement in the genre. The genre can flex as writers push against it.

AUTHORS ALWAYS CHOOSE

By definition, genres circumscribe some authorial choice, but within those limitations, authors have agency to make decisions. How they decide to conform to or diverge from expectation may be influenced by their understanding of their audience, the influence of editors or other stakeholders, or their own personal style. Most of all, authorial choice reveals rhetorical purpose: an overarching goal of the writing, a unifying message that underpins the whole of the text. I argue that even the decisions to follow convention are meaningful, communicating the author's intentions and values by indicating the conventions that they consider to be inviolable, or at least useful to their aims. The deviations from expectations stand out in sharp relief in a genre as highly conventional as the cookbook.

Deviations always come with risks. I like to use J. L. Austin's terms from the classic *How to Do Things with Words* to describe failures of language to reach their rhetorical purposes as "infelicities" or "misfires" (18). *Infelicity* suggests displeasure, like a choice that will make the audience unhappy. But *misfire* suggests missing a target or a failure at the initial launch. An argument that misfires mistakes what the audience will tolerate or what they will find convincing. It could be a misunderstanding of who is listening and what they value. An argument that misfires may never get up the logical strength to begin to be convincing. This is a failure of the content or style of the argument.

I was so interested to examine stories of suffering and pain in cookbooks because the deviation seemed to be violating an inviolable convention, taking a huge risk of misfiring. If the audience is primed for pleasure by the genre conventions, mentioning pain risks audience displeasure, putting their attention on problems or difficult emotions, potentially alienating the audience by infelicity. However, the success of this rhetorical strategy shows that audiences *can* tolerate the deviation away from pleasure and towards pain. They did not throw down Ruth Reichl's *My Kitchen Year*, a cookbook detailing the aftermath of the closing of *Gourmet* magazine where Reichl was editor and Reichl's search for comfort after being devastated by this loss. Penguin Random House lists the book as a *New York Times* Bestseller and "One of the Best Books of the Year" from a number of publications. Reichl writes extensively of the pain of disappointment and displacement and depression, but like all the other authors examined in this study, she offers pleasure in food as a balm for that suffering. The "136 Recipes that Saved My Life" provide the antidote to suffering. Clearly, mentioning pain itself is not an "infelicity" that will alienate an audience beyond recovery.

The potential for misfire is in the logic of the argument. Why is this pain being mentioned at all? What is it meant to prove? How is it being used to motivate the audience into an action or belief? For Reichl, the pain is the basis of an argument that cooking and eating can "save" a life. Food is physical and emotional comfort. To make this argument, she must first convince the audience that pain exists, then she can prove that food can comfort. That food can be comfort is a perfectly conventional argument that audiences are fully prepared to accept. The painful story does not misfire because it is the logical basis of a felicitous argument.

For southern writers, especially, pain provides a logical basis to set up an argument for southern authenticity. Audiences already share an understanding or impression that the South is a unique place with a unique experience of pain. When writers build on that shared assumption to explain the origin of their recipes, they build on a foundation of "authenticity." Authenticity itself is an argument that persuades readers to trust the source of information. But pleasure is the argument that persuades them to action in the kitchen. The promise of pleasure in all its various forms recenters the argument directly at the target audience and rhetorical goal: a felicitous argument and a sure fire.

IDENTITY MATTERS

The rhetorical triangle includes the audience and the purpose as described above, but its third point is the speaker. The ethos and identity of the speaker is perhaps the most important factor in examining the felicity of an argument that turns pain to pleasure, particularly when the pain being described is based in experiences particular to one category of identity. In each chapter of this book, I have focused on one specific experience of pain through the lens of one identity: slavery and racism as experienced by Black southerners, poverty and poor white southerners, physical agricultural labor and women. Fat and illness are relative to the norms of "ability." Grief and death affect everyone, but the rituals of death in the South fall mostly to women. You may also have noted that the people most likely to comment on those experiences of pain are members of those identity categories. Black writers write most thoughtfully and intentionally on the pain of racism. The formerly-fat and used-to-be-sick are most likely to write about weight stigma and illness. The ethos of the author is established through stories that connect them personally with the experience of pain. Those arguments are more likely to be successful because the author is speaking to and on behalf of a group to which they belong.

There are some exceptions, of course, and those reflect a riskier deviation from genre. For example, when Virginia Willis, a white writer, shares the stories of Matthew Raiford's painful experiences of racism, she risks using her relative privilege and power as author to reify that pain as essential to southern identity, an unchangeable state. However, she follows that story with her own painful experience of reckoning with her complicity in acts of racism. Because of her privilege as an established figure in southern food writing, she already has a strong ethos and the trust of her audience; she is able to successfully make this argument because of her identities and experience. She manages both to tell the truth about a painful subject and express sympathy and shame. Similarly, Vivian Howard writes about poverty from a higher class position than her grandparents. She has the privilege of access to publishing and public distribution that her poorer grandparents would never have had. Because of that privilege, she is able to speak on behalf of their painful experiences though she has experienced only a part of that pain firsthand.

INTERSECTIONALITY AND INTERPRETATION

To keep the analysis focused, I did narrow each chapter into one identity category, always intersecting with southernness as a regional and cultural identity. At some points, I couldn't help but acknowledge that other identities influenced how authors and audiences experienced and narrated stories of pain. The women experiencing the pain of agricultural labor are of course working class or poor, otherwise they would likely be engaged in some other kind of work. I focused on white southerners in the poverty chapter, and of course, their experiences of poverty are influenced by their whiteness. In the last two chapters on illness and death, the authors are white women, presumably middle class. Their experiences of their bodies as fat or sick are deeply influenced by the expectations of gender and the norms of their class. Whiteness, too, that sometimes invisible category of identity, is made more invisible, especially in the funeral cookbooks, by conflating the experiences of all southerners with that of white southerners as in Perre Colman Magness's *The Southern Sympathy Cookbook*. Whiteness is also made invisible by making Blackness a separate, hypervisible addendum as in Jessica Bemis Ward's *Food to Die For*.

However, I wasn't able to fully explore the complexities of the intersecting identities of all the writers or their subjects. Certainly race and class run throughout the book as sometimes invisible factors in how authors experience and write about pain, no matter the topic of that chapter. A certain amount of economic and social capital is required to even be able to access the marketplace of commercial publishing, particularly as a professional writer or chef. And in the South race always matters in how a person experiences southernness as a category of identity. Though the distinctions between them are sometimes artificially and self-consciously constructed in service of white supremacy, the differences are evident in lived experience and should be acknowledge in text. Gender certainly featured heavily in the chapters on women's labor, fat and illness, and death and grief, but I largely left gender unexamined in the first two chapters. Likewise, I noted how Ernest Mickler's queerness influenced his playful, campy style, but I failed to note that Virginia Willis openly identifies as lesbian. Her sexuality is well-known enough that Target invited her to post a video for Pride month in 2020 describing "what makes me feel pride" ("Virginia Willis on Coming Out" 0:27–0:39). Willis rarely, if ever, makes references to her sexuality in her cookbooks, but her identity may offer some insight into why she is invested in highlighting the diversity of the South in *Secrets of the Southern Table*. These intersections matter.

I also artificially separated books into single categories. Vivian Howard's *Deep Run Roots* is in the poverty chapter, but the book is full of stories about women's painful labor. I wanted desperately to write about images of Howard's mother Scarlett's hands, painfully curled by arthritis, and the stories Howard told of the women in her family canning and preserving food. Almost all of the cookbooks in this study make some reference to the antebellum period or ingredients introduced by the slave trade, though I only focused on Black southern writers and Willis's exceptional moment. Almost all offer some recipes for preserving, though I focused on only Lundy and Brock. A few even mention their own experiences of grief or sharing food in times of trouble, but I focused narrowly on three books devoted entirely to funeral foods. These are the rhetorical choices I made for the sake of clarity in my own argument, but this work is far from finished. In all cases, though, ethos and authority are necessarily shaped by intersecting identities.

DISRUPTING HARMFUL METANARRATIVES

I write about cookbooks because it makes me unique in my field of literary and cultural studies. I am invested materially in my own distinction here because my livelihood depends on being an expert who can contribute something special to an ongoing scholarly conversation. But I also write about them because I think they have a unique power to shape reality and lived experience. I also write about food in literary fiction. Compared to literary novels which may reach a limited audience and obscure their messages in metaphor and suggestion, cookbooks remain high performers in the book business and straightforwardly state their intentions. I know that I can look to William Faulkner and Flannery O'Connor and Jesmyn Ward and Natasha Trethewey for insight into southern identity and even southern foodways. However, these are professional writers speaking to elite audiences in highly coded and nuanced art. When I want to see what ordinary Americans think about southernness and southern foodways, I need to look at the texts they read and circulate. Cookbooks and food writing in magazines can tell me that.

Since I began my studies of southern food writing a decade ago, I can see that the field has changed. Life on planet earth has changed. The discourse of race has changed in the wake of police violence against Black citizens, Black Lives Matter movements, antiracist content for white allies, and serious consequences for white public figures who engage in racist or insensitive acts. The conversations on gender and sexuality have changed with the corporatization of Pride and new-to-most-of-us language to describe the continuums of sexual and gendered identities. The conversation about fat and ability has changed with fat positive movements like body diversity and inclusivity in advertising and fashion and "health at every size" interventions in medical discourse. Even our experiences of death and rituals of funerals in the Covid era have changed with the temporary inability to gather. The technological interventions in coordinating "meal trains" and sending food and groceries through third party delivery services may forever change the social dynamics of feeding the bereaved.

Cookbooks and popular writing about food have responded to these social changes. It is simply no longer tolerable for white writers to co-opt the cuisine of other cultures. The consequences of doing so without carefully giving credit or acknowledging origins are serious; readers respond immediately and vociferously in online forums, and the outlets that write about food and review cookbooks have huge audiences. It is not only just but fashionable for white writers to acknowledge the contributions of people of color to southern cuisine in specific and celebratory ways. Publishing houses are featuring writers of color, exemplified by Bryant Terry's editorship of a new imprint of Ten Speed Press called 4 Color Books (Maher par. 1).

Southern writers in particular are less likely to represent the South as one large and monolithic cultural unit. Even popular food writers know that the South is too large and too diverse to be essentialized into a single cuisine or culture. Falling in line with "locavore" rhetorics, writers rely on microregions and local foodsheds to define smaller and smaller regions of the South that can be more easily consumed. Cookbook writers answer the challenge to simultaneously expand the diversity of the South and contract to an "authentic" cuisine by focusing their attention on smaller southern geographies: the Mississippi Delta, the Low Country, Appalachia (and subsets of Appalachia), urban city centers, coastal port cities, rural communities, and other localized microregions. The turn to smaller regions allows writers to make a more convincing argument that the cuisine of a microregion is uniformly distinct because it is uniquely diverse in its makeup. This change is in response to social pressures to more accurately and inclusively portray the history and culture of the South.

The cookbook genre can change. It has already evolved in ways that create a more just and inclusive discourse, and it can continue to do so as long as readers (both professional readers like scholars, reviewers, and editors and ordinary readers and cookbook buyers) keep putting pressure on the industry to meet their expectations. Genre is a set of agreements between writers and readers established informally over time through the marketplace. What the cookbook will become, what the genre can tolerate in terms of serious discussion of painful subjects, is limited only by what writers are brave enough to say and what readers are interested enough to buy. Food discourse is already politically engaged in topics of sustainability and environmental impact of eating, equitable food access and the right to nutritious food for all, and even politics of identity and cultural sensitivity. These are not taboo topics in today's cookbooks because readers have voted with their clicks and page visits and purchases.

Cookbooks are no less appropriate as a medium for social change or a venue for arguments for justice than any other genre. The requirement for pleasure does pose a rhetorical challenge, but as this study has shown, savvy writers can negotiate this challenge and still open discussions of difficult topics with honesty and gravity. Pleasure itself is not an enemy of change or evidence of the absence of seriousness; rather, it is one of many powerful tools in the resistance toolbox. If writers, editors, and publishers of cookbooks are brave enough to take in hand the tools available to them and trust readers to tolerate more complexity, they may find that the cookbook can be both a commercial success and make a difference in the public imagination of who and what and where a southerner really is.

WORKS CITED

Austin, J. L. *How to Do Things With Words: Second Edition*. Harvard UP, 1975.
Brock, Sean. *Heritage*. Artisan, 2014.
Brock, Sean. *South: Essential Recipes and New Explorations*. Artisan, 2019.
Egerton, John. *Southern Food: At Home, On the Road, and In History*. U of North Carolina P, 1993.
Howard, Vivian. *Deep Run Roots: Stories and Recipes from My Corner of the South*. Little Brown, 2016.
Kord, Tyler. *A Super Upsetting Cookbook About Sandwiches*. Clarkson Potter, 2016.
Lundy, Ronni. *Victuals: An Appalachian Journey with Recipes*. Clarkson Potter, 2016.
Magness, Pere Colman. *The Southern Sympathy Cookbook: Funeral Food with a Twist*. The Countryman Press, 2018.
Maher, John. "Ten Speed, Chef Bryant Terry Launch 4 Color Books." *Publisher's Weekly*, 3 May 2021, https://www.publishersweekly.com/pw/by-topic/industry-news/publisher-news/article/86237-ten-speed-chef-bryant-terry-launch-4-color-books.
Mickler, Ernest. *White Trash Cooking: 25th Anniversary Edition*. Ten Speed Press, 2011.
Reichl, Ruth. *My Kitchen Year: 136 Recipes That Saved My Life*. Penguin Random House, 2015.
Taylor, Nicole A. *Up South: Chasing Dixie in a Brooklyn Kitchen*, Countryman Press, 2015.
Taylor, Nicole A. *Watermelon and Red Birds: A Cookbook for Juneteenth and Black Celebrations*. Simon and Schuster, 2022.
Tippen, Carrie Helms. *Inventing Authenticity: How Cookbook Writers Redefine Southern Identity*. U of Arkansas P, 2018.
Ward, Jessica Bemis, *Food to Die For: A Book of Funeral Food, Tips, and Tales*. Southern Memorial Association, 2004.

Willis, Virginia. *Basic to Brilliant, Y'all:150 Refined Southern Recipes and Ways to Dress Them Up for Company*. Ten Speed Press, 2011.

Willis, Virginia. *Secrets of the Southern Table: A Food Lover's Journey Through the Global South*. Houghton Mifflin Harcourt, 2018.

Willis, Virginia. "Virginia Willis on Coming Out." *Facebook*, uploaded by Chef Virginia Willis, 18 May 2020. https://www.facebook.com/watch/?v=239181007311978.

INDEX

Acheson, Hugh, 135, 137, 138, 149
Adams, Carol J., 44–45, 46
Adno, Michael, 102
affection, 30, 32, 35
afro-nostalgia, 55–58, 60, 64, 67, 70, 72, 76, 78
Afro-Nostalgia: Feeling Good in Contemporary Black Culture (Ahad-Legardy), 55–58, 72, 76
Afro-Vegan: Farm Fresh African, Caribbean, and Southern Flavors Remixed (Terry), 57–58
Agee, James, 96, 104
agricultural labor causing pleasure and pain, 11, 13, 121–52, 233
Ahad-Legardy, Badfia, 55–58, 63, 67, 68–69, 72, 76, 78
Alexander, Michelle, 57–58
Alford, Kathy, 46
Allen, Gus, 73
AMC (TV channel), 8
Americanization of Dixie: The Southernization of America, The (Egerton), 98
American Psychology Association, 163
And Their Children After Them (Maharidge and Williamson), 97
Angelou, Maya, 18–19, 20, 21, 24, 35–36
Appalachia, 139–40, 141, 144, 150, 152, 179, 235; Appalachian foodways, 126, 136, 137, 139, 140, 141, 207; health of residents of, 156–57; preserving food in, 138, 143
Appalachian South Folklife Center, 152
Atlantic, The (magazine), 137, 138

Austin, J. L., 230–31
authenticity. *See* southern authenticity

Bailey, Emily, 165–66
Balestier, Courtney, 126
Barton, Scott, 110
Basic to Brilliant, Y'all (Willis), 81, 166, 230
Baumann, Shyon, 89, 90, 107, 137, 217
Bee, Charmaine, 73
before-and-after narratives, 162–64, 172, 187; "Becoming a Skinny Southerner," 173, 176–77
Being Dead Is No Excuse: The Official Southern Ladies Guide to Hosting the Perfect Funeral (Metcalf and Hays), 15, 192, 198, 200–201, 203, 209, 220
Being Ugly: Southern Women Writers and Social Rebellion (Miller), 157
Belasco, Warren, 5
Belle, Effie, 67
belonging, recipe for, 206–7
Berenbaum, Michael, 42–43
Beverly Hillbillies, The, 12
Biden, Joe, 64
Big Bad Breakfast (Currence), 100
BIPOC (Black, Indigenous, and people of color), 6, 10, 100
Bitter Southerner (email newsletter), 223; Michael Adno writing for, 102
"Black, Indigenous, and people of color." *See* BIPOC (Black, Indigenous, and people of color)
"Black Joy," 38–39. *See also* afro-nostalgia

"Black Joy in the time of Ferguson" (Jahnson), 39
Bless Your Heart: Saving the World One Covered Dish at a Time (Caldwell and Wilson), 201
BMI (body mass index), 155, 163
Boden, Ian, 149
Boden, Leslie, 149–50
body fat and illness in wellness cookbooks, 13–14, 154–88, 232
body mass index. *See* BMI (body mass index)
Boiler Room, The (restaurant), 106
Bon Appetit (magazine), 59
Bon Appetit, Y'all (Willis), 81, 100, 166
Bound to the Fire (Deetz), 9
Bourdieu, Pierre, 27–28, 217
Bower, Anne, 5, 22, 24, 127
Breeden, Roshaunda L., 164
Bress 'n' Nyam: Gullah Geeche Recipes from a Sixth Generation Farmer (Raiford), 59, 60, 65–67, 83
Brewis, Alexandra, 54–55
Brock, Sean, 135–37, 139, 141, 142, 145–46, 147, 148–50, 234; arguments with Michael Twitty, 52; writing foreword to *Secrets of the Southern Table*, 83
Bryant, Chris, 144
Bunch-Lyons, Beverly, 194
Burden of Southern History, The (Van Woodward), 95

Caldwell, Patsy, 200–201
"campness" and *White Trash Cooking*, 101–2, 104, 105, 118, 233
"cancel culture," 52
cane syrup, 69–70, 105
canning. *See* preserving and canning
Carolina Gold rice, 7, 8
Carter, Lara Lyn, 165, 173–78, 179, 186, 187
Carver, George Washington, 72, 73
Cary, Nancy, 3
Cash, W. J., 94, 95–96
CBS News (TV show), 156

celebration, 56, 70, 71, 89, 108; and Juneteenth, 57, 58, 64, 73, 230; of pleasures of cooking, 78, 84, 127, 152; suffering and social justice, 3–16
Charles, Dora, 59, 62, 63, 68–71, 76–78, 80, 86, 99; and Paula Deen, 59, 71, 78
Chase, Leah, 74
Chef & the Farmer (restaurant), 106, 113
Chef's Life, A (PBS docuseries), 106, 111
Chez Panisse (restaurant), 25–26
Child, Julia, 214
Chop Shop, The (meat processing facility), 144
Christenberry, William, 104
Christensen, Ashley, 100
Cirina, Lauren, 42
cisgender, 37, 164, 198, 223
Claflin College, 63
Claiborne, Jenné, 165
Clark, Patrick, 74
Cloudcrest Farm, 144
Cobb, James C., 98
Cofer, Judith Ortiz, 40
Collins, Lauren, 52
Comer, Maria Samuella, 131
comfort food, 173, 203
communal meals, 27, 192–93, 197, 198, 205
communitas, 159, 177, 193, 195
community, belonging to, 213; distinction in community, 217–22; eating as a community ritual, 159; experiencing a Black homeplace, 223–24; place, 207–14; recipe for, 206–7; rituals around death as part of belonging to the community, 209; scripts for community, 222–24; time, 214–17
community cookbooks, 5, 102, 105, 199, 200, 207, 213–14
"Compiled Cookbook as Foodways Autobiography, The" (Ireland), 22
Compson, Quentin, 8
convenience: "culinary triangle of identity, responsibility, and convenience," 5; foods, 90, 137, 147, 169; ingredients, 100, 104, 105, 211, 215–16, 218

cookbooks, 231; as celebration, suffering, and social justice, 3–16; changes in cookbook publishing, 234–36; cookbooks and recipes as storytelling, 19, 29, 33, 205; cooking as opportunity to give and receive love and affection, 29; dealing with gardening, canning, preserving, and women's labor on farms, 13, 121–52, 232; dealing with grief and death in funeral cookbooks, 14–15, 191–224, 233–34; dealing with poverty, 12–13, 88–119, 232; dealing with racism and slavery, 11–12, 50–86, 232; dealing with wellness, 14–15, 154–88, 232; expectations of as a genre, 80; goal of, 7; historical nature of, 6–7; literary, 201; memoirs and, 21–24, 35–36, 44, 57; pleasure in, 9–10, 18–47, 187, 227, 228–29; recipe collections marketed as and suffering, 44; recipe mirroring a poem, 3–4; recipes as narrative of success, 5; rhetorical function of, 9, 11

"Cooking for Others Can Be Selfish" (Miller), 31

Cooking Gene, The (Twitty), 58–59, 60–61

Cooper, Shelley, 144, 151

Cornwall, Andrea, 124–25

"Cotton Tenants: Three Families" (Agee and Evans), 96

Country Women Cope With Hard Times (Walker), 128

Couser, G. Thomas, 23

critical race theory, 38, 40

Crohn's disease, 165–66, 181, 185

Culinary Historians of New York, 63

"culinary triangle of identity, responsibility, and convenience," 5

Currence, John, 100

Dabney, Joe, 143

Davis, David, 91, 96

Davis, Jefferson, funeral of, 194

death, social, 14–15, 199, 219

death and grief in funeral cookbooks, 3, 14–15, 191–224, 232, 233–34

"Death of Southern Heroes: Historic Funerals of the South, The" (Wilson), 194

"Debts of Pleasure" (Edge), 10

Decolonize Your Diet (Calvo and Esquibel), 5

Deen, Paula, 14, 52, 156, 165; and Dora Charles, 59, 71, 78

Deep Run Roots (Howard), 92, 106–17, 118, 134–35, 233–34

Deetz, Kelley Fanto, 9

Delta death foods, 202

democracy and simplicity (poverty foods and southern character), 90–92

Denham, Jay, 144

De Silva, Cara, 41–42, 43

diabetes, Type 2, 11, 14, 154, 165, 167, 178; author's personal story, 154–55

Dickstein, Lore, 42

diet cookbooks, 159, 160, 165, 173–78, 187; need to be value-neutral, 188

Diet For a Small Planet (Lappe), 5

digestive issues, dealing with, 163, 178–86

Diners, Drive-ins, and Dives (TV show), 50

disability and fat studies, 160; a literature review of fat studies and food studies, 161–65

disease and illness, 156–61; cookbooks for relief of symptoms, 165–66, 178–86. *See also* fat and illness

Dissen, William, 144

Distinction (Bordieu), 217

domestic work, 11, 131, 132, 183; offering satisfaction, 133

Early Girl Eatery (restaurant), 141

Easy Bistro and Bar (restaurant), 144

Eater (online publication), 46

eating as a community ritual, 159

Eating Together: Food, Friendship, and Inequality (Julier), 27

Eat My Words: Reading Women's Lives Through the Cookbooks They Wrote (Theophano), 22

Ecocriticism and the Future of Southern Studies (Vernon), 7

Edge, John T., 6–7, 10, 52, 92, 100, 114; writing foreword for *White Trash Cooking*, 101–2, 104
Egerton, John, 80, 98, 228
Emancipation Proclamation, 64, 66
Empire State South (restaurant), 135
Encyclopedia of African American Society "Funeral Rites" entry, 193–95
Enduring South: Subcultural Persistence in Mass Society, The (Reed), 94–95
Engelhardt, Elizabeth, 131
Evans, Walker, 96, 104
Exotic Appetites (Heldke), 29

Fain, Lisa, 100
family reunions, 148, 195
Farm and Ranch (magazine), 129
farm labor of women, 13, 121–52, 233–34; as painful or difficult work, 145–50, 151–52; in the South, 127–34
Farm Security Administration (FSA), 12, 96
fat and illness: body fat and illness in wellness cookbooks, 13–14, 154–88, 232; fat body case studies in pain and pleasure, 165–86; fatphobia, 164; fat studies, 160, 161–65; as a taunt, 170
Fat Studies Reader, The (Wann), 160–61
Faulkner, William, 8, 234
Feed the Resistance (Turshen), 44
Feller, Maya, 165
feminism, 132–34; Black, 38; feminine identity, 129–30; feminist theory of pleasure and pain, 13, 38, 40, 127; fourth-wave feminists, 135, 151; and the Latinx woman, 40; pleasure as resistance in, 37
Fern, Fanny, 30
Ferris, Marcie Cohen, 7, 134
Fieri, Guy, 50
flavor: difference between taste and, 29; maintaining Southern flavors and traditions, 174; Nosrat on, 32, 34; the pleasure of, 14, 25–26, 86, 148, 171–72, 177

Folwell, Emma J., 97
Food, Fatness, Fitness (blog post), 159
Food & Wine (magazine), 59
"foodies," 90, 109, 118, 137, 154
Foodies: Democracy and Distinction in the Gourmet Landscape (Johnston and Baumann), 89, 107
food insecurity, 45, 117, 134, 156, 157, 164. See also poverty
food preservation. See pickles and pickling; preserving and canning
food studies, a literature review, 161–65
Food to Die For: A Book of Funeral Food, Tips, and Tales (Ward), 198, 199–200, 201, 202, 204–5, 208, 213–14, 233
foodways: Appalachian, 126, 136, 137, 139, 140, 141, 207; southern, 7, 11, 50, 79, 92, 139, 158, 192; and southern identity, 234
Ford, Christine Blasey, 45, 46
Forson, William, 39, 40
Fortune (magazine), 96
Foucault, Michel, 37
4 Color Books, 100, 235
Frady, Marshall, 98
Franklin, Aaron, 100
Franklin, Benjamin, 23
Franklin BBQ (Franklin), 100
Fresh Start: Cooking with Virginia, My Real Life Daily Guide to Healthy Eating and Weight Loss (Willis), 158, 165, 172–73, 178
Fried Chicken (Lang), 100
Frontier Culture Museum (Staunton, VA), 139–40
frugality vs. poverty, 111, 117
FSA. See Farm Security Administration (FSA)
"Fucking Failures: The Future of Fat Sex" (White), 163
funeral cookbooks, 14–15, 191–224; case studies, 198–206; characterizing rituals beyond food, 209–10; funeral foods as expressions of local identity, 207; funeral meals binding diners together as

community, 217–22; greatest pleasures promised in, 206–7
"Funeral Fairy," 220
"Funeral Food as Resurrection in the American South" (Graham), 14
funeral rites. *See* southern funeral customs
"Funeral Tsar," 220–21

Gailey, Jeannine, 163–64
Galloping Gourmet, The (TV show), 101
Garden & Gun (magazine), 114
gardening, canning, and women's labor on farms, 13, 121–52; canning as a measure of a woman's worth, 143; as painful or difficult work, 145–50, 151–52
Gartrell, Tom and Bonnie, 71–72
Gastronomica (magazine), 127
Gay, Roxane, 154, 155
genres: author having choice within, 230–31; cookbook changing over time, 234–36; cookbooks as a pleasure-centered, 22–24, 40, 51, 80–81, 187, 227, 228–30, 231; conventions, 229–30; identifying for *In Memory's Kitchen*, 44; suffering going against expectations, 41–47
"Gentle Lentils" recipe causing upset, 52
Germany, Kent, 97
Gilliard, Jupiter, 60, 66
Gilliard Farms, 65–66, 75, 83–84, 85
Goldberg, Daniel, 161–62, 164
Golden, Zach, 26
Gomez, Asha, 6
Gone with the Wind (Mitchell), 8, 72–73
Goolsby, Bessie, 72
Gourmet (magazine), 231
Graham, Joshua, 14, 197–99, 205, 207, 213, 219
Graham, Samuel, 179
graveyards, segregated, 196
Gray, Macy, 102
Great Migration, 67, 72
Great Society programs, 96, 97
Greene, Lauren Wissner, 156

grief and death in funeral cookbooks, 14–15, 191–224, 232, 233–34; dealing with grief of children, 204
Grits (Willis), 166
Guglielmo, Letitzia, 132
Gullah cuisine, 52, 59, 63–64, 65, 75, 79
"Gullah Girl Tea" (company), 73
Gunst, Kathy, 46–47
Guterl, Matthew Pratt, 8–9

Hall, Melissa Booth, 10
Hall, Ruth, 30–31
Hallelujah! The Welcome Table (Angelou), 19–21
"Handmaiden of the Bereaved, The," 220–21
"Happy Belle," 129
Hardin, Jessica, 54–55
Harlem Renaissance, 57, 72
Harrell, Doug and Barbara, 144
Harrill, C. B., 143
Harrill, Walter and Wendy, 143
Harris, Jennifer, 30
Harris, Jessica B., 64, 73, 74
Harris, Will, 83, 230
Hawkins, Kate, 124–25
Hays, Charlotte, 198, 202, 203, 205, 206, 208–9, 210, 211, 216–17, 220–21
HBO (TV channel), 8
Healthier Southern Cooking (Jones and Jones), 165
Healthy Comfort (Smith), 167
healthy eating, 154–88; "healthy cooking" cookbooks, 165, 166–73, 182; McCormick's definition of "healthy food," 181. *See also* fat and illness
Heldke, Lisa, 217
"Hell's Own Cookbook" (Dickstein), 42–43
Heritage (Brock), 135–37, 139, 141, 142
Heritage Radio Network, 60
Hill, Grandma, 108, 111, 117
Hilliard, Emily, 144
History of Sexuality (Foucault), 37
Holloway, Karla, 194–95, 223

homecomings, 193, 195
homeplace, 135, 193, 195, 196, 198, 223–24
Homesick Texan (Fain), 100
Homeward Bound: Why Women Are Embracing the New Domesticity (Matchar), 133
Hot Grease (podcast), 60, 64
Hot Springs, Virginia Presbyterian Cookbook, 214
Howard, Vivian, 92, 106–19, 134–35, 232, 233–34
How to Do Things with Words (Austin), 230–31
Hunger and Thirst (Cary), 3
Hutchens, Sophia, 164

IACP Cookbook of the Year award, 106, 166
identity: "culinary triangle of identity, responsibility, and convenience," 5; feminine, 129–30; intersectionality and interpretation of, 233–34. *See also* southern identity
If We So Choose (documentary), 60
Igbo Landing, 65
I Know Why the Caged Bird Sings (Angelou), 18–19; compared to *Hallelujah! The Welcome Table*, 19–24
illness. *See* fat and illness
I'll Take My Stand: The South and the Agrarian Tradition, 91
imagination, 12, 23, 34, 39, 96, 206, 236; pleasure of, 33–36, 42, 47, 58, 126, 227
Imladris Farm, 143
"infelicities" vs. "misfires," 230–31
In Memory's Kitchen: A Legacy from the Women of Terezin (De Silva), 41–44
Inness, Sherrie, 9, 36–37
Instagram, 52
International Association of Culinary Professionals, 166
Intuitive Eating: A Revolutionary Anti-Diet Approach (Tibole and Resch), 52, 56, 59, 155, 186

Inventing Authenticity: How Cookbook Writers Redefine Southern Identity (Tippen), 5–6, 11–12, 13, 50–51, 115, 229
Ireland, Lynne, 22

James Beard Award, 58, 59, 100, 106, 166
Jargon Society, 100
Jaslow, Ryan, 156
"Jazz funeral" in New Orleans, 195
Jemima Code, The (Tipton-Martin), 6
Jerusalem (Ottolenghi), 100
Johnson, Javon, 38–39
Johnson, Jim, 144
Johnson, Lyndon, 96, 97
Johnston, Josee, 89, 90, 107, 137, 217
Johnston, Wendy and Steve, 152
Jolly, Susie, 124–25
Jones, Eric, 165
Jones, Heather Watkins, 73
Jones, Shanna, 165
Jones, Tangerine, 45–46
Joplin, Scott, 57–58
Joy of Cooking, The (Rombauer), 5, 208
Julier, Alice, 27
Juneteenth, 57, 58, 64, 65, 73, 230

Katzen, Mollie, 100
Kaufman, Rona, 43
Kavanaugh, Brett, 45
Kelly, Ariana, 137, 138
Kennedy, Robert, 12
King, Martin Luther, Jr., 81, 85
kin-religious gatherings, 193, 195
Knight, Ben, 109
Kondo, Marie, 52
Kord, Tyler, 227
Kwanzaa, principles of, 75

Lang, Rebecca, 100
Lange, Dorothea, 91, 96
Lasseter, Mary Beth, 10
laughter, 125–26, 143, 148
Lebesco, Kathleen, 28, 217

Lee, Edward, 144
Lee, Harper, 101
Lee, Matt, 165
Lee, Robert E., funeral of, 194
Lee, Ted, 165
Lee Bros. Simple Fresh Southern, The (Lee and Lee), 165
Let Us Now Praise Famous Men (Agee and Evans), 91, 96–97, 104
Lewis, Edna, 73, 74
LGBTQ (LGBTQIA+), 164, 196
Lighten Up, Y'all (Willis), 14, 165, 166–73, 177–78
literary cookbook, 201
Lo, Anita, 27, 31
Locklear, Erica Abrams, 207
LOFT (stores), 154
Lost Cause, 53, 90–91, 224, 228
Lu, Jessica H., 38, 39
Lundy, Ronni, 136–37, 138–41, 142–45, 146–47, 148, 149, 150–52, 234
Lynn, Loretta, 179

Magness, Perre Coleman, 198, 201, 203–5, 208, 209–11, 212–13, 215–16, 217–18, 222, 233
Maharidge, Dale, 97
Main Street Meats, 144
Making Camp: Rhetorics of Transgression in U.S. Popular Culture (Shugart and Waggoner), 102
Maor, Maya, 162, 163–64, 172
Margo, Robert A., 92–94, 97
"Maroon, The," 60
Mason, John Landis, 137
"Mason Jar, Reborn, The" (Kelly), 137
mason jars, importance of in food preservation, 137–38, 151–52
Matchar, Emily, 133–34
McCormick, Mee, 158, 166, 178–86, 187
McDaniels, Hattie, 72–73
McGhee, Trissy, 3
Meah, Angela, 27

memoirs: and cookbooks, 21–24, 35–36, 44, 57; Maya Angelou's, 18–21; pain and pleasure in *The Cooking Gene*, 58–59, 60, 76
Messina, Virginia, 44–45, 46
Mess of Greens: Southern Gender and Southern Food, A (Engelhardt), 131
Metcalf, Gayden, 192, 198, 201–2, 203, 205–6, 208–11, 216–17, 218, 220–21
Michaels, Walter Benn, 98
Mickler, Ernest Matthew, 92, 100–105, 118, 119, 233
"Migrant Mother" photo, 91
Mill, Edna Rae, 101
Miller, Adrian, 99
Miller, Betsy Minor Millsap, 221
Miller, Monica Carol, 157
Miller, Sarah, 31–32
Mind of the South, The (Cash), 94
"misfires" vs. "infelicities," 230–31
Moosewood Cookbook (Katzen), 100
Mor, Ana Francis, 125–26
Morgan, Audrey, 142
mourning, 4, 56, 62, 193–95, 197–98, 202, 206. *See also* grief and death in funeral cookbooks
My Kitchen Year (Reichl), 231
My Pinewood Kitchen: A Southern Culinary Cure (McCormick), 158, 166, 178–86

Nabhan, Gary, 140
Naccarato, Peter, 28, 217
Nashville Agrarians, 91
Near and Far (Swanson), 100
Neil, Erik, 144
Nelligan, Duane, 218–19
Nelson, Therese, 61, 62
Neville, Gwen Kennedy, 193, 195, 198, 205, 207, 213
New Encyclopedia of Southern Culture, The, entry on "Poverty," 92–94
New Jim Crow: Mass Incarcerations in the Age of Colorblindness, The (Alexander), 57

Newsweek (magazine), 42
Newton, Natasha, 165
New Turn in the South, A (Acheson), 135, 138, 149
New Yorker (magazine), 33, 52
New York Times (newspaper), 6, 42, 52, 59
New York Times Bestseller list, 231
Niewiadomska-Fils, Urszula, 27
Normans and Saxons: Southern Race Mythology and the Intellectual History of the Civil War (Watson), 194
Nosrat, Samin, 25–26, 29, 30, 31, 32, 33–35
nostalgia, 91, 98, 110, 133, 134, 217, 224; Afro-, 55–58; afro-, 55–58, 60, 64, 67, 78; in cookbooks, 57, 215; criticism of, 113; historical, 55–56; nostalgic retribution, 57, 58–59, 67, 68–69, 75; for the Old South, 54, 76, 216; pleasure as, 54, 73, 149; rhetorical purpose, 76; and suffering, 56, 68; Vivian Howard on, 112; "worry nostalgia," 54–55
Novo Nordisk, 156

obesity, 11, 134, 157, 161, 162, 168, 184. *See also* fat and illness
"Obesity Stigma: A Failed and Ethically Dubious Strategy" (Goldberg and Puhl), 161–62
obituaries, advice on writing, 210
O'Connor, Flannery, 8, 157, 234
Ohio State University, 163
Okra (Willis), 166
O'Neil, Carolyn, 165
Ottolenghi, Yotam, 100
Oxford American (magazine), 10

Pachter, Mina, 41–42, 43
pain: associated with gardening, canning, preserving, and women's labor on farms, 13, 121–52, 232; associated with grief and death in funeral cookbooks, 14–15, 191–224, 233–34; associated with poverty, 12–13, 88–119, 232; associated with racism and slavery, 11–12, 50–86, 232; becoming the identity, 126; dealing with body fat and illness in wellness cookbooks, 14–15, 154–88, 232; as evidence of authenticity, 228, 230; finding in cookbook genre, 231; of overweight people, 163, 170–71, 172–73; pleasure, pain, and play, 228–30; predicting pain, but finding pleasure, 177. *See also* suffering
Passed On: African American Mourning Stories (Holloway), 194–95
Patterson, Orlando, 219
Paula Deen Cuts the Fat (Deen), 14, 165
Paula Deen's Southern Cooking Bible (Deen), 156
Penguin Random House, 231
personal reminiscences. *See* Tippen, Carrie Helms, personal reminiscences of
Peterman, Terry, 88–89
pickles and pickling, 110, 112, 116, 135–36, 138, 142, 211. *See also* preserving and canning
Pimento Cheese: The Cookbook (Magness), 201
Pinewood Kitchen. *See My Pinewood Kitchen: A Southern Culinary Cure* (McCormick)
Play, Creativity and Social Movements (Shepard), 37–38
play, pleasure, and pain, 228–30
pleasure: of affection, 29; associated with gardening, canning, preserving, and women's labor on farms, 13, 121–52, 232; associated with grief and death in funeral cookbooks, 14–15, 191–224, 233–34; associated with poverty, 12–13, 99–117, 232; associated with racism and slavery, 11–12, 50–86, 232; associated with wellness and weight loss, 14–15, 154–88, 232; cookbook genre requirements for, 51; cookbooks as a pleasure-centered genre, 22–24, 40, 51, 80–81, 187, 227, 228–30, 231; feminist theory of pleasure and pain, 13, 38, 40, 127; and guilt, 15; of imagination,

33–36; importance of laughter, 125–26; as nostalgia, 54; pleasure, pain, and play, 228–30; pleasures of plenty, risk becoming a reward, 148–50; predicting pain, but finding pleasure, 177; of process, 26; as resistance, 36–41, 54–58; rhetoric of in cookbooks, 5–11, 12, 18–47, 86, 118, 126, 159, 205, 227, 228–29, 231, 236; sexual, 37, 124–25, 127, 163; of taste, 27–30; typology of, 4–25; urgency of, 36–41

"Pleasures of Reading Recipes, The" (Wilson), 33

Politics of Traumatic Literature: Narrating Human Psyche and Memory, The (Cirina), 42

Poole's: Recipes and Stories from a Modern Diner (Christensen), 100

"poor off" competition, 88–89

poverty, 12–13, 88–119, 232, 233; African American as an outcome of slavery, 93, 97; definition of in *The New Encyclopedia of Southern Culture*, 92–94; as essential to southern experience, 92–99, 168; and food insecurity, 45, 117, 134, 156, 157, 164; "foods," 90, 99, 118; frugality vs., 111, 117; linked to poor health of southerners, 157; and poor whites, 91, 94, 96, 97, 98–99, 105, 113, 117, 119, 232; shame and social entrepreneurship in *Deep Run Roots*, 106–17; "tour" of Robert Kennedy, 12

Poverty Politics: Poor Whites in Contemporary Southern Writing (Robertson), 95, 98

"Powerful, and Provocative Voice for Southern Food, A" (Severson), 6–7

Pratt, Mary Louise, 27

Pratt, Minnie Bruce, 224

prebiotic and probiotic focused diet, 178, 180, 181, 182, 184, 186

preserving and canning: dealing with gardening, canning, preserving, and women's labor on farms, 13, 121–52, 233; as evidence of southern authenticity, 136, 139, 151; mason jars, importance of in food preservation, 137–38; preserving food in Appalachia, 138, 143; as special women's work, 142–45. *See also* pickles and pickling

Pride month, 233

"Privilege of Rage, The" (Jones), 44–45

process, pleasure of, 26

processed foods, 108, 137, 169, 175, 180, 182

Protest Kitchen (Adams and Messina), 44–45

Puhl, Rebecca, 161–62, 164

queerness, 233

Queer Political Performance and Protest: Play, Pleasure, and Social Movement (Shepard), 37

Queer South Rising: Voices of a Contested Place (Whitlock), 196

race and racism, 11–12, 50–86, 232; Black-owned southern funeral homes, 194; pain of a southern Black girl, 18; segregated graveyards, 196. *See also* slavery and racism

Radway, Janice, 127

Raenelle (Betty Sue Swilley's sister-in-law), 102–4, 105

Rage Baking: The Transformative Power of Flour, Fury, and Women's Voices (Gunst and Alford), 45–47

Raiford, Matthew, 59, 60, 65–67, 73–76, 79–80, 83–84, 85, 230, 232

Raiford, Ulious, 67

Randall, Joe, 74

Real Southern Cook in Her Savannah Kitchen, A (Charles), 59, 78

recipes. *See* cookbooks

Recipes for Reading (Bower), 5, 22

Recipes for Respect (Zafar), 12

reconciliation, 10, 11, 74–75; and truth, 12, 80–86

Reed, John Shelton, 94–95

Reichl, Ruth, 231

Remembering Women Differently: Refiguring Rhetorical Work (Gaillet and Bailey), 132
resilience, 10, 19, 68, 123–24, 150, 228; cultural, 54; pleasure of, 12–13, 42, 88–119
resistance, 15, 45, 54, 68, 78, 95; affective, 57; Afro-nostalgia as, 57, 58; "Black Joy" as, 38–39; and cookbooks, 42, 126, 127; pain as, 56; pleasure as, 22, 36–41, 54–58, 86, 165, 236; political, 97, 99, 187; resistance or resilience, 117–19; and women's pleasure, 124–27
responsibility in "culinary triangle of identity, responsibility, and convenience," 5
rhetoric: of authenticity, 145, 160, 166, 198, 228; challenge in southern diet cookbooks, 187, 188; choices, 53; feminist, 132; focus or purpose in cookbooks, 5, 8, 9, 16, 52, 59, 70, 76, 165, 230, 231–32; laughter having a rhetorical effect, 125, 126; Lost Cause, 90–91; of pleasure in cookbooks, 11–12, 18–47, 86, 118, 126, 159, 205, 231, 236; strategies, 11–12, 50, 77, 126; triangle (audience, purpose, speaker), 232; Ricketts family, 97
Robertson, Sarah, 91, 92, 95–97, 98
Roman, Alison, 52
"Romanced by Cookbooks" (Bower), 127
Romine, Scott, 7, 8, 12
Runaway Spoon, The (blog), 201
Russell, Malinda, 140
Ruth Hall (Fern), 30–31

Salt, Fat, Acid, Heat (Nosrat), 25, 29, 31, 32, 35
Samuelsson, Marcus, 57, 72
Saturday Night Live, 156, 159
Savor the South series, 166
"Season of Lilacs: Nostalgia of Place and Homeplace(s) of Difference" (Whitlock), 196, 224
"Second Line" parades that attend burial, 195
Secret Ingredients: Race, Gender and Class at the Dinner Table (Inness), 36–37

Secrets of the Southern Table: A Food Lover's Tour of the Global South (Willis), 60, 81–85, 172, 230, 233
"Selina's Shortbread," 3–4
Severson, Kim, 6–7
sexual pleasure, 37, 124–27; and being overweight, 163–64
SFA. *See* Southern Foodways Alliance (SFA)
Shack, The (restaurant), 150
shame, 94, 113, 232; and poverty, 5, 15, 106–17, 119, 130; and slavery, 5, 15; and weight stigma, 162, 163, 164, 187
Shapiro, Laura, 42, 43
sharecropping, 62, 68, 77, 93–94, 121, 129
Sharpless, Rebecca, 127, 128–31, 133
Shepard, Benjamin, 37–38, 39
Short Stack series, 166
Shugart, Helene A., 102, 105
"sitting down someplace," 50–51, 52
size discrimination, 164
"skinny," 156, 168, 174, 176
Skinny Southern: 90 Reinvented Classics Without the Guilt! (Carter), 165, 173–78
slavery and racism: African American poverty as an outcome of, 93, 97; cookbooks grappling with, 11–12, 50–86, 232; pain and pleasure in remembering, 58–80
Slim Down South: Eating Well and Living Healthy in the Land of Biscuits and Bacon (O'Neil). *See Southern Living Slim Down South Cookbook: Eating Well and Living Healthy in the Land of Biscuits and Bacon* (O'Neil)
"small fat," 154
Smith, Andrew, 63
Smith, Art, 167
Smith, Lora, 144, 149
snacking rituals, 159
SNL (*Saturday Night Live*), 156, 159
social death, 14–15, 199, 219
social justice, 39, 44, 45, 80, 92, 107, 162; celebration, suffering, and, 3–16
"Solace" (soundtrack), 57–58

Solo: A Modern Cookbook for a Party of One (Lo), 27
Sontag, Susan, 96
Soul Food (Miller), 99
South as imagined in cookbooks, The, 9
southern authenticity, 9, 13, 14, 99, 118, 158, 160, 161, 165–66, 209, 231; being an authentic southerner and losing weight, 159–60; canning and preserving as evidence of, 136, 139, 151; and creation of belonging, 209; evidence of, 82, 136, 139, 151; in "healthy cooking" cookbooks, 165, 166; maintaining southern flavors and traditions, 74; of Mee McCormick, 179; and pain and suffering, 99, 161, 228, 231; of Pinewood, TN, 158, 179–81; source of, 14; of Virginia Willis, 82
Southern Comfort Food Diabetes Cookbook: Over 100 Recipes for a Healthy Life, The (Feller), 165
Southern Culture (journal), 194
Southern Food: At Home, on the Road and In History (Egerton), 228
Southern Foodways Alliance (SFA), 6, 10, 52, 114
southern funeral customs, 193–95; choosing the right foods for the place and attendees, 221–22; "continuing bonds theory" (using recipes of the dead), 197–98, 199; cookbooks characterizing rituals beyond food, 209–10; funeral meals, 217–22, 223; "Funeral Phrases," 209; and the Lost Cause, 224; as a place-based ritual, 195–97; postbellum funerals, 194; relatives of deceased not responsible for food, 202; rituals around death as part of belonging to the community, 209, 213; uniqueness of, 210–11; Virginia funerals, 193. *See also* grief and death in funeral cookbooks
southern identity, 223–24, 234; bringing food to those who are ill, 192; cooking as an essential southern personality trait, 168; and definition of poverty, 92–94; democracy and simplicity (poverty foods and southern character), 90–92; fat in southern cooking, 156–61; funerals as ceremonies of, 194; and hospitality, 181, 196–97; and slavery, 51–54; and southern foodways, 234; southern identity, 135–36, 192; southern women and farm work, 127–34; *Southern Keto*, 165
Southern Keto Cookbook, The (Bailey), 165–66
Southern Living (magazine), 100, 105, 165
Southern Living Slim Down South Cookbook: Eating Well and Living Healthy in the Land of Biscuits and Bacon (O'Neil), 14, 17, 159, 165
Southern Memorial Association, 199–200
Southern Snacks (Magness), 201
Southern Sympathy Cookbook: Funeral Food with a Twist, The (Magness), 15, 198, 201, 202–4, 205, 208, 210, 211, 222, 233
South: Essential Recipes and New Explorations (Brock), 135–36, 137
Spoth, Daniel, 7
Starving the South: How the North Won the Civil War (Smith), 63
Steele, Catherine Knight, 38, 39
Stefani, Gwen, 102
Stehling, John, 141
Stewart, Terah J., 164
Stigma and Health (journal), 163
stigmatization. *See* weight stigma
"Stories that Matter: Subverting the Before-and-After Weight-Loss Narrative" (Maor), 162–63
storytelling, 10, 11, 19, 29, 33, 79, 101, 198, 205
Striley, Katie Margavio, 164
SturtzSreetharan, Cindi, 54–55
suffering: body fat and illness in wellness cookbooks, 13–14, 154–88, 232; celebration, suffering, and social justice, 3–16; and farm labor, 13, 121–52, 233; and genre, 41–47, 231; grappling with poverty,

12–13, 88–119, 233; grappling with slavery and racism, 11–12, 50–86, 232; grief and death in funeral cookbooks, 14–15, 191–224, 233–34; in *I Know Why the Caged Bird Sings*, 18–19; necessity of, 54; place of in cookbooks, 9–11; and resistance, 54–56, 58; the South as uniquely prone to illness and fat, 160; and womanhood, 13, 121–52. *See also* pain
"Suicide" (McGhee), 3
Super Upsetting Cookbook About Sandwiches, A (Kord), 227
Sutpen, Thomas, 8
Swanson, Heidi, 100
Sweet Potato Soul: 100 Easy Vegan Recipes for the Southern Flavors of Smoke, Sugar, Spice, and Soul (Claiborn), 165
Swilley, Betty Sue, 102–4, 105

Tabasco Community Cookbook Awards, 200
Tailgreat: How to Crush It at Tailgating (Currence), 100
Talbot, Chuck, 144
Target (stores), 233
taste, pleasure of, 27–30
Taylor, Nicole A., 59–60, 62–65, 71–73, 80, 230
Teen Vogue (magazine), 154
Teigen, Chrissy, 52
Ten Speed Press, 100, 235
Terezin (Jewish ghetto/concentration camp), 41–42
Terry, Bryant, 57–58, 63, 64, 73, 100, 235
"Testifying, Silencing, Swallowing: Coming to Terms with *In Memory's Kitchen*" (Kaufman), 43
Texas Christian University, 89
Theophano, Janet, 22
thinness, ideal of, 162–63
This American Life (PBS radio show), 154, 155
Thomas, Edna, Lollis, 210
Thomas, Linda, 210
Tippen, Carrie Helms, personal reminiscences of, 3–4, 88–89, 234; bringing food to a funeral, 219–20; bringing food to those who are ill, 191–92; dealing with guilt, 191; health matters, 154–55; on slavery and racism, 50–51; work in the garden as a child, 121–23
Tipton-Martin, Toni, 6, 54
Tomato Clubs, 131
Trainer, Sarah, 54–55
Trethewey, Natasha, 234
Tribole, Evelyn, 155
True Detective, 8
truth and reconciliation, 11, 12, 80–86
Turshen, Julia, 44, 46
Twain, Mark, 205
Twitter battle between Brock and Twitty, 52
Twitty, Michael, 58–59, 60–62, 63, 67–68, 69, 73, 75, 76, 80; arguments with Sean Brock, 52

unhealthy southern cooking as stereotype, 156, 157, 158, 165, 167, 168, 173, 180, 187
University of North Carolina Savor the South series, 166
Up South: Chasing Dixie in a Brooklyn Kitchen (Taylor), 59–60, 62–63, 64, 65, 71, 72, 73, 230
urgency of pleasure, 36–41

Vannini, Phillip, 159
Van Woodward, C., 95
Veteto, Jim, 140
Victuals (Lundy), 136–37, 141, 147
Voyage (restaurant), 110

Waggoner, Catherine Egley, 102, 105
Walker, Melissa, 127–28, 129–31, 132, 133
Walking Dead, The, 8
Wanderer (slave ship), 65
Wann, Marilyn, 160–61
Ward, Jesmyn, 234
Ward, Jessica Bemis, 198–99, 200, 204–6, 208–10, 211–14, 215, 216, 218–19, 220–21, 233, 234
Wardi, Anissa, 196, 223
War on Poverty, 95, 97

War on Poverty: A New Grassroots History, The (Orleck and Hazirjian), 97
War on Poverty in Mississippi: From Massive Resistance to New Conservatism, The (Folwell), 97
Watermelon and Red Birds: A Cookbook for Juneteenth and Black Celebrations (Taylor), 60, 64–65, 73, 230
Waters, Alice, 25–26
Watson, Richie Devon, Jr., 194
Way to Cook, The (Child), 214
Weathers, Sanura, 73
weight loss-specific cookbooks, 159, 165, 173–78, 187; need to be value-neutral, 188; wellness focus on weight loss and symptoms of illness, 13–14, 154–88
weight stigma, 161, 162, 164, 170; study of BMI, 163
wellness as a focus in cookbooks, 13–14, 154–88, 232
Welty, Eudora, 96
West, Lindy, 155, 158, 164
What Color is Your Parachute? (Bolles), 100
What the F**K Should I Make For Dinner (Golden), 26
White, Francis Ray, 163–64
White, Milton, 144
"White Gatekeeper of Southern Food Faces Calls to Resign, A" (*New York Times*), 6
White Trash Cooking (Mickler), 12, 92, 100–105, 117
Whitlock, Reta Ugena, 196, 224
Whitt, Jonathon, 144
"Why Cooking Sucks" (Miller), 31
"Why the New South Never Became the North: A Summary" (Cobb), 98
Wiig, Kristen, 156
Williams, John, 102, 104
Williams-Forson, Psyche, 39
Williamson, Michael, 97
Willis, Virginia, 100, 175, 177–78, 179, 187, 233–34; *Basic to Brilliant, Y'all*, 166, 230; *Bon Appetit, Y'all*, 100, 166; *Fresh Start: Cooking with Virginia, My Real Life Daily Guide to Healthy Eating and Weight Loss*, 158, 165, 173–74; *Grits*, 166; *Lighten Up, Y'all*, 14, 165, 166–73, 178; *Okra*, 166; *Secrets of the Southern Table: A Food Lover's Tour of the Global South*, 60, 81–85, 230, 232
Wilson, Amy Lyles, 200–201
Wilson, Bee, 33
Wilson, Charles Reagan, 193, 194, 197, 210–11, 224
women: canning and gardening as special women's work, 142–45; "cult of true womanhood," 29; womanhood and suffering, 13, 121–52; women's labor on the farm, 13, 121–52, 233
Women, Sexuality and the Political Power of Pleasure (Jolly, Cornwall, and Hawkins), 124–25
Woodland's Pork Farm, 144
Work, Family, and Faith: Rural Southern Women in the Twentieth Century (Walker and Sharpless), 128–31
"Working Lass," 129
Works Progress Administration, 12, 96
"worry nostalgia," 54–55

Y'all Come Over: A Celebration of Southern Hospitality, Food, and Memories (Caldwell and Wilson), 201
You Be Sweet: Sharing Your Heart One Down Home Dessert at a Time (Caldwell and Wilson), 201

za'atar, 75–76
Zafar, Rafia, 12, 53–54

ABOUT THE AUTHOR

Carrie Helms Tippen is associate professor of English at Chatham University in Pittsburgh, Pennsylvania. Tippen is author of *Inventing Authenticity: How Cookbook Writers Redefine Southern Identity* (University of Arkansas Press, 2018). She is series editor of the Ingrid G. Houck Series in Food and Foodways at University Press of Mississippi and one of the hosts of the New Books in Food podcast from the New Books Network. Her academic work has been published in *Gastronomica*, *Food and Foodways*, *Southern Quarterly*, and *Food, Culture, and Society*.

www.ingramcontent.com/pod-product-compliance
Lightning Source LLC
Chambersburg PA
CBHW021837220426
43663CB00005B/291